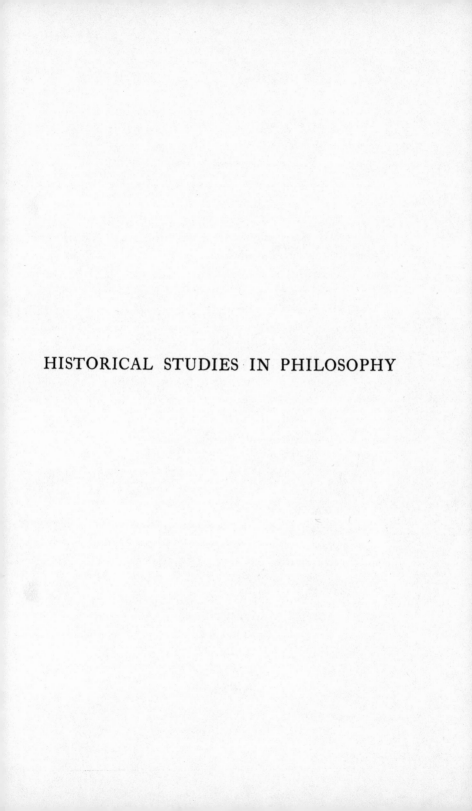

HISTORICAL STUDIES IN PHILOSOPHY

HISTORICAL STUDIES

IN

PHILOSOPHY

BY

ÉMILE BOUTROUX

AUTHORIZED TRANSLATION

BY

FRED ROTHWELL, B.A.

KENNIKAT PRESS
Port Washington, N. Y./London

129547

HISTORICAL STUDIES IN PHILOSOPHY

First published in 1912
Reissued in 1970 by Kennikat Press
Library of Congress Catalog Card No: 77-102562
SBN 8046-0722-2

Manufactured by Taylor Publishing Company   Dallas, Texas

AUTHOR'S PREFACE

THIS book, which a careful and exact translation now introduces to English readers, is a collection of studies, independent of one another, and written mostly at the express invitation of my pupils or colleagues. As I had devoted numerous lectures at the *École Normale Supérieure* and the *Sorbonne* to a minute analysis of various philosophical systems, and as I was unable to find time to set them forth in detail, the suggestion was made that I might, at all events, publish a *résumé* of the conclusions at which I had arrived. My first impulse was to decline a task which seemed somewhat ingrate and risky. Indeed, it is no easy matter to act upon the mind of the reader, unless you lead him, to some extent, along the paths you have already traversed, on to the position you yourself have reached. And even though he may not feel inclined to make your conclusions his own, he will regard them with a certain amount of indulgence if he sees that you have been at considerable pains to reach them. Frequently, too, quite apart from your results, he will fully

appreciate the investigations you have made.   As
Victor Hugo said :

. . . Dieu bénit l'homme
Non pour avoir trouvé, mais pour avoir cherché.

It may be that there are critics good enough to be less
severe than God, but if scarcely anything beyond results
are set forth, the reader will not feel inclined to show
you much indulgence !

In spite of these scruples, the reason I consented to
write these short studies, almost devoid, as they are, of
the critical basis on which they are constructed, is that
I cannot accustom myself to the idea—often tacitly
admitted if it be not openly avowed—that in dealing
with the history of philosophy all inquiry into the true
and inmost thought of a master can never be other
than premature, and that a genuine savant should
concentrate his attention upon the search after texts,
their comparison with one another, and the discussions
to which they give rise.   I am aware that Fustel
de Coulanges, one of our great historians, has said that
a single hour of synthesis presupposes centuries of
analysis.   His own admirable generalisations, however,
form a magnificent contradiction of this formal, abstract
doctrine.   Perhaps we should regard as more truly
in conformity both with the conditions of scientific
research and with the method actually adopted by
Fustel de Coulanges, the following maxim of an
eminent geographer, Professor W. M. Davis, of

Harvard University : *Invention may advisedly go hand in hand with observation.* The analytical study of the texts suggested to me a certain interpretation of the works of the masters, just as certain previous hypotheses as to the meaning of these works had served me as heuristic principles in the analytical study itself : some of the best established results are given in the present volume. I am disposed to regard them as nothing more than starting-points for subsequent research, ideas to be tested anew and revised by a comparison with facts ; still they form, in some measure, the living synthesis of several of my previous studies.

Moreover, I do not think it will ever be possible, in setting forth a system of philosophy, to content oneself with collecting extant documents, manipulating them, and finally extracting their substance, by quite mechanical processes, after the fashion of a chemist. One of our cleverest linguists, M. Michel Bréal, in his famous work, *Essai sur la Sémantique,* is altogether opposed to the opinion that language possesses an existence of its own, and is capable of being studied *per se,* independently of the living mind of man who is continually building it up and perfecting it. " Underneath the phenomena presented by language," he concludes, " we feel the action of a thought releasing itself from the form to which it is chained down . . . *Mens agitat molem.*"

A fortiori is this the case with systems of philosophy, which, assuredly, are something more than a blind impulse, an enthusiastic aspiration of the mind : they represent the methodical effort of an intelligence employing all its knowledge and dialectic power in an attempt to confine reality within clear and well-connected formulas. Still, the living mind of the philosopher is never absent from his work ; the system should never be conceived as separate from its creator, like fruit as distinct from the tree on which it has grown. Consequently, in order to understand an author's work in the way he meant it to be understood, *i.e.* to understand it aright, we must make it our constant endeavour not merely to search into the visible letter of the text and all the details of documents, but also to think and live with the author himself, to enter into his spirit. In reality, it is this interior principle of development,—which, in truth, cannot be isolated from the visible forms but rather governs them and gives them their particular aspect,— it is the active, ever-present soul of the author, that the historian should endeavour to set before us, enabling us to enter intuitively, as it were, into that soul and attain to direct participation therewith.

If this effort be made, our understanding of the work becomes as profound and adequate as we can make it. Nor is this all. Just as we must enlarge our own mind, if we would thus comprehend thoughts greater than our own, so it would seem that to cultivate the history of philosophy in this way is not only to learn to know philosophers but also to become more capable of philosophizing ourselves.   To what heights might we not aspire, what claims might we not make, if something of the genius of the masters could really live again within us and enter into our thought ! " Das ist," said Goethe, " die Eigenschaft des Geistes, dass er den Geist ewig anregt."   Is not this submission—in a happy blend of effort and *abandon*—to the potent influence of the masters, this attempt to carry on their work and message, the natural and legitimate object and end of our historical investigations ?

ÉMILE BOUTROUX.

PARIS, *March* 7, 1912.

TRANSLATOR'S NOTE

THE word *science* throughout, and especially in the essays on Socrates and Aristotle, has been frequently used both in this translation and in the original work, to render the word σοφία, as being preferable to *wisdom* and to *sagesse* alike.   It is therefore to be interpreted as connoting the highest branches of learning and philosophy.

CONTENTS

THE HISTORY OF PHILOSOPHY

ζητεῖται τὸ ἴδιον.—ARISTOTLE, *Eth. Nic.* i. 7. 1097 b 35.

THE more historical works on every subject multiply, the more difficult does it become to find agreement as to the object of history itself. Can the science studied by a Renan, when investigating the moral laws of mankind and the universe, be the same as that studied by a Fustel de Coulanges, who is ignorant as to the very existence of historical laws, and whose sole ambition is to connect a few facts with their immediate causes?

The history of philosophy cannot escape this condition of things. Hegel understands it in a far different fashion from Grote. In turn, it is philosophical, psychological, social, philological and naturalistic, nor do we clearly see what definite form it tends to assume. It has become necessary for any one who undertakes this study, unless he wishes to confine himself to some particular current of thought, to reflect upon the end of this science and examine the various definitions that may be given thereof.

What, then, is the proper object of the history of philosophy? What is the most suitable method to adopt?

Have we simply to collect and classify, geographically and chronologically, such facts as may rightly be called philosophical?

Once this selection is effected, have we to connect each of these facts with the particular environment in which it happened, and also with its conditions or causes?

Or rather, if we consider that philosophy, up to a certain point, has an existence and development of its own, and constitutes a kind of organism, shall we unravel, as it were, and follow up this autonomous development through the apparently capricious inventions of individuals? Shall we consider each philosopher as the more or less docile instrument of an immanent and universal spirit? Has our task to consist in finding and completing those parts of each thinker's work which are productive and likely to live, and neglecting those which, sooner or later, time must destroy? Is it not expected that a historian should read, study and criticise everything, so that he may relegate to the waters of oblivion such events as have no claim upon the memory of mankind?

But if we have scruples about thus judging of philosophical productions in the name of the more or less mystical idea of an eternal philosophy, should we not like, at all events, to distinguish those conceptions of a man of genius in which he is really himself and is introducing innovations or preparing the future, from those in which he shows himself nothing more, at that stage, than an echo of his predecessors?

In short, is there not a conception of the history of philosophy—a very plausible one by reason of its connection with the positive sciences—according to which it seems to be the historian's task to take philosophers, not philosophy, as the object of his investigations; and, by a process of psychological analysis, to show with reference to each of them, the line of evolution he has of necessity had to follow—taking into consideration his temperament, his education and the circumstances of his life—in the production of the ideas he has given to the world ?

Evidently each of these points of view has an interest and importance of its own, but none of them seems to be the special point of view of the historian of philosophy.

To confine oneself to the collection and chronological arrangement of philosophical manifestations would be too modest a task ; for though we may somewhere find a logical concatenation of facts along with the facts themselves, still it is in doctrines and systems that philosophy finds its realisation.

On the other hand, he would be a bold man who would affirm that some particular conception has a future before it, whereas some other has had its day. In Voltaire's time, metaphysics was an utterly exploded doctrine. Now, that was the very period when German philosophy was beginning to become known.

And what an ambition, to find the historical and unconscious origins, the mechanical genesis of a thinker's ideas ! Which of us, even the most wide-awake and skilled in analysing mental states, could correctly explain the origin of his opinions and doctrines ? Amongst the many influences under which our increasingly complex life is continually bringing us, how can we set apart those that have been deep and lasting, or state exactly in what direction they have been exercised ? Besides, why do we so strongly insist that our ideas spring only from external influences and that we ourselves have nothing to do with their production ?

Apart from these various conceptions of the history of philosophy—conceptions in turn excessively timid and

boldly venturesome—there is one of a less striking
nature, from the fact that it does not seem to be so
scientific, though perhaps it is more in accordance with
the nature of the subject under investigation. It is
also the one, unless I am mistaken, generally applied by
writers whose distinctive object is to take up the history
of philosophy, without troubling about anything else.

It consists in regarding as the subject of investigation
from the very outset, what to us are immediate data,
to wit, any particular doctrine that is one in its greater
or less complexity, any collection of ideas set forth by
the philosopher as forming a whole. Where this condition is not fulfilled, we may indeed be dealing with a
shrewd moralist or a profound, original thinker, but
certainly we are not dealing with a philosopher. The
problem to be solved is that of finding out what logical
connection the philosopher has really set up between his
ideas, which he has taken as principles, and in what
order and fashion he makes the rest depend on the main
ideas. A philosopher is a man who sets up men's
knowledge over against their beliefs, and tries to find
their relations to one another. We want to know how
a Plato or a Leibnitz conceived of these relations. And
since the philosopher is not a seer to whom truth is
revealed in a flash, but rather a patient seeker who reflects and criticises, doubts and hesitates, and listens to
reason alone, we want to know the methods, observations
and reasonings by which our author has reached his
conclusions. We are not now dealing with the unconscious, mechanical work of his brain, but with his
conscious, determined efforts to overcome the limits of
his individuality, to think in an all-embracing manner,
and to bring the truth to light.

If such be the case, it is neither philosophy in general,

throughout its development, nor the psychological evolution of each philosopher in particular, that is the immediate object of the history of philosophy : it is the doctrines that have been thought out by philosophers. To know and understand these doctrines well, to explain them—to the extent of one's capacity—as the author himself would do, to set them forth in the spirit of that author, and to some extent, in his style : this is the one essential task, to which all the rest must be subordinated.

It is, indeed, useful to consider the man, and not the work only, but it is so because, in most cases, the man helps us to understand the work. Cartesianism is indebted for more than one of its characteristics to Descartes, the man. And yet, what a mistake to insist on regarding Cartesianism as nothing more than the history of an individual mind !

It is likewise an interesting question to ask oneself : What becomes of philosophy *per se* throughout the succession of systems? Does it advance or remain stationary? This general study of philosophy, however, cannot replace that of the doctrines considered in themselves from each author's point of view : rather it presupposes it.

Let it not, then, be said that some particular portion of a philosopher's doctrines may be neglected, under the plea that it is to be found in the writings of some earlier philosopher. That is an insufficient reason. A great mind does not seek after novelty or originality ; it seeks after truth. Why should it refuse any portion thereof under the plea that it was discovered by someone else ? In the classic ages of literature, authors did not feel themselves bound to create, *ex nihilo*, after the fashion of God. A Corneille and a Molière make lavish use of the works of their predecessors. No one finds fault with their lack of originality when they take advantage of this material in writing fine and noble works. With still more reason, an Aristotle, a Leibnitz and a Kant carefully retain whatever those who have gone before have found to be of advantage. In reality, they make it their own by the way in which they use it. "When two men are playing tennis," said Pascal, "both play with the same ball, but one of them places it better than the other." It often happens that the most commonplace idea assumes a new aspect by reason of the new relations in which it finds itself.

On the other hand, some idea destined at a later period to prove an important and fruitful one, may have played only a secondary or eclipsed part in the system in which it first appeared. Though picking it up as a chance find, so to speak, or regarding it as an interesting presentiment, we must be careful not to place it in the foreground under pretence of serving the author by giving him a more modern aspect. It is not Descartes as one would imagine he would be at the present time, but the Descartes of 1644, referring every problem to the one of certainty, whom it is our object to make known.

The task in hand determines exactly the means it behoves us to put into operation. In the ulterior developments a system may have gone through, the doctrines to which it has given birth, the appreciations and interpretations of contemporaries and successors, or even the historical and biographical information regarding the author's person and works, we ought not to look for anything else than sign-posts of the problems we must set before ourselves, or material data which determine the ground on which to work. The spring and origin of the history of philosophy can be found only in the monuments left by philosophers themselves.

Each philosophical work requires to be considered both as a whole and in detail. The work of the mind is one continual oscillation from the whole to the parts and from the parts to the whole. Such is the method applied in the understanding of a drama, a poem, or a work of art. This alternate movement of induction and deduction is the origin of the sciences. In the same way, if we explain the author by himself, his general ideas by his particular doctrines and his particular doctrines by his general ideas, the probabilities are that we shall thoroughly grasp his meaning and enter into his thought.

It is not enough to discover curious—even un-published—texts. Which of us can enter completely into all an author says? What likelihood is there that a letter written to some correspondent or other, how-ever ill fitted he be to understand the philosopher, should prove of greater importance than treatises that have been slowly matured and are destined for posterity? The historian, whose aim it is not to make a collection of anecdotes, but to form a correct appreciation of a great man's work, will be less anxious to marshal and array an imposing number of disconnected texts than to become increasingly imbued with the author's thought, by reading the whole of his works not once, but many times. His aim will be to see things from the author's point of view, following him along the winding by-paths of meditation, sharing in his emotions as a philo-sopher, and, along with him, enjoying that harmony wherein his intelligence has found repose.

Systems of philosophy are living thoughts. It is by seeking in the written word for the means of reviving these thoughts within ourselves that we may hope to hear them deliver their message.

SOCRATES,
THE FOUNDER OF MORAL SCIENCE [1]

"Les mêmes pensées poussent quelquefois tout autrement dans un autre que dans leur auteur."—PASCAL.

I

AFTER the keen rivalry that has existed amongst those most capable of dissipating the clouds and mists that hang about the figure of Socrates, inquiring men of letters, shrewd moralists, philosophers of penetrating intellect, learned historians, and even doctors, whose object it has been to collect and interpret such documents as are calculated to make him known to us, is there anything left to say about him ? Is not the writer on such a theme compelled to repeat mere commonplaces if he is determined to say only what is true, to give expression to paradoxes if he claims to have anything new to advance ?

In this connection it would seem as though a distinction must be made. Doubtless, all possible light

[1] The present essay deals less with the feelings and the soul of Socrates than with his philosophy and his work. In one aspect Socrates, as a man, is an enthusiast in the literal meaning of the word, almost a mystic. He is Apollo's messenger, and feels within himself the divine afflatus. His unique originality consisted in introducing religious zeal into the preaching of rational morals. Here we confine ourselves to the consideration of the doctrine which Socrates taught his disciples and bequeathed to mankind.

has been shed on most of the details of the life and teaching of Socrates, but it is not so certain that this could be said concerning the *ensemble* of the man and his doctrine. The reader is astonished when he compares with one another those works of our contemporaries that deal with Socrates. If we would know of his life, the causes of his condemnation, the meaning of maieutics, the doctrines of virtue, or some other portion of Socratic philosophy, each of these authors gives almost identical answers. But if we ask what Socrates was in himself, the basis of his character and the root idea of his teaching : regarding this question —in which all the rest culminate—opinions are contradictory.

Thus, according to Zeller,[1] ancient physics having finally disappeared beneath the action of sophistic, Socrates regenerated philosophy by founding it upon a new principle : the general or concept, regarded as the object of science. The work of Socrates, then, was the invention of a principle of theoretical logic.

Grote, in a series of life-like sketches, presents Socrates as a religious missionary, appointed by the oracle of Delphi for putting the would-be wise on the rack and inducing them to confess their ignorance. Socrates is the god of debate, "an elenchtic or cross-examining god." [2] His work, religious in its inspiration, is a living dialectic in itself.

Fouillée regards Socrates as a speculative philosopher, who substitutes final causes for physical ones in the explanation of all phenomena, both physical and moral. He is the creator of spiritual metaphysics.

Lévêque considers that Socrates endeavoured to

---

[1] *Die Philosophie der Griechen*, 3rd edit. vol. ii. p. 93-94.
[2] *History of Greece*, vol. viii. p. 566.

bring about the moral and political reform of Athens, and, with this end in view, established morals as a science independent of the physical sciences.

Janet's brief though important sketch in the *Dictionnaire philosophique* shows us Socrates as a philosopher above all else ; he mentions two main characteristics of his : the moral sentiment, which dominates his personality and appears throughout his doctrine ; and maieutics, from which the Platonic dialectic was to originate.

In a short work, published in 1881, Gustave d'Eichthal considers the outstanding feature of the Socratic doctrine to be religious instruction. Socrates, he says, with a view to checking the evils he saw ravaging his country, wished to give his fellow-citizens what, to him, was the principle of all virtue and the first condition of every reform, namely, religious faith, especially faith in divine Providence.

Finally, Franck, in an article that appeared in the *Journal des savants* on d'Eichthal's book, likewise admits that Socrates was not only a reasoner and a philosopher, but more than all else a profoundly religious soul, in the real meaning of the word, a soul in whom faith in God, admiration of his works, the certainty of his kingdom throughout nature and of his providence over men, were tinged with a certain degree of mysticism.

All these interpretations, moreover, are based on texts of the greatest importance. Thus, confining ourselves to the three of our contemporaries who have written most about Socrates, Zeller, in support of his position, quotes that clear, precise passage in Aristotle [1] where it is mentioned that Socrates seeks the τί ἐστί,

---

[1] *Met.* xiii. 4. 1878 b 23 *sqq.*

the general essence, though without regarding this essence as existing apart, as Plato did. Grote draws his conclusions from the *Apology*,[1] which, indeed, mainly shows us Socrates as having received from the gods the mission of convincing men of their ignorance. And lastly, the statement of Fouillée [2] appears inspired by those luminous passages of the *Phaedo*,[3] in which we find Socrates reproaching Anaxagoras for omitting to take into account, in his explanation of the details of the world, that ordaining and regulating intelligence he had so wisely proclaimed to be the universal cause ; considering, for his part, that any purely mechanical explanation was superficial ; and satisfied only with such explanations as, in the ultimate analysis, were given by final causes.[4]

But why is it that each of these authors has taken up some particular text in preference to others ? In all likelihood, personal preoccupation or different mental habits may give a partial explanation. An old Hegelian like Zeller, whose object above all is to find out the place occupied by men and doctrines in the general development of the human mind, was bound to take, as his main guide, Aristotle, who emphasises in his predecessors just those ideas that have paved the way for his own. Grote, the historian, who would point out the part played by famous men throughout the entire social and political life of their times, was bound to rely mainly on the *Apology*, a life-like picture, it would seem, of Socrates as he appeared to his fellow-citizens. Lastly, Fouillée, the eloquent and profound interpreter of the theory of Ideas, was naturally disposed

---

[1] Grote, *History of Greece*, viii. 565.
[2] *La Philosophie de Platon*, vol. i. p. 17 *sqq.*
[3] Ch. xlv. *sqq.*
[4] *Phaedo*, ch. xlvi. p. 97 B.

to regard Socrates as the precursor of Plato, and to
find in his doctrines the germ of Platonic metaphysics.
It is not surprising that he should take as his starting-
point those passages in which Plato himself connects
his theory of Ideas with the speculations of his master.

In these investigations into the real character of
Socrates, Zeller appears to have adopted the standpoint
of absolute mind, Grote that of a cultured Athenian of
the fifth century, and Fouillée that of Plato. What
would be the result were we to adopt the standpoint
of Socrates himself, asking ourselves what Socrates
must have been, not in the eyes of others but in his
own ? The apostle of the γνῶθι σαυτόν must have
been acquainted with himself. We should regard ourselves as having sufficient knowledge of him were we
acquainted with him to the same extent.

But then, how can we enter into the soul of Socrates,
since he left nothing in writing ? Is it not this very
difficulty of adopting his point of view which induces
historians to seek one from without ?

Perhaps the difficulty is partly artificial. It showed
itself most prominently when Schleiermacher advanced
the principle that, for an exposition of the Socratic
doctrine to be a faithful one, it must above all else
explain how Plato came to regard Socrates as the
promoter of his philosophic activity. From this standpoint a comparison was made between the Socrates of
Xenophon and the Socrates of Plato and Aristotle, and
the two were found to differ widely. Naturally, the
followers of Schleiermacher adopted the views of Plato
and Aristotle, and so the authority of the only one of
our witnesses who was a historian by profession, and
who had made it his business to tell us what Socrates
had really been in his own person, was discredited.

A change, however, has come about since then.
Whilst the champions of Xenophon and Plato were
wrangling over Schleiermacher's theory, a less biassed
criticism compared the testimonies of Xenophon, Plato
and Aristotle with one another. Now, these testimonies
have been found to agree as regards the main issue.[1]
Henceforth, to an impartial critic, the authority of
Xenophon was restored. The charge might still be
brought against him that he set forth the person and
teachings of his master more or less incompletely, though
not that he presented them in a wrong light. If such be
the case, the historian of the present day has the right,
not only to invoke the testimony of Xenophon, along
with those of Plato and Aristotle, but even to assign
the greatest importance to this testimony, for Xenophon
is the only one of the three who does nothing more
than repeat what he personally knew. True, the
immediate object of his work would appear to have
been to refute the harangue of Polycrates, the rhetor,
about the year 393 B.C. ; none the less, Xenophon
must have brought to his task those qualities of fidelity
and impartiality that distinguish his strictly historical
narratives.

Of course, we must not repeat the mistake made by
the historians of old, who, reading Xenophon in a very
superficial manner, saw depicted only the account of a
simple-minded moralist ; we must allow Plato and
Aristotle to breathe life into and complete the picture
sketched by Xenophon. Still, it would be wise to use
the contributions of the two former only as a scholar
uses a hypothesis, that is, in stating or asking questions,
not in solving or answering them. To analyse the
data of Xenophon, interpreting and developing them

[1] Such is the opinion of Zeller, Grote and Fouillée.

according to a scientific induction whose leading ideas are to be supplied by Plato and Aristotle : such seems to be the method we must pursue, if we would know Socrates in a really historical fashion.

Along with Xenophon's *Memorabilia* we must consider Plato's *Apology*, which most critics [1] look upon as trustworthy with regard to facts ; also certain portions, difficult to define, it must be confessed, of the *Crito*, *Phaedo*, *Laches* and *The Banquet*.

Now, what is the root thought of Socrates, regarded, as far as possible, from his own point of view?

II

The first result we obtain, if we take the *Memorabilia* as the main source of the history of Socratic thought, is a confession of ignorance as to what happened previous to the last ten years of the philosopher's career. The temptation is almost irresistible to seek in other works for some means of going back to an earlier year in Socrates' life than the *Memorabilia* allow. For instance, Fouillée believes he has found, in the famous passage of the *Phaedo* on the early philosophical reflections of Socrates,[2] and the coincidence of this text with the *Clouds* of Aristophanes, the proof that Socrates, before devoting himself to moral research, passed through a previous stage, in which he was engaged in speculations on nature. Disappointed in this direction, he would appear to have fallen back on morals for a solution of the very problem of ancient Greek philosophy : that of the explanation of the universe. Besides the fact, however, that the *Memorabilia* contain no indication

[1] Schleiermacher, Zeller, Überweg and Grote.
[2] Ch. xlv. *sqq.*

whatever of such a starting-point, the statement of the
Socrates of the *Phaedo* contradicts the formal declarations of the Socrates of the *Apology*, where it is affirmed
that he never studied physics.[1] The objection may be
urged that the character of Socrates in the *Clouds* must
rest upon some historical basis. But it is precisely
when speaking of the *Clouds* that Socrates makes this
solemn declaration in the *Apology*. True, the question
is decided by dismissing the *Apology*, under the pretext
that it is a speech, and alleging that the text of the
Phaedo itself gives one the impression of historical
reality. Such preference, however, is unjustified. As
it is the object of the text of the *Phaedo* to show us the
origin of the theory of ideas, which theory, moreover,
is likewise attributed to Socrates, it is best to attribute to
Plato himself the reflections with which this exposition
commences. The *Apology* is certainly possessed of
historical value, as is proved, along with other details,
by the strange prediction Socrates made to the judges,[2]
that, when he was dead, the Athenians would find a far
greater number of censors (ἐλέγχοντες) rising up against
them, and these would be all the more unpleasant
because they would be younger. This prediction,
which does not appear to have come to pass, would
certainly have been omitted in an apology invented by
Plato himself. But if Socrates indeed challenged his
listeners to prove that he ever even mentioned physics,[3]
how could we affirm the contrary? Shall we set the
fiction of a comic poet above the testimony of Socrates
himself?

Consequently, we will abandon the attempt to discover what ideas Socrates held in youth and even in

[1] Ch. iii. p. 19 C D. [2] Ch. xxx. p. 39 C D. Cf. Grote.
[3] Ch. iii. p. 19 D.

mature age.   Besides, we have ground to suppose they were in conformity with those he held at the end of his life, for Socrates, in the *Apology*, tells his listeners that the reason they are prejudiced against him, and look upon him as a physicist and a sophist, is that ever since they were children they have been deceived by his enemies regarding himself.[1]   At all events, to claim to throw light on the Socrates of his latter years by the Socrates of the *Clouds* period is trying to explain the known by the unknown.

The starting-point of the established doctrine of Socrates we shall find in his critical reflections on the two disciplines which then occupied men's minds : physics and sophistic.

Socrates never applied himself to physics.   The testimony of Plato [2] and Aristotle [3] is a proof of this, without mentioning that of Xenophon.   There can be no doubt, however, that he had studied the subject, though it was principally as a philosopher that he was interested in it.   It was not the details of the science, the particular theories which in all probability were the main object of research on the part of the ancient physiologists, that he cared about, but rather those general principles that controlled all the rest, the mechanical or dynamical conceptions of nature which led philosophers to explain everything without having recourse to supernatural powers.   Is being one or multiple ; is it in motion or at rest ; is it subject to a state of becoming and destruction, or is it exempt from generation and corruption ?   Such were the philosophical questions that physiologists asked themselves.[4]

Socrates wasted no time in examining one by one

[1] Ch. ii. p. 18 c.
[2] *Apol.* ch. iii. p. 19 D.
[3] *Met.* i. 6. 987 b 1.
[4] Xenophon, *Mem.* i. 1. 14.

the different doctrines to which the idea of natural physics had given birth. He condemned them *en bloc*, as being useless, barren and sacrilegious.

Physics was useless, for physicists were unable to agree on a single point. Some maintained that being is one, the rest that it is infinitely multiple ; some that everything is in motion, the rest that everything is for ever motionless, and so on.[1] Now, contradiction is a sign of ignorance.

And it was barren as well. Do those who trouble about such matters, said Socrates, imagine that when they have discovered the law of necessity according to which everything is produced, they will be able to make the winds, waters and seasons at their own pleasure ?[2]

And these two features were themselves the result of a radical vice : to wit, the sacrilegious nature of the task. All that is, said Socrates, may be divided into two categories,[3] human things (τὰ ἀνθρώπεια), such as pious and impious, beautiful and ugly, just and unjust, matters dealing with civic life and authority,[4] and divine things (δαιμόνια), such as the formation of the world,[5] or even the distant and final consequences of our actions.[6] Now, the gods have given us power to know the former by reasoning ; the latter they have reserved for themselves.[7] Physicists, when speculating on things divine and neglecting the human, invert the order set up by the gods themselves : they disdain knowledge which the gods have placed within our reach, and try to acquire that knowledge the gods have reserved for themselves.

It is noteworthy that Pascal makes a similar dis-

[1] Xenophon, *Mem.* iv. 2.
[2] *Ibid.* i. 1. 15.
[3] *Ibid.* i. 1. 12.
[4] *Ibid.* i. 1. 16.
[5] *Ibid.* i. 1. 11.
[6] *Ibid.* i. 1. 8.
[7] *Ibid.* i. 1. 7-8.

c

tinction. He also[1] divides things into human and divine, and accuses men of having perverted the order established by God when they use profane things as they ought to use sacred ones, and *vice versa*, that is to say, when they consider profane things with the heart and divine ones with the mind. To Pascal, however, it is physical things that are profane and moral ones that are divine.

Both this resemblance and this difference enable us all the better to understand the thought of Socrates. The same religious spirit, both in Socrates and Pascal, sets a limit upon human reason. To the Hellene, however, man himself is his own master ; it is nature, with its mysteries and remoteness, that is divine. To the modern man and the Christian it is the infinitude of the interior life that is divine, and nature, brute, passive matter, that is the object set before human activity.

The original cause of Socrates' condemnation of ancient physics may be found in the stock or fund of ideas peculiar to his nation. Greece could not wholly adapt herself to those speculations on the principles of things into which physiologists had plunged. Doubtless the power of reasoning, the ingenious subtilty and wonderful sense of harmony displayed by these profound investigators, were a good thing, but the immediate application of these mental qualities to material objects most foreign to mankind was opposed to the genius of a race that was essentially political, and mightily enamoured of fine speeches and noble deeds. Besides, how could one reconcile a philosophy which undertook to explain physical phenomena by perfectly natural causes with a religion which everywhere introduced the immediate action of the gods? Certainly

---

[1] *De l'Esprit géom.* 2nd frag.

they were Greeks who had planned these beautiful systems in which nature was subject to the laws of thought ; still, they were citizens of the colonies, and had dealings with the Egyptians, Phoenicians and Babylonians. They had created the form : the East had supplied them with the matter. To detach human affairs from the totality of things, to make them the proper domain of man's activity and intelligence, and at the same time to restore physical phenomena once more to the gods, was to place oneself again in the position of the Hellene : more especially of the Athenian. This was quite natural for the philosopher who never left Athens except to fight in the ranks of his fellow-citizens.

Socrates' judgment on physics, therefore, is no fortuitous accidental fact ; it is not the outcome of a positive, a prosaically utilitarian mind. It is not even altogether that depreciation of the past, habitual to innovators, that antagonism to a rival idea : the condition of the realisation and development of the new idea which claims the right to exist. Socrates' objections to physics are the philosophic expression of that antipathy of a religious, artistic people to a mechanical explanation of things, whereof Aristophanes set himself up as the interpreter in the *Clouds*. The real Socrates flouts the Socrates of Aristophanes, as do the people. The only difference is that he knows better why he does so.

But this very discernment of his prevents him from altogether condemning the work of the physicists. Though declaring it useless, barren and sacrilegious, he yet discovers in it a principle which he is jealously anxious to adopt. This principle is the form and mould, so to speak, of Hellenic thought into which the physiologists cast the matter they borrowed from the East : it is the consciousness, henceforth acquired by the human mind, of its need of unity and harmony ; the notion of an impersonal truth, distinct from opinion and fancy ; the abstract idea of science. When Socrates asks the physiologists [1] if the reason they undertake to speculate on divine things lies in the fact that they think they know enough of human things, he evidently retains of ancient physics the general idea of science as being a special, a superior mode of knowledge, whilst leaving on one side the object to which this idea has hitherto been applied.

And so the general idea of science does not spring forth all at once in the mind of Socrates, with the intuition of genius, as one might imagine from Schleiermacher's profound though abstruse dissertation. Nor is it the reaction of subjectivism against objectivism, a reaction which was evidently determined by the excesses of objectivism itself, in accordance with the general law of the development of the human mind, as appears to be admitted by the former Hegelian, Zeller. This idea of science is nothing else than the proper share of the Hellenic genius in the formation of ancient physics. Socrates' work lies in freeing it from the foreign elements with which it was confused, owing to a subtle distinction between matter and form which the different opponents of the physiologists had been unable to draw. In this he was doubtless aided by his power of invention, as well as by his singularly Hellenic turn of mind. In him the Greek genius recognised its own good fortune through the scientific form that the physiologists had given to the practical knowledge or astronomical speculations of the Orientals.

Though Socrates concerned himself with physics, he paid even more attention to sophistic. Here he dis-

[1] *Mem.* i. 1. 12.

tinguished two things: the end and the means. In his opinion, the end or object of sophistic was to make men capable of speaking and acting well, of managing efficiently the business of city and home, in a word, of being useful to others as well as to themselves.[1] The means consisted solely of exercise and routine, the immediate practice of that action the capacity for which it is one's object to acquire, and so the Sophist, in the mind of Socrates, is the man who identifies the means with the end, who considers, for instance, that, in order to learn to speak well, all that is necessary is to hear others speak and to speak oneself, without taking the trouble to study theoretically the conditions of eloquence. Practice is sufficient in itself. Talent is like some physical aptitude which men acquire by being shaped and drilled to acquire it.

Socrates approved of the object of this discipline, though he condemned the method employed.

It was not ironically that he called the sophistic art the finest and greatest of them all, a truly royal art.[2] If we consider nothing but the end set up for human activity, we find that Socrates is not only in agreement with the Sophists, he is himself one of them. Like the Sophists, he considers that man should trouble himself about none but human affairs. Like them, he thinks that, apart from and above men engaged in special professions and trades, carpenters, pilots, and doctors, etc., there is man, pure and simple, who calls for and deserves distinct culture and training. Evidently Socrates does not limit philosophy to the study of human things for the same reason as do the Sophists. The latter extolled mankind because they denied the existence of the gods. Socrates sees the proof of the

[1] *Mem.* iv. 3. 1 ; iv. 2. 11.   [2] *Ibid.* iv. 2. 11.

existence and greatness of the gods in the very limits
imposed on man.   Socrates and the Sophists arrive at
the same conclusion, though along different paths.

In this comparison between Socrates and the Sophists
there is nothing disparaging to our philosopher if we
form a correct idea of sophistic.   The Sophists were
something more than the destroyers of whom Zeller
speaks, something more than that impersonal echo of the
prevailing morals that Grote would have us believe.   It
fell to the creators of sophistic, men like Protagoras and
Gorgias, to be the first to conceive of the legitimacy
and utility of intellectual culture of a general nature,
applied not to some particular faculty, but to the man himself, in such a way as to make him capable of acting nobly
under all circumstances.   To gymnastics the national
education had now added music, or the teaching of
knowledge which moulds the intelligence.   The Sophists,
however, rose to a loftier conception of education, the
end of which they regarded as being not only the introduction into the mind of more or less determined
knowledge, but also the creation of universal aptitudes.
In doing this it may be said that they brought within
the sphere of consciousness the principle which had
long controlled the practical life of the Hellenes, and
which showed itself in a strange admiration for men
fertile in expedients, and skilled in getting out of a
difficulty under all circumstances : men like Ulysses,
Themistocles or Alcibiades.   The special form the
Sophists gave to their principle indicates even more
clearly its Hellenic nature, for it was essentially in the
ability and skill to speak and debate that they placed a
man's peculiar worth, it was to develop this virtue in
their pupils that they established what might be called
intellectual gymnastics.

No wonder Socrates approved of whatever there was in sophistic that was lofty and in conformity with the genius of the race. But he did not therefore accept the principles of the Sophists.

Indeed, the thought came to him to find out if performance came up to promise, and if the Sophists really carried out that intellectual and moral education the excellence of which they well understood. It must be confessed that the process he adopted to assure himself thereof was that of a man prepossessed in favour of a contrary doctrine, rather than that of an impartial critic who unreservedly sees things from the point of view of his interlocutors. He did not trouble about seeing people at work, or trying to discover if the pupils of the Sophists behaved as clever politicians, just, clearsighted men. He started with the idea that the proof of ability was knowledge, and that the proof of knowledge was the power to explain to others what one knows.[1] Then he went about the town, questioning the Sophists and their pupils, calling upon them to tell him what piety, justice, courage and virtue were, and satisfactorily to answer all possible questions thereon, without ever contradicting themselves. Not one came successfully out of this test ; so Socrates concluded that, though the Sophists made fine promises, their performances were not in conformity with them.

Now, what but the method employed by the Sophists could be the cause of their failure ? This method consisted of practice left to itself and rejecting all theory as vain and useless ; it was art considered as its own means and end.

Here Socrates saw a double error. In the first place, art cannot be an end unto itself. Consider bodily

---

[1] *Mem.* iv. 6. 1 ; iii. 3. 11. Cf. *Laches,* 190 c.

gymnastics. If you admit this to be an absolute end, you will be led to attach as much importance to tricks of strength which deform the body as to the well-planned exercises which make it supple and strong. It is the same with intellectual gymnastics. In itself it is quite as likely to make men more unjust and wicked as to make them more just and noble.[1] Will it have the same value, then, in both cases?

There is more than this, however. Not only cannot art be an end unto itself; it cannot come into being from exercise and practice alone. If art for art's sake is dangerous, art by means of art is impossible. Is it imagined, as Aristotle says later on, that, according to Socrates' meaning, in teaching a man the trade of a shoemaker, it is sufficient to place in his hands a collection of ready-made shoes?[2] To call forth art itself is a very different thing from imparting the products of art. A pupil trained by external means can, more or less faithfully, reproduce whatever he has seen his master do, but he has not within him that general, self-sufficing ability which constitutes true art. Art is independence, whereas such a pupil is his master's slave.[3]

Art by means of art is, in a word, routine, ignorance, chance. Now, a man must be very simple-minded if he thinks that, whereas it is impossible to become a carpenter, pilot, or general unless one possesses special knowledge of these different professions, all the same, skill in the general conduct of life can spring up within us as the result of mere chance.[4] Take any mental quality you please, if, in acquiring it, you restrict yourself to practice alone, you can never be certain you will

[1] *Mem.* iv. 3. 1.   [2] Arist. *Soph. Elench.* 184 a 1.
[3] *Mem.* iv. 7. 1 : αὐτάρκεις ἐν ταῖς προσηκούσαις πράξεσιν.
[4] *Ibid.* iv. 2. 2 *sqq.* ; iii. 5. 21 *sqq.*

not end in the very opposite of what you are aiming at.
Take justice, for instance. The man who has learnt it
by nothing but practice and routine will regard it as
consisting of certain determined modes of action : *e.g.*
never stealing or deceiving another. Deceit is just, when
you are dealing with enemies ; and so is pillage, when
it is the foe you are plundering.[1]

But if art is insufficient unto itself, where can it find
the rule and principle it needs ? Nowhere but in just
ideas on the use of mental qualities, and on the conditions of these very qualities : in a word, it can find
them only in science. The Sophists missed their goal
because they were too eager, and made straight for it,
instead of proceeding along the winding path which
alone could have led them to it. Before laying claim
to skill in practical speech or deed, one must acquire
that theoretical knowledge which alone confers general
ability.[2] We are good at the things with which we are
acquainted, and bad at those we know nothing about.[3]
Art implies science : a thing the Sophists did not see.

Such were the views of Socrates regarding physics
and sophistic. One judgment was the reverse of the
other. He blamed the physiologists for not having
that sense of human affairs which he praised the
Sophists for possessing : he blamed the Sophists for
being without that conception of science which he
found in the physiologists. The latter had applied the
form of science to something that goes beyond it: the
Sophists had omitted to apply it to the thing that requires and admits of it. Physics was science isolated
from art and practical life, losing itself in empty speculations; sophistic was art isolated from science and so
reduced to dangerous routine.

[1] *Mem.* iv. 2. 14 *sqq.*   [2] *Ibid.* iv. 3. 1 ; iii. 9. 4.   [3] *Laches,* 194 D.

Such an appreciation of physics and sophistic naturally led Socrates to collect and combine the principles which to him appeared viable in each of these two disciplines, *i.e.* scientific form, on the one hand, and exclusive preoccupation about human things, on the other. By applying to the object of sophistic the scientific form invented by the physiologists, there would be established a wisdom as useful as art and as universal and communicable as science, capable of moulding man and influencing his morals, capable also of being self-sufficient and defending itself against objections, in a word, proportioned to the forces and the needs of human nature.

This idea of a union of science and art is the very germ of Socratic philosophy. Socrates does not first cultivate science and art separately, and make them serve each other afterwards. To his mind, each strays from the path whenever it claims to be journeying alone. In their close co-operation, their mutual penetration, lies the condition of their existence and success.

Here we find determined the general object of Socrates' investigations. This object is the domain he clearly discerned and circumscribed between things divine and the mechanical arts, *i.e.* human nature in whatever it offers of a general and definable character ;[1] it is real and substantial human happiness, as distinct from imaginary, fragile and delusive happiness ;[2] it is the art of using men and human things well, not only under certain circumstances and by chance, but with certainty and under all circumstances ;[3] in a word, it is all that is necessary and sufficient for the making of an honest man.

Such was his idea when he went about repeating the Apollonian maxim : Γνῶθι σαυτόν. According to

---

[1] *Mem.* i. 1. 16.   [2] *Apol.* 36 D.   [3] *Mem.* iv. 1. 2.

Socrates to know oneself was not simply to be conscious, under all circumstances, of what one is or is not,
capable. It meant entering deep into one's own soul,
beyond the particular and the fleeting, to find the one
identical, permanent substratum. It meant finding that
secret nature we carry about everywhere with us, and
which contains within itself the conditions of our wisdom
and happiness far more than do external things. In a
word, the Socratic maxim is an exhortation to become
conscious of whatever in us is general.

Socrates does not consider the Γνῶθι σαυτόν as simply
the first step in the search after the whole of truth. He
does not mean that knowledge of self is the condition of
attaining to all other knowledge, and that once it is
acquired we shall be in a position to enter upon the
search for all the rest. The Γνῶθι σαυτόν is the end
as well as the beginning of science ; there can be no
other science for man to acquire than that of himself.

True, we read in the *Phaedrus* of Plato [1] that Socrates
regards it as ridiculous to trouble about other things,
when one is still ignorant of oneself ; this passage would
seem to indicate that Socrates merely postpones physical
and theological research, not that he rejects it. Here,
however, he is speaking ironically. To his mind, the
time will never come for taking up the science of
universal being, because man will never know himself
completely. Probably no one, before the time of Socrates,
was as conscious as he was of the infinite complexity and
the unfathomable profundity of man's moral nature, as
we see from the passage just quoted in the *Phaedrus* :
" I am trying to find out," he says, " whether I am
more complicated and wicked than the serpent Typhon,
or if I am of a simple nature, participating in divinity."

[1] 229 E.

How could Socrates recognise research—even so far as to postpone it—which had not man for its object ? Apart from human things, there are none but physical or divine things and the mechanical arts. Now, the former are beyond man's reach,[1] and the rest, such as the art of the shoemaker, the carpenter, the wrestler, and the pancratiast, are practised very well by special men, without the aid of theoretical science.[2]

Moreover, wisdom, when thus restricted to man, is that which is of the greatest interest to him. Indeed, what most dignifies human nature if it be not freedom, independence with regard to other men and external matters, and the possession of everything necessary for good conduct and happiness ? Now, what kind of occupation is capable of conferring on us this divine independence ? Not the mechanical arts, subjected to the needs of the body ; not advanced astronomy and geometry, difficult and useless sciences, whose object is quite foreign to the human soul.[3] Close investigation will reveal to us the fact that, under all circumstances, it is one and the same thing that makes man dependent and a slave, to wit, ignorance of real good and evil, ignorance of himself.[4] Therefore, what is to set man free and enable him to be sufficient unto himself, under all circumstances,[5] is science, not any particular science, but the knowledge of what we are and of what tallies with our nature.

Thus, Socrates regards the science of human things as the object most worthy of man's powers. Great is the distance, however, between the idea of such a science and its realisation. The scientific form, as we find it in ancient physiology, is not adapted to things dealing with

[1] *Mem.* iv. 7. 6.   [2] *Ibid.* iii. 5. 21 ; iv. 2. 12.
[3] *Ibid.* iv. 7. 2.   [4] *Ibid.* iv. 2. 22-23 ; i. 1 16.   [5] *Ibid.* iv. 7 1.

the moral life, nor does art, as the Sophists conceived it, lend itself to scientific development. For the physicists science consisted in knowing the generation of things, in being able to say whether there is only one substance or several, whether everything is immovable or in motion. How can these categories be applied to intellectual and moral things? On the other hand, for the Sophists there is nothing fixed or universal in human nature, good and happiness are entirely relative to individuals. Human things offer for our study only an infinite number of particular cases unconnected with one another. How can such material be an object of science?

The idea, then, of a moral science such as Socrates had conceived it, called forth a double task. On the one hand, the idea of science had to be elaborated so that it might be adapted to moral things ; on the other, moral things had to be looked upon from such a bias, so to speak, as to make them appear fit to become objects of science. A mould suited to the matter had to be made, and the matter rendered capable of flowing into the mould. The mind of Socrates was directed to the solution of this double problem. The results of his reflections on both points may be grouped together under the terms *dialectic* and *ethic*. Still, we must not attribute to Socrates a dialectic and an ethic distinct from each other. The characteristic of his dialectic is that it is built up with a view to his ethic, and the characteristic of his ethic is that it is the working out of his dialectic. They are only two phases of one and the same discipline : the more or less artificial duplication of the " Moral Science."

In this sense, in what do the dialectic and ethic of Socrates consist ? In the details of his philosophy shall we find those characteristics that seem to us to have indicated his general conception of human wisdom ?

III

Both Zeller and Schleiermacher maintain that Socrates, far from being a merely popular moralist, does not limit himself to moral philosophy : he follows after true science, the science of the essence of things. First of all, he forms a universal conception of science, regarding it as consisting of the methodical determination of the concept or the expression of the general element of the things given. Then, in accordance with the law of the human mind, he applies this universal form to the particular incomplete object with which experience supplies him. This object happens to be human life. The subsequent task of the Socratics consists in applying this very form to the other domains of reality.[1]

According to this interpretation, the Socratic theory of science would appear to have a distinct existence. Logically, if not chronologically, it would seem to be anterior to and independent of the Socratic ethic ; a system of symbols which the philosopher had created from quite an abstract point of view, and without considering the peculiar nature of the things he had undertaken to investigate.

It cannot be denied but that this interpretation accords with the destiny of Socratic philosophy. Indeed, we find Plato and Aristotle applying to the whole study of nature a method analogous to the one employed by Socrates in the investigation of moral questions.

---

[1] Schleiermacher, *Werke*, iii. 2, p. 300 *sqq.* ; Zeller, *Phil. d. Gr.* 3rd edition, vol. ii. 93 *sqq.*

But does an interpretation need only to be in
agreement with the historical fortune of a philosophy
for us to regard it as the faithful expression of the
thought of the philosopher himself? To find out what
a thing is in its true nature by what it subsequently
becomes is a method dear to Hegelians. Indeed,
to their mind, creation is being itself. It does not
seem, however, to be without reason that Pascal said :
"Sometimes the self-same thoughts develop quite
differently in others from the way in which they
develop in their author." How many principles
expand or shrink, become modified or transformed,
when they pass from one mind to another which
examines them from its own point of view ! We
could not say with Schleiermacher and the Hegelians :
" To know what Socrates was, we must above all find
out how Plato came to regard him as his master."
For Plato may have applied the Socratic method to
objects for which it was not meant.

Now, if we consider the main elements of this
method, one by one, we shall find that, in the form
in which they appear in Socrates' speeches, they can
be explained only by a continual preoccupation upon
the moral object to which they are to be applied. We
shall not find Socrates determining the idea of science
for itself, and afterwards applying it to morals. Science,
he imagines, can be separated from morals only in a
totally abstract manner, in language, if you will, never
in the nature of things. In a word, we shall find
Socrates stating the logical problem in the following
terms : of what should science consist, in order that
virtue and happiness may become objects of science ?

First of all, the criterion of science, in the mind of

Socrates, is agreement with itself, and the power to get accepted infallibly by all, what one thinks he knows.[1] Socrates does not show himself anxious to confront philosophical doctrines with the nature of things as this nature is capable of existing in itself, independently of the conceptions of the human mind. According to him, the necessary and all-sufficient condition of certainty lies in the double agreement of man with himself and with the rest of mankind ; in other words, in the agreement of the human mind with itself.

Now, this principle, new to philosophy, would indeed be strange were the knowledge of being and of the universal principles of nature the object of philosophy. In that case, if we would understand Socrates' doctrine, we should have to infer that he was already identifying human thought with the principle of being in general. But such identification was possible only when several regions had been distinguished in the human mind, and the existence of an eternal reason had therein been found. Such an analysis was the distinctive work of Plato and Aristotle. Socrates, for his part, clearly distinguishes opinion from reasoning, but he goes no farther ; he considers that our power of reasoning cannot claim to know the first principles and final ends of things.

On the other hand, it may well be understood that the agreement of the human mind with itself should be looked upon as the criterium of truth, if we are dealing only with truth in moral affairs. For it is quite natural to admit that, innate in the human mind, there is the general idea of what is suitable for man, and that this intellectual substratum is the same in all individuals. It is this that is called common sense, a sure guide so

---

[1] *Alcibiades I.* iii. D-E ; *Mem.* iv. 6. 1 and 15.

long as we are concerned with the conduct of life, but pregnant with error when dealing with the knowledge of the laws of the universe.

Now, to what object must one apply oneself to realise that agreement with oneself and the rest of the world which forms the condition of certainty? In other words, what is the matter proper to science?

Here we find what constitutes the essence of the logical doctrine of Socrates, that original and fruitful principle which was to remain the guide of the human mind for two thousand years. Science, asserted Socrates, has for its object that which is *general*. There is no science of the individual, of the accidental, of particular things as they are presented to us. The object of the science of courage, for instance, is not courageous deeds, it is that which is common to all courageous deeds, it is the answer to the question : τί ἐστιν ἡ ἀνδρεία ; it is, as Plato says later on,[1] τὸ διὰ πάντων περὶ ἀνδρείας πεφυκός.[2]

This maxim is the very one advanced to prove that Socrates considered science in itself, apart from the matter to which it must be applied. But though it is true that the maxim of Socrates became after his time a logical and even metaphysical doctrine superior to any particular domain, it does not therefore follow that it was so to himself. This will be evident if, instead of considering it separately, it is replaced in the *ensemble* of the Socratic philosophy.

The whole work of Xenophon[3] clearly shows that Socrates never sought the general except in human things.

Consequently the matter at issue has less bearing on the question of fact than on that of right.

---

[1] See *Mem.* i. 1. 16.   [2] *Laches,* 192 B.
[3] See principally *Mem.* i. 1. 16.

What was it that Socrates meant by the general, and why did he see in it the only object that admitted of scientific knowledge ?

By the general, Socrates did not mean the simple permanent element which may lie hidden in the compound things that strike our senses. In reality, that is not the general ; it is rather substance, that is to say, the very object which physicists had considered and which Socrates regards as inaccessible. On the other hand, the general is not yet to him what it will be to Plato and Aristotle : the normal type of a species, the natural being as it would be if the cause peculiar to it were acting alone without being opposed, as happens in the sensible world, by outer influences. The general, of which Socrates speaks, is not related to the material world, nor even to an intelligible world : strictly speaking, it is the common substratum of men's speeches and actions. Socrates starts with the idea that the reason we use one and the same word, justice, to designate quite different modes of action, such as doing good to one's friends and doing evil to one's enemies, lies in the fact that we have in mind a certain notion which is single in its nature, and the object of which we find in the various actions we designate as just. And as men, when they talk to one another in good faith, come sooner or later to agree as to the use of their words, the ideas represented by these words are bound to be identical in the minds of all.

And now, why does Socrates make the general, thus understood, the proper object of science ?

Because he finds in it the necessary and sufficient condition of that agreement with oneself and others which, in his mind, is the mark of knowledge.

Apart from these determined, fixed notions, which

form the foundations of words, there is no guiding-mark for the mind in its reasonings, and therefore no means of coming to an understanding with oneself and others. On the other hand, it is sufficient to make one's discourse conform to those general notions on which all men are agreed, to be sure of obtaining the assent of one's interlocutors. Why does Homer call Ulysses an orator sure of success? Because Ulysses, in his discourse, is guided by ideas which all men accept : διὰ τῶν δοκούντων ἀνθρώποις.[1]

Francis Bacon, the modern legislator of the sciences of nature, said, not without reason, that from human language one can deduce only words, not things, if we would know the nature of the external world ; but human language is certainly the first testimony that must be consulted if it is desired to become acquainted with the thoughts and wishes of the human mind. There is nothing to indicate that the categories of language reproduce those of things ; but it is evident they are an image of the categories of our thoughts and actions. The discourse of men can supply the physicist only with an altogether provisional *ensemble* of signs and conjectures. Such language, when dealing with moral philosophy, is the very thing we have to fathom.

If we now consider in detail the method of Socrates, we find that it consists of two parts which may be designated by the names of exterior form and logical substratum. The former consists of dialogue along with certain features peculiar to Socrates, such as irony and maieutics, as well as the leading *rôle* assigned to self-possession and love. Logical substratum consists

---

[1] *Mem.* iv. 6. 15.

of definition and induction.   Each of these parts, according to Socrates, has a special aspect.

Zeller says that the reason Socrates makes use of the dialogue form is that he is conscious of his own ignorance, because of the contradictions he finds in the various systems of philosophy, and that it is his desire to escape from this state of ignorance.   Hence, according to Zeller, his disposition to appeal to others, with the object of discovering if perchance they are in possession of the very science he lacks.

This explanation is not altogether satisfactory.   In the first place, Socrates does not consult his interlocutors on things in general, but only on what concerns mankind : he expects to learn nothing from the dialogue form—any more than from any other method of investigation—about physical things.   Then, too, Socrates does not see in the dialogue form merely a convenient and suggestive method of philosophising ; to his mind dialectic cannot be distinguished from wisdom itself.

Though investigation into the causes of the world is a matter of solitary speculation, it is not the same with investigation into the conditions of human life.   How can man be known, except by conversing with men ? And if science consists in discovering the points on which all men are agreed, and which form the substratum of all their judgments (τὰ μάλιστα ὁμολογούμενα), what shorter and more certain method can one have than to bring together men's opinions and compare them with one another ?   In a word, if science must be used for instructing men and persuading them of things of which we have become certain, once for all, is not methodical conversation, from its beginning right on to its end, an integral part of philosophy and wisdom ?

Consequently, it is not from modesty, from deference to the science of others, that Socrates constantly speaks of examining things in common, κοινῇ βουλεύεσθαι,[1] κοινῇ σκέπτεσθαι, κοινῇ ζητεῖν, συζητεῖν : this form of investigation is implied in the very object he has in view. For a dissertation on the principles of nature, writing is sufficient ; but to know men and succeed in convincing them, one must converse with them.

Socratic dialogue frequently assumes the form of irony. Socrates puts his questions without ever answering them,[2] and thus brings his interlocutor either to the point of contradicting himself or coming to a dead stop, and acknowledging his ignorance of the very things he thought he knew.[3]

Now, the use of such a method is far more comprehensible when dealing with the knowledge of human things than when dealing with that of nature. How, when dealing with external things, can a man confine himself to questioning others without bringing their assertions face to face with reality itself ? In order profitably to undertake such questioning, would not a man need previously to have shown himself competent in both physics and metaphysics ? And again, would not the listeners also need to be specially competent if their judgment on the discussion is to be of any value ? But when dealing with human things, every one is competent, for he bears within himself just the touchstone needed for the testing of opinions. In conversation itself, the questioner may find all that is needed for proving that his interlocutor is not only in flagrant contradiction with himself, but with the very nature of things as well. Moreover, is it not especially such human qualities as

---

[1] *Mem.* iv. 5. 12. [2] Arist. *Soph. el.* ch. xxxiii.
[3] Plat. *Repub.* i. 337 A E ; *Sophistes*, 183 B.

piety and justice, courage and virtue, with whose nature every man thinks he is acquainted, though really such is not the case? The physiologists would not have accepted the contest to which Socrates invited his interlocutors. Only such men as were occupied in moral affairs could submit to such a mode of questioning : only they, in fact, did so.

It is the same with maieutics. Socrates would have us think that he is barren as regards wisdom ; but by his questions he helps others to bring to birth what they bear in their own mind, and that unconsciously. Then, after thus eliciting the secret ideas of his interlocutors, he carefully examines whether the offspring of their soul is nothing but fancy, or fruit that is real and capable of living.[1] What must we think of such a method?

Socrates, we are told, considers himself barren as regards wisdom. What kind of wisdom is here meant, if not practical wisdom, which indeed has the strange characteristic of being, in one aspect, incapable of communication, of existing within us only if it is ourself, of being produced within our person only if it springs forth from our own inmost nature ?

How is Socrates able to generate, in the minds of his interlocutors, ideas likely to be true and capable of living? This doctrine is a very strange one, if we are dealing with physical or metaphysical truths. That audacious doctrine which identifies the mind of man with the principle of things is nowhere to be found in Socrates : if it happens that he predicts the future[2] it is not by the might of his intelligence alone, but owing to a mysterious and quite supernatural revelation. Maieutics, however, is a very reasonable and legitimate method, if our object is to bring moral truths before

---

[1] *Theaet.* 149, 157 C. [2] *Mem.* i. 1. 5.

men, for these truths are nothing but the expression
and reflective knowledge of human nature : and human
nature is what every man has within himself. The
fiction of *Meno* is a Platonic and paradoxical extension
of Socratic maieutics. Socrates, for his part, elicits
from the minds of his listeners only knowledge that
relates to piety, justice, temperance, courage, urban
government, and everything that goes to make up an
honourable man.[1]

Finally, how can Socrates, who professes to be ignorant, rightly estimate the true value of the fruit which
he assists human intelligence in bringing forth ? Are
we not here dealing exclusively with those moral and
practical ideas upon which every man, in his human
capacity, is competent, when in forming his judgments
he imposes silence on his distinctive tastes and passions
and puts himself just at that point of view, superior to
the individual, which Socrates had defined ?

Dialectic, besides, possesses two very remarkable
moral conditions : self-possession and love : ἐγκράτεια
and ἔρως.

" To those who are self-possessed, and to them only,
is it given to investigate the best in everything, and,
distinguishing things by a dialectic of actions and words,
according as they belong to the good or the evil, to
choose the one and abstain from the other." [2] It is
because dialectic has for its object the determination of
the value of things, from the moral and human point
of view, that self-possession is its essential condition.
Indeed, the true moral value of things lies in the interest
they offer to human nature in general, not to the individual, regarded from the standpoint of his tastes and
passions, which are superficial and fleeting. Now, it is

[1] *Mem.* i. 1. 16.   [2] *Ibid.* iv. 5. 11.

owing to self-control that man, in his judgments, lays his individual and accidental preferences on one side.

And finally, love, ἔρως, plays an important part in the dialectic of Socrates. The same may be said regarding all the Socratics. Not only Xenophon and Plato, but also Euclid, Crito, Simmias and Antisthenes, have written on the subject of love. What is the love that is here meant? Doubtless Socrates does not mean friendship, pure and simple, but rather affection mingled with sense attraction. It is a kind of spiritual ardour that enters the whole man, causing in him an emotion that has nothing to do with mere friendship. Evidently Socrates disparages physical love, though not in all its elements. He retains its soul-uplifting charm, which is lacking when the intelligence alone is at play. He keeps, one might say, its vital impulse, if not its object.[1]

This love, moreover, could not go to the point of passion and frenzy, like the love of which Plato speaks in *Phaedrus*. Even here self-possession is still a superior, inviolable duty. The Platonic distinction between good and evil frenzy would have been rejected by Socrates, to whom all frenzy is slavery.

How is the rule that governs such a mental state to be explained?

Certainly Socrates does not dream of investing love with the *rôle* that Plato assigns to it, and which consists in introducing us into the world of beauty, as into the vestibule, as it were, of divine, transcendent truth. In order that love might appear as endowed with such power, it would have to be a state of rapture and ecstasy, whereas Socratic love is inseparable from self-possession. Already Socrates condemns poets for writing poetry

[1] Xen. *Banquet*, ch. viii.

not by science but by enthusiasm, a kind of divine inspiration.[1] With all the more reason would he have condemned as sacrilegious the claim that the secrets the gods have removed from our mental grasp could be reached in a state of frenzy.

In investigations upon human things there is room for a kind of love which combines sense attraction and self-possession. In accordance with the principle of maieutics, the soul must bring forth its wisdom from itself, just as the body brings forth from itself the fruit to which it gives birth. Therefore the soul, as well as the body, must be impregnated. Love here intervenes for the purpose of playing a part similar to that it plays in physical procreation. Intelligences impregnate each other, as bodies do. By the influence of noble love the soul becomes big with noble thoughts and feelings. " Orestes and Pylades, Theseus and Pirithous, and several other demi-gods are famous . . . because, admiring one another, they performed together the most glorious deeds." [2] Moreover, it was a familiar idea amongst the Greeks that the mutual love of youths exalted their courage, and made them capable of mighty actions.

And so we find that dialogue, irony, maieutics, self-possession and love, all of which are elements of the Socratic method, if regarded not as abstract formulas but rather in their historical aspect, testify to a reflective and exclusive preoccupation to establish the science of morals. But, so far, these are nothing but the externals of the method. What must we think of that which constitutes their basis, to wit, of the process of refutation which, in some way, makes up the negative method, and of the processes of definition and induction

---

[1] Plat. *Apol.* 22 B-C.   [2] Xen. *Banquet*, ch. viii.

of which the positive method consists? Does it not appear that here, at all events, we have to do with instruments that are really of universal importance, and with conditions, not merely of the science of morals, but of science in general, whatever be its object?

Of what does the Socratic refutation consist? Socrates begins by eliciting or drawing forth from the problem in question the very datum he presupposes.[1] For instance, if he is told that any one man is a better citizen than another, he asks his interlocutor what, in his mind, constitutes a good citizen. When the other man has replied, Socrates asks him additional questions, dealing with cases to which the term " good citizen " is generally applied. By this method he makes him give answers that are incompatible with the original reply : the result being that the definition put forward was either too restricted or too wide, or defective in some other way.[2]

Socrates applies this method of refutation to the judgments either of ordinary men, politicians, poets and artists of renown,[3] professors of eloquence and virtue, or of sophists ; in a word, he applies it to all ideas that deal with morals ; but we do not find that he made use of it to refute physical or metaphysical doctrines. As regards the latter, he contents himself with emphasising the contradiction that prevails between the various ideas of philosophers.

Naturally, the Socratic method of refutation may be employed under all circumstances, but its most legitimate use is in regard to morals. If we carefully notice, we find that Socrates bases the truth of any given particular asser-

---

[1] *Mem.* iv. 6. 13 : ἐπὶ τὴν ὑπόθεσιν ἐπανῆγεν ἂν πάντα τὸν λόγον.

[2] For instance, *Mem.* iv. 2 : Conversation between Socrates and Euthydemus.

[3] *Apol.* ch. vi. to viii.

tion on knowledge of the general principle relating to that assertion. Now, such a method is incomprehensible, if we are dealing with the order of physical realities, where the particular is given before the general. Is it conceivable that, when affirming we see the sun turning round the earth, we should be interrupted and asked whether, before expressing ourselves in this way, we have assured ourselves that we know what sight and movement are ? All philosophies—even ancient philosophy—have necessarily subordinated knowledge of the principles of physics to the facts and appearances that have to be explained, not the existence of facts or appearances to a knowledge of the principles. In the moral order of things, however, the particular is not "given" : it is to be sought for. Aristides is not "given" to me as a virtuous man : I ask myself if I ought to declare him to be so. The conduct I should observe if I would practise piety is not "given" : it is to come, it is only possible. And how can it be determined except by starting from the general idea of piety? Socrates is therefore right in subordinating the truth of particular judgments to the knowledge of the general, if he is specially considering the moral domain ; for here the particular is nothing more than we make it ; and we make it of such or such a nature only by virtue of the ideas inherent in our own mind. Now, universal principles exist in most men only under the form of habits or blind instincts ; hence the principitancy and inconsistency noticed in their judgments. It is the very object of the method of Socrates to substitute deliberate, resolute maxims for these blind, wavering opinions.

But we have not yet entered upon the two Socratic processes, which, more than all others, appear to be of universal, theoretical application : definition and induction ; [1] definition, the supreme object of dialectic ; induction, the methodical march leading to definition.

Definition is the adequate expression of that general essence which is the object of science. The Socratic definition possesses this in particular : it does not confine itself to offering a distinctive sign of things ; it claims to set forth the necessary and all - sufficient condition of their existence. It not only states what the thing is, seen from without, it even tries to discover what is capable of producing it. For instance, to call a just man the one who does just things is not to define him. It is possible to do just things by chance, not by justice; and one may be just without manifesting justice within oneself. On the other hand, to say that the just man is he who knows what the laws ordain with reference to men, is to offer a true definition. For we do not find that men ever do anything else than what they think they ought to do, and those who know justice will necessarily do just things under all circumstances.[2] They have within themselves the universal capacity for justice.

Thus the Socratic definition consists of the declaration of the inner capacity, of which the thing to be defined is the outer manifestation.

Now, where, in the first place, is this distinction between the concrete, particular thing and the invisible, general power to be found, if not in man? And does not this search after a metaphysical essence—justified, if we are dealing with the human soul, by consciousness itself—become extremely rash and dangerous if we claim to practise it with regard to the outer phenomena of nature.

---

[1] Arist. *Met.* xiii. 4. 1078 b 25.   [2] *Mem.* iv. 6. 6.

Why, too, does Socrates regard the capacity, or total principle of the action as reposing in an idea, in the knowledge, pure and simple, of the conditions of action, leaving aside the force necessary to realise it? The reason is that, in man, force or activity is ever present, and is always determined conformably with knowledge. Such, at all events, is the opinion of Socrates regarding will. Will is, as it were, a constant datum which it is practically needless to mention. It would not be so were we dealing with the production of physical phenomena, for in the latter case the nature of the generating causes and their mode of action are unknown and inaccessible.

To arrive at definition, thus regarded, the method Socrates uses is induction. This operation consists of two parts, which may be called invention and discussion.

To discover the general essence, Socrates takes as his starting-point a certain number of instances of the thing to be defined. These instances, however, do not consist of natural facts, directly observed : Socrates takes them exclusively from human discourse. Language, opinions, ordinary judgments or even nature seen through man : such is the material of which his induction is formed, such the ground in which it must germinate. From the outset Socrates interests himself preferably in the feelings of men regarding paltry matters and commonplace pursuits.[1] Initiation into the lesser mysteries, he says, must precede initiation into the greater. This is the reason he is constantly speaking of shoemakers and smiths, carpenters and drovers : a reproach brought against him by his enemies.[2]

To observation, as thus understood, Socrates adds

---

[1] *Gorgias*, ch. li. p. 497 B-C.   [2] *Mem.* i. 2. 37.

analogy. He appeals to things his interlocutor knows; and, showing him the resemblance between these things and those that form the subject of conversation, he draws him on to the discovery that even the latter were not really unknown to him.[1] What, for instance, constitutes a just man? We know that a carpenter is a man who knows carpentry ; a musician is one who knows music ; a doctor, one who knows medicine. Our conclusion, by analogy, will be that the just man is the man who knows justice.[2] The usual and, as it were, essential theme of these analogies consists in the transition from mechanical, special arts to moral and general art ; in a word, the transition from things of the body to those of the soul.

Still, observation and analogy give only provisional results : discussion alone affords decisive ones. Having once invented a general formula by means of carefully chosen cases, Socrates considers the greatest possible number of cases and applies his formula to all these instances, retaining it unmodified if it emerges successfully from the test, and suitably modifying it if it does not. Not only does he vary, he even reverses the experiment, trying to find a definition for the contrary object, and ascertaining whether this new definition is to the former what negation is to affirmation.

Such is Socratic induction. Now, all the details of this process are applicable to human things, whereas they are inapplicable to physical or metaphysical things.

To take as one's starting-point the language and discourse of ordinary life, and not external facts, is a method that may rightly be regarded as meaningless and fantastic if our object is to know the absolute essence of being and of things ; but it is a very natural

---

[1] Xen. *Economicus,* 19. 15.   [2] *Gorgias,* 460 B.

and legitimate method if our object is to find out what lies at the bottom of human judgments. It is also quite conceivable that the philosopher should bestow particular attention upon common and ordinary things, if his express purpose is to know man, for it is in this order of things that human nature appears as it really is, stripped of the mask of convention and false knowledge.

The complaisant use of the method of analogy and the fact that this mode of reasoning is regarded as proof, would indicate anything but a scientific mind if one's investigation were compelled to cover every domain of reality. But if we are to move in one and the same domain only, and that the domain of human things, then analogy is a useful method to follow. For then, its action is limited to passing from one species to another in the same genus, and that, too, in the order of things most familiar to us, in which we need only retire within ourselves to find points of reference at each step.

In short, the Socratic process of discussion and control is a very uncertain and inadequate method, if we would have knowledge of the things of nature. Socrates endeavours to verify his induction by examining every instance that offers itself. But how can one gather together all the instances of one and the same genus in the order of physical and material things? How can we call up at will the manifestations of the essence contrary to the one whose definition we are seeking? Doubtless modern experimentation must have realised these conditions to some extent; but the ancients had no idea whatever of such a method of investigation. On the other hand, they must have thought that, in human things, the conditions in question were quite realisable. Though it is foolish to claim to know all the different cases in which cold and heat, generation and destruction may be met with, it would seem easier to set forth a complete list of such actions as we call just and of those we call unjust. The number of names representing these actions is limited and they are all at the disposal of man, for they are his work. This possibility of comprehending the entire domain of moral things must, above all, have been recognised in a nation where the conditions of human life were relatively simple, where the totality of human duties naturally clustered round a few precise, concordant ideas, and there was entire ignorance of those conflicts between the individual and society, conscience and public interests, family and country, country and humanity, physical comfort and lofty culture, that have introduced inextricable confusion into the moral life of modern nations.

The logical method of Socrates is limited to induction and definition as thus understood. Aristotle finds fault with this dialectic, which is carried on exclusively by a process of questioning, because it pins its faith to common opinion, and goes no farther than probability. His appeal is to special, direct intuition, the indispensable condition of a complete, infallible demonstration. Aristotle's reproach is comprehensible, if our object is to go back to the first principles of all things. But if we have only to find in human nature a rule for human judgment and conduct, to discover and set forth the principles applied by human reason when tranquil and free from routine and passion, with the object of discovering in these principles, which are now objects of clear consciousness, a weapon against routine and passion themselves ; in a word, if we have to set man free by enabling him to know mankind, we can understand why Socrates contented himself with the observation of human phenomena, and made no attempt to pierce, by metaphysical intuition, into the mysteries of absolute thought.

IV

Thus we see that the nature and import of the Socratic method are in exact proportion to the object Socrates had in view, which was nothing less than the constitution of ethics as a science. Conversely, the concrete doctrine of Socrates, his conclusions on things and on man himself are exactly what might have been expected from the use of such a method. Matter responds to form as form responds to matter.

It may seem, if we cast a general glance at the teaching of Socrates, that the science of which it consists does indeed go beyond the limits marked out by his method, and, in a sense, includes not only human but also physical and divine things.

Is not his reason for throwing overboard the mechanistic physics of the ancient philosophers, that he wishes to substitute therefor a teleological system of physics ?[1] Though he condemns cosmological theology, the investigation into the way in which the gods formed the universe, does he not extol what may be called moral theology in his endeavour to demonstrate the existence of a divine intelligence and providence? The considerable importance given, in the *Memorabilia*, to speculations of this kind, the originality of Socrates' views on these matters, have induced several critics to regard them not only as significant parts of his

[1] *Mem.* i. 4, iv. 3.

E

philosophy, but even as its very centre and ground-work. Thus, to Fouillée, Socrates is essentially the promoter of a system of teleological metaphysics, whereas to Franck[1] he is above all else a theological philosopher.

But in order to discover if teleology and moral theology form an integral part of the object of science according to Socrates, it is not sufficient to examine and see whether Socrates advanced profound ideas on these subjects or not. We must also ask ourselves what relation these ideas bear to the fundamental principles of his philosophy.

Now, one can, it would appear, divide the teleological and the theological ideas of Socrates into two parts ; the one overstepping the limits of ethics, though at the same time offered us as the fruit of supernatural inspiration superior to science ; the other, of a more scientific nature, though connected with ethics as its source and *raison d'être*. When Socrates speaks of his daemonic sign and of the power it sometimes affords him of foreseeing the future ;[2] when he speaks of the divinity that is not far from each one of us and is ready to utter a warning call to the man who listens in silence ; when he declares that to fear death is to believe oneself wise without really being so, for it is to believe that one knows what one does not know,[3] he is evidently speaking of those things which, as they are beyond our power to control, are also beyond the reach of our science.[4]

When, on the contrary, he deals with physical and divine things in a scientific method, we see him pre-occupied about considering things, not in themselves,

---

[1] *Journal des Savants*, October 1881.

[2] *Mem.* i. 1. 3-5.   [3] *Apol.* 29 A.   [4] *Mem.* i. 1. 9.

but from without and with reference to man. Thus, he constantly tends to substitute for the gods the daemons, who are nearer to ourselves, and for the daemons the mere daemonic phenomena or visible signs of the gods, perceived directly by man.[1] He believes that we cannot see the gods ; that we see nothing but their manifestations to us.[2] The order and harmony the gods have introduced into things consists in the appropriation of these things to our needs.[3] In this way, physical or teleological objects are brought within the compass of moral and human ones.

These conjectures on the adaptation of the outer nature to the needs of man, besides the fact that, in the case of Socrates, they spring naturally from a very sincere and deep religious sentiment, are called for, or required, by his ethical doctrine, in accordance with which the happiness of man depends on himself, on nothing whatever but self-knowledge. Since, in spite of his efforts to suffice unto himself, man cannot free himself from physical nature, he must admit, if he claims to be good and happy without occupying himself with externals, that the gods are occupied with them on his behalf, and control them so as to meet his needs. Teleology and the doctrine of providence were the necessary postulates of Socratic morals.

This very *rôle* shows us that they are complementary, not essential parts, of the philosophy of Socrates.

The proper object of this philosophy, not only in theory but in fact, is the one that the Sophists had brought into credit ; that is, art, or practical skill, understood, however, in an original manner, which we have now thoroughly to investigate.

Art, in the mind of Socrates, is not the search after

[1] *Apol.* 27 B, E.   [2] *Mem.* iv. 3. 13.   [3] *Ibid.* iv. 3. 1, 4.

absolute good, the power to regulate our actions by
the whole of the consequences which must result therefrom, so as to perform only those whose consequences,
even the most far-reaching, are in conformity with our
wishes. The gods have reserved to themselves the
knowledge of the final result of our actions. Does the
man who plants an orchard know who will gather the
fruit thereof? Does he who builds a house know who
will dwell in it?[1]

On the other hand, however, art worthy of the
name resembles no special profession such as that of
the carpenter, the shoemaker, or the armourer. These
men have in mind the realisation of some particular
material object; whereas art pursues a general, immaterial end, viz. the happiness and good of man.
This is what the Sophists had already taught, and
rightly taught. But though they had the idea of what
may be called the moral end, they were mistaken as to
the manner of attaining to it. They imagined this
could be effected by regular practice, similar to that
which proves successful in special professions. But,
even in these latter, regularity or routine is far from
being sufficient. Every good artisan possesses not only
the practice but also the science of his trade, in so far
as his trade is capable of being an object of science. A
well-drawn analogy will lead us to think that moral art
also must be a science, according to the acceptation of
this word in the moral domain.

To sum up, moral art, occupying a position midway
between religion and the special professions, art which
has for its aim the present good and happiness of man,
and for its province the science of human things : such
is the object of Socrates' reflections.

[1] *Mem.* i. i. 8.

It is this object that exactly answers to his idea of science. Science tries to discover that which is general, and which forms the material for the discourse of men ; *i.e.* the categories in which they place particular things. But is it not in moral things that we find a perfect instance of that relation of genus to species, of principle to application, of latent to manifest knowledge, which such an idea of science implies? Moral things do not contain within themselves the absolute, the one in itself, the supreme principle of being and knowing ; but then, Socratic science does not aim so high as that. On the other hand, however, and in contradistinction to the opinion of the Sophists, in human nature itself there are certainly fixed, solid points, which enable one to gain a satisfactory science of the general.

Moreover, is it not moral things that form the usual matter of human discourse ? Is it not on these questions that each man has acquired experience and is capable of advancing an opinion worthy of consideration? If so, then it is along this line that there will be the best chance of success for a science that seeks its various elements in the discourse of men, even of the humblest and most ignorant.

When considered with a view to the knowledge of moral principles the Socratic method thus reacts on the conception of moral things themselves. In the light of the idea of science, Socrates found in human nature that substratum of common and invariable notions that had escaped the notice of the Sophists ; thereupon, everything human was invested with new dignity in the mind of the philosopher.

This reaction of method on object appears no less clearly in the details of Socratic morals.

Here two essential parts may be distinguished : 1st,

the general principle : all virtues are sciences ;[1] 2nd, the deduction of the virtues, which deduction is supplied by this principle.

In what sense did Socrates claim that all virtues are sciences ?

According to Zeller,[2] the science here in question is evidently science in general, the science of the nature of things. But in none of the texts dealing with our question do we find this abstract expression : science. They all state more or less explicitly: the virtues are sciences.[3]

Consequently, virtue is not identified with science in general, but with some particular science. Now, what is this science ?

Fouillée[4] says that the science of which Socrates speaks is probably the science of good in itself, *i.e.* the science of the real and absolute worth of things.

Such an object, however, would go beyond the end aimed at. When, says Socrates, one is thinking of becoming a good shoemaker, or pilot or musician, the science each man regards as indispensable is that of shoemaking, ship-management or music: that special science alone, in each category, makes the man competent. Now, competency is also what Socrates extols in moral matters. The analogy he is constantly drawing between the special professions and the practice of virtue shows that he places the condition of this new competency not in a universal and necessarily vague science, but in the science of virtue itself. Though Socrates does not agree with the Sophists, who made too close a comparison between moral art and the mechanical

[1] Aristot. *Eth. Nic.* vi. 13. 1144 b 28.   [2] ii. (3rd edit.), 93, 117.
[3] *Mem.* iii. 9. 5, iv. 2. 22, iv. 6-7 ; Aristot. *Eth. Nic.* vi. 13. 1144 b 17.
[4] *La Phil. de Socrate*, i. 177, 281, 285.

arts, he yet does not go so far as to abolish all analogy between these latter arts and the former. Virtue is still a special, determinate art ; just men as well as artisans have their own distinctive work.[1]

Science, thus determined, *i.e.* the special science of virtue, is, according to Socrates, the very definition or essence of science. Socrates means thereby that it is its necessary and all-sufficient condition.

It is the necessary condition of virtue. If competency is necessary in mechanical arts, how can it be superfluous in an art that is surely more delicate and complicated, since it has to work upon things that are invisible, accessible to the understanding alone ? The masses are wrong when they think that nature in moral matters is all-sufficient. In vain did the Sophists substitute practice for nature. He who is ignorant of the definition of good may, by a happy chance, sometimes meet with it, but he will never be certain that he has not altogether passed it by. He will even run the risk of taking evil for good, and *vice versa*. For instance, if one does not possess a definition of justice, one may regard it invariably as unjust to deceive and injure others, whereas it is just to deceive the enemies of the State, and to reduce an unjust nation to a state of subjection.[2] Again, if one is without this definition, one will stop to examine such a question as the following : " Who is the more unjust : the man who wittingly deceives, or the man who unwittingly deceives ? " One will be astonished at finding arguments in support of both positions, whereas, at bottom, the question is an absurd one, since the terms " unjust " and " unwittingly " immediately exclude each other. Science renders certain actions good, which, without it, would be indifferent or even evil ; for

[1] *Mem.* iv. 2. 12.   [2] *Ibid.* iv. 2. 14-15.   [3] *Ibid.* iv. 2. 19.

instance, the use of money. By science and science alone does skill in speech and action become a virtue : this skill, if left to itself, might readily cause men to become more unjust and maleficent than nature made them.[1]

Science is not only necessary, it is all-sufficient for the engendering of virtue. This doctrine is what may be called the Socratic paradox. Perhaps the paradox is not so pronounced as it at first seems.

It would, indeed, be strange for Socrates to attribute such efficacy to science, if we were dealing with a purely theoretical science, or even with the science of good in itself and of the rational value of things. At the outset the objection will be made that such knowledge supplies a law to the intelligence, but that it does not determine the will.

The science, however, of which Socrates speaks, is distinctly the science of the suitability and utility of things from the human point of view ; it is the knowledge of the relation that exists between things, and the end that man follows of his own accord, naturally and of necessity. "In order to be obeyed by my subordinates," said a cavalry officer to Socrates,[2] "will it suffice if I show them that I am their superior ? " "Yes," was the answer, "provided you prove that obedience to you is safer and more beautiful for them than the contrary (κάλλιόν τε καὶ σωτηριώτερον αὐτοῖς)." Socrates reasons in this fashion : it is acknowledged that men invariably do what they believe they ought to do, i.e. what they look upon as most profitable to themselves. If, then, it is demonstrated to them that virtue is most profitable, they will infallibly practise virtue. In a word, our philosopher transfers to the science of

---

[1] Mem. iv. 3. 1. [2] Ibid. iii. 3. 10.

the good the practical efficacy he usually notes in the mere opinion of the good. More than this : the science of the good seems to him as though it must be even more efficacious in determining the human will than the mere opinion of the good can be, because science is immovable, whereas opinion is at the mercy of circumstances.

Fouillée [1] considers that the Socratic paradox consists essentially in the negation of free-will. It rather consists in the claim to demonstrate that virtue is always that which is most advantageous to man.

As regards free-will, Socrates neglects to take it into consideration rather than denies it. And, indeed, free-will is almost useless in a doctrine which only requires man to decide in the way he considers most beautiful and advantageous. This method of determination, according to Socrates, is that of the masses ; it is quite spontaneous, and does not imply the consciousness of being able to determine in favour of the opposite course of action.

True, the objection may be advanced that, for a man to regard as insufficient the mere opinion of good, and try to discover the constituents of real good, he must make an effort which involves the intervention of free-will.

Socrates is far from denying the necessity of such an effort ; though he connects it with self-control and temperance, which latter is itself, in his mind, a science, and the most important of them all.[2] The obligation of self-control and temperance is demonstrated in the same fashion as that of all the other virtues : by its useful effects. It by no means follows that, in acquiring this virtue, the first condition of all the rest, free-will

[1] *La Phil. de Socr.* i. 173.   [2] *Mem.* i. 5. 4.

has no part to play. The negation of free-will might be deduced from the doctrine if Socrates distinctly set up self-control (ἐγκράτεια) between science (σοφία) and temperance (σωφροσύνη) as being a consequence of the former and nothing more, as Fouillée [1] states. Socrates, however, regards self-control as both a condition and a result of science. " Do you not think," he says, " that lack of self-control (ἀκρασία) turns men away from science (σοφία), the greatest of all things, and drives them to its opposite ? " [2] " Only to such as are self-possessed," he says in another place, " is it given to practise dialectic." [3] It is, therefore, no abstract science, but a living science, action and knowledge combined, which is the root of virtue.

Thereby we find clearly determined the relation Socrates sets up between science and practice. He maintains that science engenders virtue to which it plays the part of an efficient cause ; but he also maintains that the search for science has, for its province, the desire to attain to virtue, and thus virtue plays the part of final cause, as regards science. Science is both cause and means, virtue both end and result. Between the two terms there is solidarity, mutual action. It must be granted that such a relationship raises difficulties for him who would understand it thoroughly. Socrates, however, must have found it tolerably clear, at a period when neither the efficient nor the final cause had yet been studied for themselves and no clear line of demarcation drawn between will and intelligence.

Though such is the Socratic doctrine as to the relation between science and virtue, Socrates, doubtless explicitly, went beyond the stand-point of ordinary

---

[1] *La Phil. de Socr.* i. 173.   [2] *Mem.* ix. 5. 6.
[3] *Ibid.* iv. 5. 11.

morals which merely sets forth isolated precepts without connecting them with any principle. He also went beyond that of the ancient sages, as well as of the great writers of his time, who confined themselves to deriving, direct from their own consciousness, maxims that were frequently profound, without attempting to demonstrate them scientifically. He was the first to make science an integral element of morals ; the first to bring action, which appears as individual, within the compass of true knowledge, which is universal.

But this does not mean that he applied to morals the universal idea of science, and not merely that idea of a science of man which appears as the term of his dialectic. Where can Socrates obtain the rational knowledge of good and virtue, which is all that he here means by science, except in the discourse of men, that immediate testimony of their desires, their needs and experience ? What more certain method of giving a practical definition of things, expressing the interest they offer to man, than that of using the analogy and induction which take human facts themselves for their basis, and interpret them in the light of human reason ? Likewise, what science will have most chance of acting upon the will, what science will better merit those bold words of praise : οὐδὲν ἰσχυρότερον φρονήσεως,[1] than that truly living science which Socratic maieutics evolves from our soul, and which is, at bottom, only the consciousness of our own nature ? If care be taken, the details of the doctrine of the relations that exist between virtue and science, coincide, step by step, with the details of dialectic ; in such fashion that, the latter being posited, the former necessarily follows.

Dialectic, sprung from the general and still vague

[1] *Eth. Eud.* vii. 13.

idea of moral science, reacts upon this idea and
determines it.   Moral science is but dialectic in action.

We reach a similar conclusion if we examine the
second part of Socratic morals, to wit, the deduction of
the virtues, supplied by the general principle of morals.

What are the chief maxims of this science of good
which is the necessary and all-sufficient condition of
virtue?

In this connection Socrates distinguishes between
good in general and particular good.

Good in general is the truly useful as distinguished
from the pleasant.[1]   The whole of morals consists in
distinguishing what distinctly constitutes our own good
from what seems to do so, though in reality giving us
only passing pleasure, perhaps even loss.   Why is in-
temperance evil?   Because, says Socrates, it turns man
aside from useful things (ὠφελοῦντα) and inclines him
towards pleasant things (ἡδέα).[2]

Though Socrates makes a broad distinction between
what is good in appearance and what is good in reality,
we do not find that he is thinking of an absolute good,
of which the good of man would seem to be only one
particular manifestation.   He appears to have completely identified the good with the useful,[3] and the
reason he recommends the acquisition of science, the
practice of justice, soul-culture and the attainment of
the loftiest virtues, is that he regards them as useful for
man's happiness.   Even when he prefers death to
shame, the reason he gives is that, in the absence of the
daemonic sign which usually warns him whenever he is
about to do something destined to injure him, he is
convinced death will do him no harm.[4]

<hr />

[1] *Mem.* iv. 6. 8.   [2] *Ibid.* iv. 5. 6.   [3] *Ibid.* iv. 6. 8.
[4] *Apol.* cc. xxix. *sqq.*

Clearly, this doctrine, in the Socratic philosophy, is the reaction of form on matter. Matter was first the vague idea of pleasure and well-being, as found in the reasonings of the Sophists concerning the goal of our actions. Now, science, according to Socrates, is the search after the general. Therefore, when brought into contact with the idea of science, the idea of well-being becomes two-fold, engendering, on the one hand, the idea of pleasure, pure and simple, or a chance, fleeting enjoyment, incapable of becoming an object of science, and, on the other hand, the idea of true utility and happiness, corresponding, in its generality, with the conditions of dialectic. True utility is that object, at once stable and human, the type and standard of which each of us bears within himself and which it is for maieutics, induction and definition to find out and determine.

Now, what is the teaching of Socrates regarding particular good?

Socrates is sometimes represented as deducing *a priori* particular good from the idea of absolute good, and judging custom and legality in the name of reason and justice. This is by no means his method of procedure. Instead of criticizing tradition and the positive law in the name of reason, it is in the traditional and the positive that he seeks the expression of the rational. According to Socrates, particular good consists of those things that men are agreed in regarding as good : health and strength of body and soul,[1] easy domestic circumstances,[2] useful knowledge,[3] family and friendly relations,[4] civil society and the country's prosperity,[5] good repute,[6] and, speaking generally, skill in the management of life.

[1] *Mem.* iii. 12. 4, 6.   [2] *Ibid.* ii. 17.   [3] *Ibid.* iv. 2. 23-35.
[4] *Ibid.* ii. 3. 19.   [5] *Ibid.* iii. 7. 9.   [6] *Ibid.* ii. 1. 31.

Socrates distinctly identifies justice with legality, and piety with the observance of the religious laws of one's country. φημὶ γὰρ ἐγώ[1] τὸ νόμιμον δίκαιον εἶναι . . ., τὸ αὐτὸ νόμιμόν τε καὶ δίκαιον : "I say that justice consists in the observance of the law ; that the just and the legal are both the same thing." After all, what is law ? It is what the citizens, gathered together, have decreed, in writing, as something that must either be done or avoided.[2] Piety itself is nothing else than the knowledge and practice of those laws of one's country which refer to the gods : τὰ περὶ τοὺς θεοὺς νόμιμα.[3]

True, Socrates also speaks of divine, unwritten laws.[4] By these he means not laws of an abstract, universal nature, but laws that are quite as positive (νόμιμον) as human laws. These laws are written in the soul, though they may not be found on material tablets. When Socrates wishes to cite examples thereof, he speaks of the recommendation to honour the gods, the prohibition from marrying one's own children : maxims that partake of the nature of particular and positive statutes. In his own words : "In the divine as in the human order of things justice is identical with legality."[5]

The doctrine of Socrates regarding particular good is, however, not limited to this. To common, traditional morals as matter he connects the idea of science as form ; and, by contact with this new element, morals is completely transformed without this appearing, externally, to be so.

The first function of science is to justify, to deduce what common sense and tradition offer to us only as independent facts.

---

[1] *Mem.* iv. 4. 12. [2] *Ibid.* iv. 4. 13. [3] *Ibid.* iv. 6. 4.
[4] *Ibid.* iv. 4. 19. [5] *Ibid.* iv. 4. 25.

This deduction is effected by demonstrating that all actions which common sense and tradition prescribe to us are calculated to procure advantages for us, whereas the opposite of these actions must sooner or later do us harm. For instance, temperance is a good thing, because it is the condition of pleasure, helps us to bear privation, and makes us esteemed by our fellow-beings. If a general, a tutor, or a steward is wanted, the temperate man, not the intemperate, is the one who will be chosen.[1] The observance of civil laws is a good thing, for, under all circumstances, those who observe the laws are the ones best treated in the State ; in public or private life it is they who inspire most confidence.[2] The same reasoning holds regarding unwritten laws. It is good to observe them, for the man who violates them is punished : thus, parents who marry their own children have misshapen offspring.[3] In this sense Socrates affirms that what is legal is likewise just. A law is just, in so far as its observance procures advantages, whilst its violation has disastrous consequences.[4]

Science thus deduces and justifies the established laws. Nor is this all. As the wise man, by means of science, searches into and understands the rational value of tradition and legality, and thus learns to conform with the laws of his country, not blindly, as do the masses, but by reflection and reason, he regards action inspired by science as superior to that emanating from instinct or custom. Science no longer seems to him merely to confirm the positive rules of morals : it becomes itself an indispensable condition of virtue, the root of all virtue : virtue *par excellence*. To act under the

---

[1] *Mem.* iv. 5.   [2] *Ibid.* iv. 4. 17.   [3] *Ibid.* iv. 4. 19 *sqq.*
[4] *Ibid.* iv. 4. 25.

influence of nature alone, like prophets and soothsayers,[1] means not only exposing oneself to continual failure in some direction or other, it likewise means having nothing but the mask of art or virtue. He alone who is virtuous through science (σοφία) truly merits the title of virtuous. Nothing blind or inconsiderate could be really good : on the other hand, once a man acquires self-possession, his actions are of necessity good. And so Socrates, when accused, refuses to move his listeners to compassion, because compassion is a blind sentiment.[2] On the other hand, he declares that, as he has never, willingly and knowingly (ἑκών), done wrong, he is certain he has never really done wrong at all.[3]

The mental state which immediately corresponds to science, because it is both its condition and first result, is self-control (ἐγκράτεια) or freedom (ἐλευθερία). Self-control thus becomes the first of all virtues,[4] the one whose possession is both necessary and all-sufficient for the performance of good under all circumstances. To know how he ought to act, the wise man has definitively only one question to ask himself : is this particular line of conduct seemly in a free man, or not?

On several puzzling occasions, this doctrine explains the line of conduct adopted by Socrates. The reason he refused to accept money from his listeners, was not liberality on his part or the fear of slanderers, it was because he considered that to receive money from another was equivalent to acknowledging that man to be one's master.[5] The reason he extolled manual work was not from sympathy with the occupations of the humble, but because he saw in such work a source of independence and easy circumstances from a material

---

[1] *Apol.* 22 B.   [2] *Ibid.* 35 B.   [3] *Ibid.* 37 A.
[4] *Mem.* i. 5. 4.   [5] *Ibid.* i. 5. 6.

point of view.[1] If it is true that, on one occasion, he
walked barefoot on the ice, and on another, remained
standing for a whole day and night in the self-same
spot,[2] this was not done in a spirit of folly or boasting,
though it might have been an instance of mystic contemplation ; perhaps, too, these experiments were made
for the purpose of seeing how far his independence of
the external world could be carried. Again, the reason
he endured the peevish temper of Xanthippe his wife,
was not from resignation or good temper, it was because his wife offered him a splendid opportunity for
practising self-control. The reason he delighted in
banquets and feasts, conversed in perfect freedom with
Theodota, the courtezan,[3] considered it quite right that,
in the relations between the sexes, one should obey
the promptings of nature, provided one is caused no
embarrassment thereby,[4] acknowledged so strange and
dangerous a kind of love between young men ; was to
be found in the fact that he saw nothing in all this,
irreconcilable with self-possession, nothing but a witness
to or an instrument of freedom.

In this dignified conception of life, the positive and
traditional rules of morals are by no means neglected ;
but from the *rôle* of principles they descend to that of
matter or external conditions. The wise man has self-
possession, and that is enough for him ; after all, he
speaks and acts like the rest of mankind. He is conscious of his freedom in the very act of observing the
laws and customs of his country. These laws govern
his outward actions, just as science governs his inner
disposition, and harmony between the two disciplines
is all the better established in that self-possession, the

[1] *Mem.* ii. 7. 4. [2] Plat. *Banquet,* c. xxxv-xxxvi.
[3] *Mem.* iii. 11. [4] *Ibid.* i. 3. 14.

F

supreme command of the inner law, becomes reconciled of itself with the most multiple and diverse modes of outer action. Besides, it is evident that amongst the various positive disciplines conceivable, the wise man will decide for that of his own nation. What, indeed, could be more favourable to the inner freedom after which he aspires, than to live in harmony with those around him? What, on the other hand, could be more prejudicial to quiet and self-possession than that disturbing, harassing conflict with things which makes us lose control of ourselves?

The whole of this doctrine was summed up in two famous aphorisms : " Virtue is one in itself," and " Virtue can be taught."

By the oneness of virtue, Socrates did not mean, after the fashion of the mystics, the elimination of all particular virtues in favour of some transcendent perfection. He simply meant that all virtues have one common root, to wit, the science of good, as he understood it. To the wise man, the diversity of virtues held in honour amongst men is nothing but the multiplicity of the aspects shown forth by the one sovereign virtue, according to the various objects to which it applies. Thus, virtue was neither absolutely one nor altogether multiple : it was unity in multiplicity, self-possession and the science of good realised in the virtues sanctioned by tradition.

Socrates claimed that virtue is taught, but he by no means meant thereby that it is taught by purely theoretical teaching or speculation, like the doctrines of the physiologists. Nor, in his opinion, is it taught by practice alone, as the Sophists had imagined. Virtue is taught, said Socrates, by instruction combined with exercise or practice ($\mu\acute{a}\theta\eta\sigma\iota\varsigma$ and $\mu\epsilon\lambda\acute{\epsilon}\tau\eta$). All the

texts dealing with this doctrine [1] clearly show that
Socrates invariably employs these two words together.
This is the natural outcome of the intimate union of a
theoretical and a practical element in the very science
which is the principle of wisdom.

If such is the doctrine of Socrates upon particular
good, it bears the impress of the Socratic dialectic, as
does his doctrine of the good in general. Scrupulous
respect for tradition and for the laws of one's country
is in conformity with this method, which places the
starting-point of knowledge not in pure reason, but
rather in general ideas. The philosopher, without
contradicting himself, could not turn against these
ideas the very principles he extracted from them.

On the other hand, the dialectician must go back as
far as possible into antiquity when seeking the general
principles implied in human discourse. Now, in the
accomplishment of this task, Socrates comes to regard
the essence of virtue as existing not in external acts
that conform with legality but in self-possession and
the science of good, which form the common, permanent
substratum of these acts. Self-possession and the science
of good bear the same relation to good actions that
definition does to the class of objects to be defined.

In short, the special sense in which Socrates teaches
that virtue is one and can be taught, exactly answers to
the nature of the general in Socratic dialectic. This
"general," indeed, has by no means a distinct existence,
it is only what is continually assumed in human
discourse ; and, since it is drawn from the common
ideas relating to social and private life, it possesses,
of necessity, both a practical and a theoretical nature.

[1] *Mem.* iii. 9. 2 ; iv. 1. 3 ; i. 2. 19. Cf. *Laches,* 190 E.

V

Thus do Socratic dialectic and ethic interpenetrate and determine each other. The idea of moral things as an object of science, leads Socrates to invent a scientific method applicable to such an object. On the other hand, the use of this method reacts on the object itself, giving it a new aspect. From the elaboration of the form with a view to the object arose the theory of practical induction and definition ; from the elaboration of the object by means of the form arose the doctrine of virtue, dwelling in the free and deliberate observance of positive laws and maxims.

The expression " moral science " thus would seem to characterize the invention of Socrates exactly and fully, provided we mean by these words, not morals founded on the science of things in general, but rather an effort of the human mind to build up a science without leaving the circle of moral facts themselves, and confining itself to the fertilisation of moral experience by an appropriate mode of reflection.

Here, indeed, is the centre of Socrates' doctrine, the principal mobile of his thought.

It is because he institutes a new order of investigation that he rejects and dismisses the investigations of his predecessors. All innovators possess this disdain of the past : it forms part of their faith in their own mission.

Because his conception of science is exclusively calculated with a view to the reasoned knowledge of human things, he says, along with Protagoras, that science does not attain to things divine. Stricter in his reasoning, however, he has not the impertinence to suppress a given object, under the pretext that our intelligence cannot grasp it : on the contrary, he acknowledges the limits of our faculties as soon as he discovers their powers ; and, faithful to his country's religion, he trusts to the gods in regard to everything beyond the reach of human understanding.

The belief of Socrates in an Apollonian mission and in the supernatural warnings of a protecting divinity can be perfectly reconciled with this doctrine, which both respects the domain of the gods and takes possession of that of men.

That it was the ambition of Socrates to restore the political fortunes of his city by a moral reform, was only natural and legitimate for one able to distinguish the principles of virtue and of success in human things, and whose very philosophy gave him a fresh motive for gratitude and attachment to his country.

Finally, that Socrates submitted to death rather than renounce the testing of the Athenians for the purpose of convincing them of their ignorance, is, as he says himself, the logical consequence of a doctrine which looks upon self-examination as the principle and condition of all things good, and expects the gods to complete what human wisdom began.

Of Socrates' many preoccupations, the idea of setting up morals as a science is the principal one ; for it alone brings harmony and light into this apparently strange, contradictory character. It alone explains how Socrates is both a believer and a free thinker ; positive and speculative ; a man of his own age and country, ever disposed to adapt himself to his environment, and yet one who retired within himself, was ever master of himself, obstinately jealous of his freedom and independence ; an aristocrat attached to the past, contemptuous towards popular caprice, and at the same time a revolutionist, demanding that the functions of the State be given to the best instructed citizens ; in a word, to sum up everything perhaps, it alone explains how he was both a philosopher and a man of action.

The idea of Socrates is not only novel and original, it has occupied a prominent place in the intellectual and moral history of mankind. This *rôle* has been a double one : showing itself both in the order of the practical and in that of the theoretical sciences.

In vain did Socrates scrupulously confine himself to the study of human things ; the productiveness of his method in this domain, and its conformity with the Greek genius, quickly caused it to be regarded as applicable to all objects, physical and metaphysical. Plato and Aristotle set forth the principle of Socrates : " The only science is that of the general," as including not merely the science of human things but also universal science.

The syllogism, or deductive reasoning in qualitative matter, the final definitive form of the Socratic method, was regarded as the expression of the connection between things in nature herself. From Aristotle this method passed on to the Schoolmen, who misinterpreted it, substituting for the living discourse of men which the Greeks had taken as the starting-point of their discussions, the mute, rigid text of some particular book, which was looked upon as being truth itself. Nevertheless, positive science gradually developed. On attaining to self-consciousness, so to speak, it declared, with Bacon, that syllogistic science was nothing but a science of words ; and with Descartes, that the general essences of the Socratics were only empty fiction, that science had as its object not quality or the general, but quantity or the relations of dimension. The progress of science has proclaimed Descartes to be more and more in the right, and one is nowadays tempted to ask oneself whether the Socratic principle : " The only science is that of the general," when applied, as it has been, to the investigation of the laws of nature, has not rather bewildered and unsettled the human mind than helped it.

Even were such to be the case, Socrates, who denounced all investigation into moral causes, and claimed only to build up moral science, would not be responsible for it. This extension of the Socratic method, however, was by no means an aberration of the human mind. Before knowing things in themselves, they must be known in their relations to us, and it is this indispensable provisional knowledge that we obtain from Socratic induction and definition. It may be that in all things the element of quantity is the ultimate object for which science ought to look. But it could not attain to this all at once : it must first define the qualities which form its support. In every department of knowledge, classification and induction must precede the application of mathematical analysis.

Anyhow, the Schoolmen with their syllogistic science, even Plato and Aristotle, in so far as they place being, strictly so called, in forms expressed by our concepts, are not the true successors of Socrates. Those he would have recognised as such, are the philosophers who, taking as their starting-point the observance of the moral facts of human nature, have endeavoured to set up morals as a distinct and self-sufficient science. The purest and finest fruit of the Socratic method consists of the *Nicomachean Ethics*, in which, without appealing to the physical sciences or demanding of metaphysics anything else than an ardent flow of the mind and general views on finality and activity, Aristotle condensed in a series of maxims the very thought of those who have experience of life think vaguely regarding the conditions of virtue and happiness.

Nor is the influence of Socrates, along this line of investigation confined to antiquity. When the Christian religion, after proving adequate to the moral needs of men for fifteen centuries, began to lose its power over their souls, the Socratic study of man was restored to favour. They were not content with finding the secret springs of human actions in any particular case, after the fashion of the moralists. Morals was proclaimed anew as a distinct and separate science, with an object and a method of its own. So great an advance was made in this direction that a daring system of philosophy, that of Kant and Fichte, not content with claiming a place for moral science, began by making a clean sweep of the whole of metaphysics, in order that morals might establish itself, unchecked, in its own fashion ; nor would this philosophy acknowledge that theoretical reason had any other rights than those admitted by moral science, thus organised. And soon afterwards, just as in former times Plato and Aristotle had built up a metaphysical philosophy on the basis of Socratic morals, we find Fichte, Schelling, and Hegel founding a new philosophy of the absolute on the morals of Kant.

Moral science, though for a brief space compromised by the excess of its claims, now that it has been restored within the limits marked out for it by Socrates, has acquired fresh precision and vitality at the present time. Even nowadays, there are many who consider that the time has not yet come—if it is ever to come—for morals to assume the same scientific form as physics or even the natural sciences, and yet they consider that it admits of something else than the particularities, in which the moralist confines himself, or the oratorical developments that suffice for the man of action. The truth in this matter would seem to be, even nowadays, that morals has a distinct domain, *i.e.* the sum total of the moral facts of human nature, a method proper to itself, to wit, qualitative induction and definition, and that, by modestly confining itself to its own domain and scrupulously adapting its means of investigation to the object under study, it can attain, more certainly than by any other means, to the twofold end it has in view : the knowledge and the direction of human activity. The man whose ideas are most instinct with life in contemporary society, is Socrates.

ARISTOTLE

Τὸ πρῶτον οὐ σπέρμα ἐστίν, ἀλλὰ τὸ τέλειον.

ARISTOT. *Met.* xii. 7. 1073 a 1.

IF it be true that the genius of a people is sometimes incarnated in certain men, and that these mighty, comprehensive minds form, as it were, the act and perfection in which a whole world of virtualities finds its goal and completion, then Aristotle, more than any one, was such a man : in him the philosophic genius of Greece found its universal, its perfect expression. It is therefore something more than the thought of a single individual, far-reaching and profound though it be, that we now summon forth ; it is the spirit of Greece itself, which has reached the highest pitch of its intellectual greatness. It will be conformable to the analytical temperament of the philosopher with whom we are now dealing, and also practically indispensable to set up numerous divisions in so vast a subject, and consider its different parts one after another.

I.—BIOGRAPHY [1]

Aristotle was born at Stageira, a Greek Ionian colony of Thrace, situated on the coast of the peninsula

---

[1] The ancient writers who deal with the life of Aristotle are the following : (1) Diogenes Laertius, v. 1-35 ; (2) Denys of Halicarnassus, letter to Ammaeus, 1. 5 ; (3) the anonymous author of a biography of Aristotle,

of Chalcidice, in the year 384 B.C. He died, aged sixty-two, at Chalcis, in Euboea.

His father, Nicomachus, was a doctor, as also were his ancestors. They traced their descent back to Machaon, son of Aesculapius ; and, like many others, were called Asclepiads. Nicomachus was physician to the king of Macedonia, Amyntas II., Philip's father. This circumstance may have brought it about that Aristotle was summoned to the court of the king of Macedonia to undertake the education of Alexander. It is probable that, as an Asclepiad, Aristotle was instructed in anatomy at an early age.

When about seventeen years old, he lost his parents. Being now independent and in possession of a large fortune, he was attracted to Athens. He went to this city the following year. Plato, who had founded his school there about 387 B.C., was then absent ; he had started for Syracuse, 368 B.C., left that town three years later, and returned about 360 B.C. Aristotle joined Plato's pupils, remaining with them for twenty years, until the master's death. Here we find refuted the story of a quarrel, which was alleged to have arisen between the master and the disciple long before the death of Plato, and to have been caused by Aristotle's ingratitude and lack of consideration. It is said that Plato, having remarked Aristotle's zeal and keenness of mind, called him " the reader," and " intelligence." In

---

published by Ménage in the second volume of his edition of Diogenes Laertius ; (4) the Pseudo-Ammonius ; (5) the Pseudo-Hesychius ; (6) Suidas, under the article, 'Αριστοτέλης. These texts may almost all be found in vol. i. of the edition of Aristotle's works undertaken by Buhle, between 1791 and 1800. The relative importance of these different sources cannot be determined a priori. All that is possible is the separate examination of each hint or indication from the standpoint of its internal and external probability.

all probability he studied not only Platonism at Athens, but also the other systems then in vogue.

Long previous to the death of Plato, he gave proof of his independence of thought and action. Quite possibly, as a member of the Platonic school, he had already taught on his own account. At all events, he began to write at that period, and though his early works were Platonic in form and substance, none the less did they contain, even then, objections to the theories of ideas along with the affirmation of the eternity of the world. He tells us that it is with regret, and because of his zeal for the superior interests of truth, that he thus opposed his master. Moreover, he set an example of respect for the genius of Plato. In a poem which has come down to us, he celebrates his master as one whom the wicked have no right to praise, and who showed, both by his life and his teachings, how a good man is also a happy man.

The death of Plato (347 B.c.) begins a new period in the life of Aristotle. He left Athens, accompanied by Xenocrates, and went to Atarnea, in Mysia, to his friend and fellow-disciple, Hermias, the ruler of that town, whose sister, or niece, Pythias, he subsequently married. Later on, he married a woman named Herpyllis. After the fall and death of Hermias (345 B.c.) Aristotle went to Mytilene. From there he would seem to have returned to Athens and opened the school of rhetoric, in which he set up as an opponent to Isocrates. In 342 B.c., he responded favourably to the summons of Philip, king of Macedonia, who requested him to undertake the education of his son Alexander, at that time about fourteen years of age. He remained at the court of Macedonia until Alexander undertook his expedition into Asia (334 B.c.). Without losing himself in pursuit of an ideal too far removed from the conditions of practical life, Aristotle appears to have instilled generous qualities in the mind of his pupil. Throughout his life Alexander retained feelings of respect and love for his master, though after the death of Callisthenes, Aristotle's nephew, in 325 B.C., all relations between the two were discontinued.

In 335 B.C. or 334 B.C., Aristotle returned to Athens, and at Lycaeum opened what was called the Peripatetic School, probably on account of the master's habit of walking about with his disciples as they talked of science and philosophy. In the mornings, relates Aulus-Gellius, Aristotle gave, to a chosen body of hearers, *acroamatic*, or esoteric, instruction, dealing with the most difficult portions of philosophy, mainly dialectic and the philosophy of nature. In the evenings he gave *exoteric* instruction to all who offered themselves, dealing with rhetoric, topics and politics. His teaching took the form both of classes and lectures ; and his school, like that of Plato, was a band of friends who assembled on fixed days, and took their meals in common.

Wealthy himself, and able to rely on the assistance of the king, Aristotle was in a position to obtain all the scientific resources the society of the times could offer. It is said that Alexander sent him eight hundred talents to enable him to complete his *Historia animalium*. It is even related that he placed at his disposal millions of men, whose duty it was to seek out animals of every kind, especially fishes, to maintain in perfect order aviaries and gardens filled with animals, and to keep the philosopher informed on such observations and discoveries as were calculated to advance science. These are, doubtless, mere inventions, though facts were at the bottom of them. Certainly Aristotle gathered together all the documents of every kind it was possible for him to obtain. He was the first to form a large collection of books.

Although Aristotle had broken off all relations with Alexander in 325 B.C., none the less did the king's death, two years afterwards, prove an occasion of peril for him. When the Lamian war broke out, he was looked upon as a friend of the kings of Macedonia and Antipater, and was prosecuted on the charge of atheism. He left Athens, so that the Athenians, as he said, might not a second time be guilty as regards philosophy. He fled to Chalcis, in Euboea, where he fell sick and died in the summer of 322 B.C., a few months before Demosthenes, who was born in the same year as himself. He was sixty-two years of age.

Though early attacked by his political and scientific opponents, he would appear from his writings to have been of a noble, humane, and loyal nature, and we are acquainted with no actual proved fact to the contrary. His life bears the impress of moral philosophic dignity. Aristotle was both a creative and a universal genius, and an indefatigable worker. He is devoid of the ardent buoyancy of Plato. With mind bent on the reality presented to him, whatever bears no relation thereto he looks upon as fantastic ; he does not bury himself in the facts of the sensible world, however, but is always looking for the intelligible. In all things he recommends moderation, the golden mean. A moderate fortune, government by the moderate classes : such, to his mind, is the best condition both for the individual and for society.

We are told that he was short and thin, with small eyes and an ironical expression playing about his mouth. By Pythias, his first wife, he left a daughter of the same name ; and by his second wife, Herpyllis of Stageira, a son Nicomachus, whose name we find in the *Nicomachean Ethics.* In his will he speaks affectionately of both his wives and of his two brothers and their children ; he also refers in sympathetic terms to his friends and distant relatives.

II.—Aristotle's Writings

The story of the preservation of Aristotle's works is but little known. According to Strabo and Plutarch, the writings of Aristotle and Theophrastus, after the latter's death, fell into the hands of Neleus, who took them to his home in Skepsis, Mysia. There they would appear to have been hidden away in a cellar, where they were discovered by Apellicon, in the time of Sylla. The latter is reported to have had them transferred to Rome. Whatever degree of truth there may be in these anecdotes, the texts that had been preserved were revised and classified in the first century before Christ by Andronicus, a Peripatetic philosopher of Rhodes, who published a complete edition about 60-50 B.C. It is this text of Aristotle, more or less remodelled, that we now possess. In all probability our collection contains everything authentic that existed in the time of Andronicus, and we have good grounds for regarding as apocryphal the works mentioned by Diogenes Laertius, that are absent from this collection. Most likely, however, all that is contained in the so-called Andronicus edition, is not by Aristotle ; even the authentic works themselves are not free from additions and changes. There have also come down to us the titles of works that are certainly authentic, and yet are lacking in our collection, having apparently been lost at the time of Andronicus. All the same, it would appear that the most important works on Aristotelian philosophy and science have been preserved.

Which of the works we possess are to be laid aside as unauthentic? In many cases the question cannot be answered with any degree of precision or certainty. The following are the results reached by Zeller in his *Philosophie der Griechen*, 3rd vol. 3rd edition. The authenticity of the following works is either inadmissible or very doubtful :—*De Xenophane, Zenone et Gorgia ; De animalium motu ; De plantis ; De coloribus ; De audibilibus ; De mirabilibus auditis ; Physiognomonica ; Mechanica problemata ; De indivisibilibus lineis ; De mundo ; De respiratione ; De virtutibus et vitiis ; Oeconomica ; Rhetorica ad Alexandrum.* The *Eudemian Ethics* and the *Great Ethics* are alterations of the *Nicomachean Ethics.* Such fragments of letters as we possess have undergone considerable additions and changes.

The works left by Aristotle may in all probability be placed in the three following categories :—

1st. Books of instruction and science properly so called : summaries and treatises of which he made use in his classes. He did not publish them, but merely imparted their teachings to his pupils.

2nd. Published writings : intended for the masses of the people. They were written, we are told, with considerable fluency and charm, and were partly in the form of dialogues.

Using Aristotle's own terms, the unpublished writings have been called *acroamatic* or *acroatic*, and the published ones *exoteric*. These expressions clearly answer to a fundamental distinction in Aristotle's philosophy. In his mind, there are two modes of instruction, proportioned to the two degrees of knowledge. That which is cognizable as necessary and

absolutely certain is a matter of demonstration strictly
so called ; that which is cognizable as being only likely
is a matter of dialectic. In his classes Aristotle taught
complete science ; he gave demonstrations ; the pupil
had nothing to do but to listen. Apart from these classes,
however, Aristotle directed dialectic conversations, in
which reasoning from probabilities, and from considerations more or less foreign to the subject in question, was
carried on ; to these conversations others were admitted
as well as pupils. Such is the significance of the words
acroamatic and *exoteric*, used with reference to the
teaching of Aristotle. He himself does not apply
them to his works, though such application may well
be made.

3rd. To these two categories must be added a third,
viz., notes intended for the personal use of Aristotle.
These latter writings may be called *hypomnematic.*

Last of all, Aristotle left behind him speeches, letters
and poems. Of these three classes, only the first have
come down to us, and a few fragments of the second
and third. Amongst the lost works, the most important
are, in the first category : the *Treatise on Plants*, *Anatomy*,
Astrological Theorems; in the second : the *Dialogues*,
and the *History of Rhetoric;* in the third: extracts from
some works of Plato, and writings on the Pythagoreans
and other philosophers. In this third category, evidently,
we must place the *Constitutions* (Πολιτεῖαι), in which
were to be found all kinds of information about 158
Greek and foreign cities, a lost collection of which we
possess many very interesting extracts. The treatise
entitled *The Constitution of the Athenians* was recently
discovered on a papyrus, and published in 1891.

We may classify as follows the scientific, properly
so called, or unpublished writings, in our possession,

G

representing, in a probably complete manner as regards essentials, the philosophical work of Aristotle :

1st. Works on logic, collected at the Byzantine period only under the name of ὄργανον : Κατηγορίαι (categories), partially added to and altered ; Περὶ ἑρμηνείας (on speech or propositions) — this appears to be the work of a Peripatetic of the third century before Christ ; Ἀναλυτικὰ πρότερα (Prior Analytics), dealing with syllogism ; Ἀναλυτικὰ ὕστερα (Posterior Analytics), dealing with demonstration; Τοπικά (Topics), dealing with dialectic, or reasoning in probabilities. The ninth book of this work is usually given as a special work, entitled Περὶ σοφιστικῶν ἐλέγχων (On Sophistical Refutations).

2nd. Works on natural philosophy : Φυσικὴ ἀκρόασις (Physics), in eight books, the seventh of which, though edited from Aristotelian notes, does not appear to have been written by Aristotle ; Περὶ γενέσεως καὶ φθορᾶς (On Generation and Destruction) ; Περὶ οὐρανοῦ (On the Heavens) ; Μετεωρολογικά (Meteorologics) ; Περὶ ψυχῆς (On Soul), and divers treatises referring thereto, entitled *Parva Naturalia* ; Περὶ τὰ ζῶα ἱστορίαι (Animal History), in ten books, a work that has undergone considerable changes and the tenth book of which is not authentic ; Περὶ ζώων μορίων (The Parts of Animals) ; Περὶ πορείας ζώων (The Motor Organs of Animals) ; Περὶ ζώων γενέσεως (On the Generation of Animals), a work that has been considerably changed.

3rd. So-called metaphysical works, dealing with what Aristotle calls first philosophy (πρώτη φιλοσοφία) : the work called *Metaphysics*, in fourteen books, is a collection made, in all probability, shortly after the death of Aristotle ; it comprises all that his papers

contained referring to first philosophy. These writings
owe their present name (Τὰ μετὰ τὰ φυσικά) to their
position after physics in the edition of Andronicus.
The substance of these writings is comprised in Books
i., iii., iv., vi. to ix., x. (numbers of the Berlin edition).
Book ii. and Book xi., from chapter viii., 1065, a, 26,
are unauthentic.

4th. Works on the practical sciences : Ἠθικὰ
Νικομάχεια (Morals addressed to Nicomachus, or Nicomachean Ethics) ; Πολιτικά (Politics), an unfinished
work. According to Zeller, Books vii. and viii. of
the *Politics* ought most probably to be inserted between
Books iii. and iv. ; Τεχνὴ ῥητορική (Rhetoric) ; Περὶ
ποιητικῆς (On Poetry).

With regard to the didactic works, the question of
chronology is only of moderate importance. Indeed,
they were all written during the last twelve years of
the philosopher's life (335-322), they make references
to each other, and, in their *ensemble*, offer us the completed system, without any proof of progress. So far
as can be judged by the paltry indications that may be
obtained from historical testimony and the examination
of the works in themselves, Aristotle first wrote the
works on logic (except the notes from which the Περὶ
ἑρμηνείας were compiled, and which appeared after the
Περὶ ψυχῆς). Then the writings on natural history
appeared, followed by the physiological and psychological works and those relating to the practical
sciences ; last of all, most probably and in any case
subsequent to the physics, the collection called metaphysics. Thus Aristotle appears to have proceeded
from the abstract to the concrete, and, in the domain
of the concrete, from changing being to immutable
being.

III.—THE *ENSEMBLE* OF ARISTOTLE'S WORK

As indicated by the very title of his writings, universality is the first characteristic of Aristotle's work. Theory and practice, metaphysics and the science of observation, erudition and speculation, his philosophy includes everything. It is, or would like to be, knowledge in its totality. The idea of science, considered as the loftiest object of activity, stands out in Aristotle as more precise than in Plato and more general than in Anaxagoras and Democritus. It is not the curiosity of a scholar, it is the ambition to enter into the very essence and cause of things. Without exception, everything that is, even what appears mean and insignificant, calls in this sense for the philosopher's investigations. He knows he will find the divine and the intelligible in all the productions of nature, even those that are apparently the humblest.

It was thus that he approached everything accessible to human intelligence ; and, provided with all the positive knowledge it was at that period possible to acquire, a philosopher of penetrating intuition and strict reasoning power, he either created or constituted most of the sciences which the genius of mankind was subsequently destined to develop. The list of the sciences he thus organised is but the list of those he himself studied : the history of philosophy, logic, metaphysics, general physics, biology, botany, ethics, politics, archaeology, literary history, philology, grammar, rhetoric, poetics and the philosophy of art. In each of these sciences Aristotle is at home ; for each of them he lays down special and appropriate principles. A pure ethicist when dealing with justice and friendship, he is a professional naturalist when dealing with zoölogy.

Are we then to conclude that Aristotle comprises many human beings in himself, so to speak ; is his vast work nothing but the juxtaposition of the most diverse labours, such as might result from the collaboration of many learned men ? Such an appreciation would certainly be a superficial one. First and foremost, there is community of spirit and method between the different works of Aristotle. This common substratum might be defined as a harmonious blend of idealism, observation and logical formalism. Aristotle always seeks for the idea in the fact ; for the necessary and the perfect in the contingent and the imperfect ; everywhere he endeavours to substitute fixed conceptions and definitions for the fleeting data of sensible observation. Nor is this all ; according to him, the different parts of knowledge hold a fixed relation to one another, and this relation he very clearly defines. Speaking generally, the superior is known only after the inferior, and that only by the help of the knowledge of this inferior ; at the same time, however, the true cause and *raison d'être* of the inferior is to be found in the superior. For instance, the soul can be known only after the body, which is its basis and the condition of its existence. But the body exists only for the soul ; from this latter it obtains the regulated movement which constitutes its being. This principle of Aristotle's will assist us in classifying the many forms of his philosophical activity.

IV.—CLASSIFICATION OF THE SCIENCES

Without attaining to precision or even permanence in detail, Aristotle was none the less the first to conceive of science from an encyclopaedic point of view and to endeavour to discover a principle for the complete classification of knowledge.

In the first place, science stands clearly out from the very things to which it relates. It consists of the conception of things as necessary, and admits of different degrees according as the object under consideration itself admits of necessity or only of probability.

Science, in its *ensemble*, follows a double line of direction, according as the human mind adopts as its starting-point that which is first from its own point of view, or that which is first absolutely. These two steps are the very opposites of each other : for facts are what is first to us, and, in the internal order of nature, facts are what exists in the last resort ; and *vice versa*, what is first in itself consists of principles, and principles are the last thing to which we can attain.

Philosophy, in the broad sense of the word, is science in general. In the first place, it comprises first philosophy or the science of unconditioned principles ; in the second place, the totality of the particular sciences, the chief of which are : mathematics, physics, ethics and poetics. Philosophy is one, thanks to first philosophy, which is the common reservoir whence all particular sciences draw their principles.

This division, although fundamental, does not always reappear in Aristotle's classifications of the sciences. In certain places he divides the propositions, after the fashion of the Platonists, into *ethical, physical* and *logical*, these latter comprising the very propositions that refer to first philosophy.

More frequently he divides the sciences into *theoretical, practical* (or relating to action) and *poetical* (or relating to production by means of matter) ; placing, from the logical and absolute point of view, theory before practice, and practice before poetics. Then he subdivides the theoretical sciences into *theology*, *mathematics* and *physics*. Theology may be brought under first philosophy, of which it forms the summit. Mathematics deals with essences still stable though not separable from matter, except by abstraction. Physics deals with sensible—*i.e.* movable and perishable —substances. The practical sciences, or sciences of human things, are subdivided, if we proceed from potency to act, *i.e.* from that which is first for us to that which is first in itself, into *ethics*, *economics* and *politics*. In fact, economics is often given by Aristotle as included in politics. Rhetoric is more particularly set forth as an auxiliary science to politics. Poetics includes all the arts, the most important of them being poetry and music. No mention is made of logic in this classification, doubtless because the latter embraces only the sciences dealing with realities, whereas logic deals with concepts.

V.—METHOD AND THE POINT OF VIEW

The object Aristotle has in view is essentially theoretical. To know in order to know, to understand, to adjust things to the intelligence : such is the end of all his efforts.

All men, he says, have a natural desire to know. We love science quite apart from any advantage to be gained thereby. Wisdom is independent of utility ; in fact, the greater it is, the less useful it is. The highest science is that of the goal or end, in view of which, beings exist. This science alone is truly free, because it alone exists solely in view of knowledge itself. It is the least necessary of all sciences, and therefore the most excellent. Science enables us to become acquainted with the intelligible reasons of things. The ignorant man, who all the same observes, is astonished that things are as they are, and this very astonishment is the beginning of science : the wise man would be astonished were things otherwise than as he knows them.

How does Aristotle proceed in order to acquire science, thus understood ? Aristotle is neither the dogmatic idealist that Bacon supposes, building up the world with nothing but the categories of language, nor the empiric that many moderns see in him. He is both an observer and a constructor: speaking generally, he closely allies and combines the scrupulous study of facts with the effort to make them intelligible. For him, facts are the starting-point, but he does not stop there : he tries to distil from them the rational truths he knows beforehand to be contained therein. The end he has in view is the knowledge of things in demonstrative form, i.e. in the form of a deduction in which the properties of the thing are known by its very essence.

Most frequently, and especially when dealing with metaphysical or moral matters, before entering upon the study of things in themselves, he investigates and discusses all the opinions of others thereon. This is the dialectic method ; drawing its arguments not from the essence of the thing, but rather from the admissions of one's interlocutor, it does not go beyond probability. In using this method, Aristotle frequently begins with popular conceptions : he finds a philosophical meaning in them and utilises it in constructing his theory. He also starts with language which, for him, is a sort of intermediary between things and reason. He pays special attention to the doctrines of his predecessors, carefully going over all the opinions they have upheld ; and even when rejecting these opinions, he tries to find out the reason they were held and the degree of truth in them. His philosophical dissertations are generally composed as follows: 1st, he determines the object of investigation, so as not to be exposed to misunderstanding, as is the case with Plato ; 2nd, he enumerates and estimates the indications and opinions held on the matter in hand ; 3rd, he investigates and examines as completely as possible the difficulties or ἀπορίαι offered by the question asked ; 4th, considering things in themselves, and utilising, in his reasonings, the results of the foregoing discussions, he seeks for the solution of the problem in the determination of the one eternal essence of the object in question.

VI.—ARISTOTLE, THE HISTORIAN

We see from the preceding that Aristotle is a historian above all else. He began by learning as much as possible. According to report, Plato called him the *reader*. But history was not a final end for him, although he manifested extraordinary curiosity regarding facts ; it was, however, an indispensable means to an end. It supplied the mind with materials without which it would have nothing to work upon. Aristotle gave himself up to profoundly historical studies in every domain of science.

As regards the history of philosophy, he wrote mainly on Platonism and the Pythagoreans. The whole of the first book of the *Metaphysics* is full of historical research: it is a summary of the principles set forth from the time of Thales to that of Plato. But as the object he has in view is dogmatic, he makes previous systems fit into the framework of his own philosophy. He tries to find their perfect form, the idea within each, their end and completion ; he is determined to understand them more profoundly than even their authors did, and he summarises them into rules created by himself, which rules are used as stepping-stones to his own system. When he classifies doctrines, he does so according to the resemblances and differences they offer from his own point of view, not according to the influence they have had upon one another. Thus, the summary contained in the first book of the *Metaphysics* is intended to prepare the ground for the Aristotelian theory of the four causes. Aristotle shows that, before his time, the material, motive and formal principles were more or less discerned and rightly estimated, but that the final cause was spoken of as though by accident, as something unessential. Anaxagoras, who had caught a glimpse of the final cause, stands out, says our author, as a sensible man amongst men who speak at random. Chronological investigations have little to do with these considerations. Aristotle, likewise, troubles himself little with the relations of master to disciple. He notes the services rendered by each of his predecessors to philosophy in general, as he conceives it ; he points out anything of a lasting nature that each thinker has found, and mentions the inventors and promoters of ideas that have played some part in the development of science and appear to him deserving of examination. In a word, making no attempt to find out the historical origins of the systems, he all the same elicits from the crude mass of facts, the logical formation of definitive philosophy.

With political history are connected the famous πολιτεῖαι in which Aristotle set forth the constitutions of 158 Greek and foreign cities. This collection

of treatises belonged to what we call archaeology and
the history of civilisation. In them were to be found
many a striking national custom, and even the proverbs
and popular songs of different peoples. According
to certain Greek commentators, the order of the contents was alphabetical. Diogenes says that the constitutions were classified according as they resembled
democracies, oligarchies, aristocracies or tyrannies. We
can nowadays form some idea of the πολιτεῖαι, thanks
to the recently discovered treatise on the *Constitution of
the Athenians*. The first part of this treatise is an
explanation of the political transformations of Athens
from its historical beginnings. The second describes
the political and administrative organisation of Athens
about the time of the Crown trial (330 B.C.).

In the literary order of things, Aristotle had written
the history of rhetoric and poetry. This history, which
has not come down to us, was greatly praised by Cicero.
" Aristotle," he said, " had noted down all the precepts
given by the rhetors, and that, too, with such a degree
of perfection that these precepts were found to be more
clearly set forth by him than by their authors themselves ; so that when one wished to become acquainted
with them, it was in Aristotle's works that search was
made."

He had also drawn up chronological lists of dramatic
performances as well as lists of the victors in the Olympic
and Pythian games. These works are lost.

As may be seen, Aristotle's curiosity is insatiable and
embraces every department of nature. Still, he is
determined to know and understand, not to amuse himself with the mere statement of facts : history for him
is nothing but an instrument of science, and a fact has
no value except as the vehicle of an idea.

VII.—Logic

Aristotle is determined to become acquainted with facts, not only as regards what they are, but as regards what they ought to be ; he wishes to resolve the contingent into the necessary. First, then, he has to find out under what conditions the mind conceives something as necessary ; in other words, he has first to consider science in its form, putting on one side its content : this is the object of logic.

Logic is the determination of the laws of reasoning and of the conditions of science. In knowledge Aristotle makes a distinction between form and matter, he regards form as possessed of an existence and laws of its own. Its existence lies in the reality of stable concepts, or general, single ideas, exactly determined both as regards their comprehension and their extension. Its fundamental law is the principle of contradiction : " It is impossible for one and the same attribute to belong and not to belong to a given subject, regarded in one and the same connection." Moreover, according to Aristotle, there is proportion as well as agreement between thought and being ; consequently, our philosopher does not object to the introduction into his logic of many elements of a metaphysical nature.

Aristotelian logic is the rational analysis of the conditions which any reasoning must satisfy for its conclusion to be regarded as necessary. The thing is not to know how, as a matter of fact, we reason in ordinary life, but rather how reasoning must be built up in order that the necessity of the connection it establishes may appear immediately and irresistibly evident. This is why the problem of the psychological analysis of natural reasoning, indicated by Locke, could be substituted for that of Aristotle only by admitting the reduction of the necessary to the contingent, the ideal to the real, precept to fact, and art to nature.

It is advisable to distinguish between : 1st, the instruments of thought ; 2nd, the *rôle* and value of these instruments in the constitution of science.

The instruments of thought are : notions, propositions and reasoning.

The general heading of *notions* includes the predicables, the categories and the notions of logical relations.

The *predicables*, which Aristotle, it would seem, calls the genera of problems, are the universal notions that relate to the general modes according to which one thing may be enunciated with reference to another. These are what are called the universals, viz. genus, species, difference, property and accident.

The *categories* are the irreducible genera of words, and consequently of things, for classes of words are the classes of the things themselves. These are the ultimate genera. The categories are ten in number : 1st, essence, for instance, man, horse ; 2nd, quantity : two ells long ; 3rd, quality : white ; 4th, relation : double, half ; 5th, place : at school ; 6th, time : yesterday ; 7th, position : to be seated, lying ; 8th, possession : to be shod, armed ; 9th, action : to cut, to burn ; 10th, passivity : to be cut, burnt. The categories are divided into two classes, essence alone forming the first, and the nine other categories constituting the second.

This table of categories seems to have been drawn up empirically by comparison of the words with one another. It differs fundamentally from Kant's, which sets forth the different ways of connecting, *a priori* and necessarily, the various elements of an intuition in general, *i.e.* of bringing this scattered matter under the unity of transcendental apperception.

The different *logical relations* of terms to one another are identity and opposition, the latter including contrariety, contradiction and the relation between deprivation and possession.

The general principle with regard to opposition is that two terms opposed to each other always depend on one and the same science.

Propositions result from the union of concepts. They are affirmative or negative, universal or particular. They alone admit of truth or error, whereas isolated concepts are neither true nor false. The result is not the same, when two judgments are contradictory to each other, as when they are simply contrary. Two contrary judgments cannot both be true, though they may be false, whereas one of two contradictory judgments is of necessity true and the other false : this results from the principle of excluded middle, a particular expression of the principle of contradiction.

Propositions admit of conversions or inversions of subject and predicate, the rules of which are determined by Aristotle.

Reasoning consists essentially of syllogism. The theory of syllogism and of demonstration, or perfect syllogism, is called by Aristotle *analytics*. Aristotle claims to have invented it. He affirms that, previous to his time, there existed nothing on this subject, that he had not merely to improve but to invent, and that he attained his end by dint of laborious attempts. Kant said regarding the theory of the syllogism that, ever since the days of Aristotle, it had not moved a step, either backwards or forwards.

The syllogism is a process of reasoning in which,

certain things being posited, something different necessarily results. The property of the syllogism is that it makes evident the necessity of the conjunction. This result is obtained by the use of elements adapted to an exact application of the principle of contradiction. These elements are terms regarded as holding to each other the relation of the part to the whole. Granted that A contains B and B contains C, it necessarily follows, in accordance with the principle of contradiction, that A contains C. This is the type of the syllogism, and the three terms it implies are therefore called *major*, *middle* and *minor*. This relation of extent is regarded by Aristotle as equivalent to the relation between general and particular. The genus is a kind of definite circle, containing the various species.

The syllogism is perfect or imperfect, according as it conforms immediately to the type we have just indicated, or becomes conformable thereto only by the aid of transformations or reductions.

The origin of this theory may be found in mathematics. It consists in an adaptation to the qualitative notions of the relations of dimension. It was natural that Aristotle should seek, in an analogical imitation of mathematics, for the means of demonstrating necessarily in qualitative matter ; since it was acknowledged by all that mathematics realised that necessity in the concatenation of the terms, which he had in view. In the syllogism the instrument of necessary connection is the middle term.

Of the particular cases of syllogism, the most important is *induction*, or the reasoning which proceeds from particular to general. The following is an instance of this reasoning : " The man, the horse and the mule live long. Now the man, the horse and the mule are animals devoid of gall. Therefore, all animals devoid of gall live long." The condition of the legitimacy of the conclusion lies in the convertibility of the minor premise. Here, for instance, for the proposition : " The man, the horse and the mule are animals devoid of gall," we should have to be permitted to substitute : " All the animals devoid of gall are man, the horse and the mule." The legitimacy of this substitution is no longer a matter of logic. In fact, the series of animals devoid of gall is an infinite one. But the essence of the animal devoid of gall is entirely in each animal devoid of gall. The question is to discern this essence, to find the type of the animal devoid of gall, so as to distinguish the characteristics belonging to animals devoid of gall, in this particular condition of being devoid of gall, and separate them from the characteristics belonging to them independently of this condition. To effect this, we consider a certain number of animals devoid of gall, compare them with one another, find out what they have in common, and so what there is in them that is essential and necessary. In other words, we consider the beings of nature not only with the senses, but with the νοῦς—the seat of the essences—which is capable of finding and recognising them in the data of the senses.

Aristotle's induction thus aims at the classification of beings and facts, and also at a *natural* classification. In so far as it is applied in distinguishing necessary relations from contingent ones, it makes prediction possible, and thus supplies us with true laws, in the modern sense of the word. This possibility of prediction, however, is restricted to the facts that proceed immediately from a determined essence ; it does not extend to the facts that result from the mingling of several essences. There is no necessary reason for the mingling of the essences ; this is something purely contingent. The genera, according to Aristotle, are radically separated from one another ; each of them is an absolute. In this doctrine of the independence of genera, the Aristotelian theory of induction is opposed both to Cartesianism, which reduces physical laws to mathematical determinations, the heterogeneous to the homogeneous ; and also to evolutionism, which recognises the present existence of species, though attributing to them a natural genesis in the past, starting from one common origin.

Syllogism, properly so called, and induction are to each other, says Aristotle, as the order of nature and that of human knowledge. In itself, syllogism is the more intelligible ; to us, induction is the more distinct. A syllogism starts from the general. Now, it is impossible for us to have knowledge of the general except by induction. Not that general principles rest on sensation and induction as their foundation ; it is rather that induction discovers these principles for us and supplies us with the intelligible elements which the νοῦς acknowledges to be both necessary and true.

Such are the instruments of science. How, by means of them, is science formed ?

Science is the knowledge of things in so far as they are necessary. A thing is known scientifically when we know that it could not be otherwise than it is. Now, this knowledge is realised when we succeed in connecting the given thing with its cause.

In nature there are three kinds of connections : 1st, conjunctions that are always realised, for instance : the relations of astronomical phenomena ; 2nd, conjunctions that are usually realised, for instance : the relations of physical things to one another, and, even more so, of moral things ; 3rd, chance, *i.e.* the coincidences that are but seldom, or never, reproduced. The first kind of connection admits of perfect science ; the second, of imperfect science, limited to probability ; the third is outside of the domain of science. There is no science of what is passing away.

Neither opinion nor sensation can produce science, for as they are both incapable of perfect determination and finity, they cannot grasp the finite and immovable. Platonic dialectic, too, is powerless to afford us science, for as it consists of questions and answers, it relies only on the consent of the opponent, not on truth in itself. Starting from hypothesis, it does not go beyond a purely formal and logical inference. It is by demonstration that we arrive at science. *Apodeictic*, or the theory of demonstration, differs essentially from dialectic.

Demonstration is effected by direct syllogism of the first figure. *Reductio ad absurdum* and syllogisms of the second and third figures are not yet demonstration, which has its starting-point in a principle that is not only granted by the opponent, but is necessary in itself. This is how the mathematician reasons.

Demonstration comprises three elements : 1st, the subject ; 2nd, the predicate, which has to be linked to the subject by a bond of necessity ; 3rd, the general principles on which demonstration is based. These latter are the principle of contradiction and its derivatives. Though indispensable, they are empty and insufficient in themselves. It is in the nature of the subject that the basis of demonstration lies.

There are, in effect, principles proper to the subject, for instance the continuous, inherent in extent ; and the discontinuous, inherent in number : it is these special principles that have a content and are productive. On these principles it is good to rely, and, in deduction, we should never pass from one genus to another unless the one is properly subordinated to the other. Thus, geometry could not be explained by arithmetic ; it would be impossible to adapt to dimensions of extension demonstrations proper to number. When this rule is violated, we have for our guidance none but the principles common to all sciences ; and so the connections established are known only as accidental and contingent, not as essential and necessary : we have been proceeding by analogy, not by demonstration. The impossibility here seen by Aristotle was at a later date removed by Descartes and Leibnitz.

Proper principles cannot be proved like common ones. To claim to demonstrate everything would be to condemn oneself either to progress *ad infinitum* or to the argument in a circle. Thus each science has its special irreducible principles.

Whence come these principles? They are neither innate, nor received purely and simply from without. There is within us a disposition to conceive them ; and, as the result of experience, this disposition passes into action. It is in this, after all, that induction consists, and so it is by induction that we know the first principles proper to each science.

Demonstration implies definition. There must be undemonstrable definitions : otherwise we should proceed *ad infinitum*. There is no definition, either of the individual or of the accident—or the indeterminate general—but only of intermediate species between the

general and the individual. Definition is effected by
indicating the next genus and the specific differences.
In order to constitute a definition, we must proceed
from the particular to the general and verify this induction by a deduction proceeding from genus to species.

To sum up, a thing is known as necessary when
connected, by deduction, with a specific essence.

Below apodeictic, which teaches how one comes to
know a thing as necessary, stands *dialectic*, or the logic
of the probable : we find it set forth in the *Topics*.
The domain of dialectic is opinion, a mode of knowledge admitting of truth or of falsehood. The
dialectician takes, as his starting-point, not definitions
necessary in themselves, but opinions or theses pro-
pounded either by philosophers or by common sense ;
he tries to discover which of these divers opinions is
the most probable. Proceeding by means of questions
and answers, he contradictorily examines the yes and
the no regarding each subject. Thus, he arranges his
questions in such fashion as to present first a thesis,
then an antithesis ; afterwards he discusses both propositions. This discussion consists in examining the
difficulties that arise, when we wish to apply the proposition to particular instances. The dialectician
reasons syllogistically, though he starts with the probable. The probable, taken as the given, is in reality
the purely *generic* essence, not yet determined by the
specific difference. Only by the addition of the specific
principle to the generic principle could the conclusion
be made necessary. The specific principles, however,
cannot be deduced from the generic ones, for every
genus admits alike of different species.

The *rôle* of dialectic is important : it is the only
possible mode of reasoning in things which do not

admit of necessary definitions. And in the search after necessary truths themselves, dialectic is the indispensable preliminary of demonstration.

What dialectic is in logic, *rhetoric* is in morals. If the former seeks after the probable, the object of the latter is to commend it to acceptance. And so rhetoric and dialectic go well together, or rather, as practice is to theory what the particular is to the general, so rhetoric is a part of dialectic. The mode of reasoning proper to rhetoric is the enthymeme, a syllogism in which one of the three propositions is left unexpressed, and the reasons are not obtained from the essence of things, but from probabilities and signs. The main element of the enthymeme that rhetoric uses, is analogy, or the induction which proceeds from particular to particular.

Finally, a distinction must be made between dialectic and *eristic*. Whereas the former has to deal with things that are general and ordinary, without being necessary, the latter deals with pure accident, and that deliberately. Eristic contents itself with a probability that is accepted by the hearer; consequently eristic reasonings are pure sophisms. Aristotle minutely exposes and describes them.

Below things that always happen, which depend on an essence both generic and specific and are capable of being known as necessary, even below things that usually happen, which depend on a simply generic essence and are capable of being known as probable, there are those that happen accidentally, apart from any rule at all. As things that usually happen result from the mingling of *species*, so isolated phenomena result from the mingling of *genera*; but whereas that which is not determinable by species is still determin-

able, to some extent, by genus, the common substratum
of several species, that which is not even determinable
by genus is no longer determinable at all, since, above
genera, there are none but universal principles, which,
as they apply to everything, determine nothing. There
is no science, then, of hazard, as such, the meet-
ing with the two genera. Only the elements of which
the fortuitous phenomenon consists can be known as
necessary or possible, in so far as they are connected
with their respective specific or generic essences : the
union of these elements, which, properly speaking,
constitutes the fortuitous phenomenon, is without
reason, because genera, as such, are without mutual
connection.

Aristotelian logic held undisputed sway down to the
time of Bacon and Descartes. From the beginning of
modern philosophy, it has been attacked and battered
on every side ; either reproached for being the logic of
exposition, and not that of invention, or else regarded
as artificial and illegitimate. Discussion bears mainly
on the value of the concept or general idea, the basis of
the theory. The empirics, in particular, to whom ideas
are only traces of sensation, estimate the value of
generalities by the number of ascertained facts they
represent ; they maintain that, as the truth of the
major premise of a syllogism implies that of the conclusion, the syllogism is necessarily an argument in a
circle.

Here the thing to discover is whether a concept
is anything else than a collective idea, or a static or
dynamic unity, valid for an indefinite series of past,
present and future facts. But even should the Aristotelian concept not exactly coincide with the nature
of things, as would be the case were continuity the

fundamental law of being, the logic of Aristotle would none the less retain real value. Not only would it subsist as an analysis of the conditions of ideal knowledge for the human mind, but it would be legitimate in proportion as there exist species in nature. Now, these do exist, if not in an eternal, primitive fashion, perhaps, at all events in actuality and at the present time. Superior beings, especially, form relatively stable groups. Even though continuity were the fundamental law, none the less would it be necessary to recognise in nature a tendency to discontinuity and specification. Aristotelian logic would answer to that part or side of nature which is governed by the law of specification. Deprived of the metaphysical and absolute value its founder attributed to it, it would retain a relative and experimental value.

VIII.—Metaphysics

Whereas each science considers some particular species of beings ; physics, for instance, considers being in so far as it has matter and motion ; mathematics, the form of mobile being in so far as it is isolated by abstraction from the matter in which it is realised ; first philosophy, as Aristotle calls it, considers being, in so far as it is being, τὸ ὄν, ἦ ὄν, and in this way tries to discover its principles.

Aristotelian metaphysics has been set up as opposed to Platonic philosophy. Thus, we find Aristotle beginning his exposition by a criticism of his master. Plato, he says, seeks both the object of science and being, in so far as it is being, in the general essences conceived of as existing apart, outside of things and also outside of one another. Now, here, the true is confounded with

the false.   Plato clearly saw that the general alone can
be an object of science and that the sensible world as
such cannot, therefore, be known scientifically.   But he
was mistaken in thinking that genera can exist apart, that
they are themselves principles and substances.   Genera
exist only in individuals.   We get entangled in inextricable difficulties if we insist that they exist *per se*.
Under this hypothesis, what will be the relation of
things to their respective genera ?   Will it be one
of participation ?   Then how can this participation
be conceived ?   Besides, how many substantial genera
will there be ?   How can the idea, the one substance,
be met with in an infinite number of individuals ?   If
the general idea is substance, either there are no
individuals or there is only one.   In addition, the
general cannot be principle and substance, because it
is devoid of force and cannot exist *per se*.   The general
is always an attribute, a predicate : substance, on the
other hand, is a subject, a thing existing apart.   Therefore, it is quite true that the general alone is an object
of science ; substance, on the contrary, can be only
individual.

Here, however, a difficulty arises.   If, on the one
hand, all science rests on the general, and, on the other,
substance can be only something individual, how can
there be a science of substance ?   Does not our theory
end in the following result : a science whose object is
not in being ; a being which cannot be an object of
science ?

To solve this difficulty, we must enlarge our notion
of science.   All science does not rest on the general.
Science has two modes, two degrees.   There is science
in potency and there is science in act.   The former has
the general for its object, but it is not so with the

latter, which has for its object the perfectly determined being, the individual.

In this doctrine we find the central idea of Aristotelianism. The general is not the constitutive principle of being, it is nothing but the matter thereof. Though determined in one direction, it is indeterminate in another : every general type may be realised in divers ways. A real being, a substance, is a completed being, which, in every respect, is this and not that : consequently, in any real being whatsoever, there is something more than in any general idea. The entire science of the general could not build up the individuality of Socrates. There are necessarily two things outside of this abstract science : accidents, because they are below the general ; individuals, because they are above it. The knowledge of individuals is effected by an intuition, which, immediately, grasps the substantial unity that could not be deduced.

This irreducibleness of the individual to the general will be seen through the philosophy of Aristotle. By virtue of this principle, abstract speculation will be powerless to enable us to know nature ; to do this, experience will be necessary. And in the moral order of things, laws will be inadequate to bring about the reign of justice ; the magistrate must be brought in, empowered by law to apply general rules to the endless diversity of individual cases.

What are the principles of being ? Being, which is given to us, is subject to a process of becoming. Now, becoming, in so far as it exists, implies principles that have not been generated : a halt must necessarily be made in the retrogression towards causes, when we have to find out what are the integral elements of present existence.

What are the principles required in order to explain becoming ? They are four in number : 1st, a substratum or matter, the scene of change, *i.e.* of the substitution of one mode of being for another ; 2nd, a form of determination ; 3rd, a motor cause ; 4th, an aim or end. For instance, the principles of a house are : the timber, as matter or material, the idea of the house, as form, the architect, as motor cause, and the dwelling to be realised, as object or end.

These four principles, in turn, may be reduced to two : matter and form. In fact, the motor cause is nothing more than form in an already realised subject : thus, the motor cause of the house is the idea of the house, as conceived by the architect. And the final cause is also the form, for the final cause of each single thing really consists of the perfection or form towards which it is tending.

And so matter and form are definitely the two non-generated principles that are necessary and sufficient to explain becoming. Matter is the substratum. It is neither this nor that ; it is capable of becoming this or that. Form is that which makes of matter a determinate (τόδε τι) and real thing. It is the perfection, activity or soul of the thing. As Aristotle interprets it, the word *form* has quite a different meaning from ours. For instance, in Aristotle's phraseology, a sculptured hand possesses the *figure* and not the *form* of a hand, because it cannot perform such functions as are proper to the hand.

There is a scale of existences from lowest matter, which has no form at all, to highest form, which is devoid of matter. Absolutely indeterminate matter is non-existent. Form without matter is outside of nature. All the beings of nature are compounds of matter and form. The opposition of matter and form is relative. That which is matter from one point of view is form from another. Timber is matter in relation to the house, and form in relation to uncut wood. The soul is form with regard to the body, matter the intelligence.

Aristotle does not content himself with this reduction of the four principles to matter and form ; he attempts to bring together these two principles themselves. To effect this, he brings them within the scope of potency and act. For him, matter is not mere receptivity, as it is for Plato : it has a propensity to receive form, it desires form. The latter is not something heterogeneous as regards matter : it is its natural completion. Matter is potency, potency that is capable of two determinate contraries. The logical mechanism of the substitution of forms in inert matter thus resolves itself into a metaphysical dynamism. There is an inner action in the transition from potency to act. This is no longer a juxtaposition or separation of inert, pre-existing elements : it is a spontaneous creation of being and perfection. If a force of determinate quantity, says Aristotle, is needed to produce a certain effect, the half of this force, applied separately, does not produce this effect at all. Were it not so, given a ship which several men, with united effort, set in motion, a single man would be able to communicate a certain amount of motion to the ship, but this, as we know, is contrary to experience. Any particular part, which produces motion when united with the whole, if taken separately and acting alone, becomes altogether powerless. Truth to tell, the part has no existence as a part in what is really a whole : a part exists only potentially in the whole from which it may be taken.

As we see, the Aristotelian concept of potency and act is very empirical. Aristotle takes it for granted that the effort of a single man produces no result on a ship, because he does not know that the work which does not become manifest in the form of movement, at all events, generates heat. None the less is the push of a single man really ineffective, so far as actual removal from one place to another is concerned. Even at the present time, there is a school of chemists who reason like Aristotle, and do not regard hydrogen and oxygen as existing in water in act, but, relying on experience, these scientists say that hydrogen and oxygen exist in water in potency, in this sense that, if water is subjected to certain conditions, hydrogen and oxygen may be obtained.

To sum up, becoming, according to Aristotle, originates neither in absolute being nor in absolute non-being; it originates in being in potency, midway between being and non-being.

From this being in potency, or matter, proceeds all that is indetermination and imperfection in the world. Matter is the principle of brute necessity or ἀνάγκη, which is mechanical and blind causality, in contrast with the motor cause which acts with a view to an end. If such necessity exists, it is because nature is compelled to employ material causes in its creations. Now, in a sense, matter is resistant to form. That is why the creations of nature are invariably imperfect ; there are even produced many things that are devoid of purpose, in so far as they come into being by the action of mechanical forces only. Slaves, for instance, whose actions are regulated often, nevertheless, act on their own account, quite apart from regulations. Matter is the principle of the contingence of future events.

As regards the future, the position of a determinate alternative is alone necessary : the realisation of either term of this alternative is indeterminate. From matter proceeds hazard. In any given being, those phenomena are fortuitous which do not spring from the essence of that being, but are the result either of its imperfection or of the influx of extraneous causes. Hazard manifests itself by the rarity of the event. The fortuitous event is mechanically necessary, though necessary only from this point of view : in relation to finality it is indeterminable and uncognisable. Matter is the cause of the imperfection of beings as well as the cause of evil. It is likewise the cause of the multiplicity of species, for, in all their infinite variety, the beings of nature are only more or less complete realisations of one and the same type supplied by the form. Animals are only incomplete men, arrested at a certain stage of their natural development. From the presence of matter in natural things, it follows that these things cannot be the object of perfect science, i.e. they cannot be known as fully determined. In itself, the material element of things does not admit of science.

Such are the proximate causes of being when submitted to a process of becoming. We could not have a full explanation of this being, however, were we to confine ourselves to a consideration of its elements. Being in process of becoming finds its ultimate explanation only in an eternal being.

The existence of God is already proved, in a popular way, by the gradual perfection of beings and the finality that reigns throughout nature. Scientifically it is proved by the analysis of the conditions of motion. This is what is called the argument of the prime mover.

Motion is change, the relation of matter to form. In this sense, the motion of the world is eternal. Indeed, time is necessarily eternal; now, without motion or change, time could not exist. But motion implies both something movable and a moving principle. Motion, then, in so far as it is eternal, presupposes something eternally movable and an immovable first mover. The "eternally movable" moves in a circle; this is the first heaven, the heaven of the fixed stars. The immovable first mover is what men call God.

This proof may be generalised as follows. The actual is always previous to the potential. The first, in the absolute, is not the germ, but rather the completed being. Besides, actuation could not take place were not pure act already in existence. God is this pure act.

In a word, demonstration of the existence of God is based on the following dual principle: 1st, act, from the point of view of the absolute nature of things, is anterior to potency; 2nd, the conditioned presupposes the unconditioned.

What is God? His nature is determined by his *rôle* as first mover. God is pure act, *i.e.* he is exempt from indetermination, imperfection and change. He is both immovable and immutable. He is thought which has thought—and nothing else—as its object (ἡ νόησις νοήσεως νόησις). He sees not the world, for when we are dealing with imperfect things, not to see them is better than to see them: the dignity of an intelligence is gauged by the perfection of its object. He is eternal, all-excelling life, and therefore supremely happy.

To this thought which thinks itself the world is suspended, as a thought which does not think itself and tends to do so. This is how God moves the world. What is desired and thought moves without oneself moving. It is the intelligible that determines intelligence, not intelligence that determines the intelligible. Now, God is the supremely desirable and the supremely intelligible. God, therefore, moves the world as final cause, without himself moving. God is not the ultimate product of the world's development; logically, he is anterior to the world. Nor is he immanent in the world, as order is immanent in an army : he is out of the world, as a general is distinct from his army.

The immediate effect of divine action is the rotatory motion of the whole universe, which gives rise to the motions or changes of perishable things. The world is one, because God is one. Because God is intelligent, the world is a harmonious whole, a well-composed poem. Everything therein is arranged with a view to a single end. The relation of the various beings to the whole is all the closer from the fact that these beings are higher in the scale of nature ; just as, in a well-ordered house, the actions of free men are more regulated than those of slaves. God, moreover, to whom the world is as though it did not exist, intervenes in no single detail of his own events.

This theology is an abstract monotheism. All the beings and facts of nature are wholly referred to natural causes. It is only nature, regarded in its entirety, that is made contingent on divinity. There is neither special providence nor supernatural reward in another life. The only thing in popular religion that Aristotle admits to be true is the general belief in divinity and in the divine nature of the sky and the stars. To his mind, the rest consists of nothing but mythical additions, the explanation of which a philosopher finds either in the tendency of men towards anthropomorphic conceptions, or in the calculations of politicians.

IX.—GENERAL PHYSICS

The object of first philosophy was immovable and incorporeal being ; the object of physics, or second philosophy, is movable and corporeal being, in so far as the latter has within itself the principle of its motion. Φύσις is spontaneous motion, in opposition to that which results from compulsion.

Does nature exist as such ? Is there, in the universe, an internal principle of motion, a tendency to an end ?

According to Aristotle, it is the fundamental principle of physics that God and nature do nothing in vain ; that nature always tends towards something better ; that, as far as possible, it always brings to pass what is to be the most beautiful. The existence of finality in the universe is proved by observation. In the smallest as in the largest things, if we take notice, we find there is reason, perfection, divinity. Nature converts even its own imperfections to good.

But if order and harmony exist throughout the universe, does it follow that the universe is the product of a φύσις properly so called, a divine creative power ? Is not there some other possible explanation of this order and harmony ? Why, for instance, should we not say : Jupiter does not send the rain in order to make the corn grow ; the corn grows because it rains. Necessity makes the rain fall, and when this pheno-menon takes place, the wheat profits thereby. Necessity likewise makes the organs of animals, and of these they make use. Whereas everything appears to take place with a view to an end, it is really only things that survive, because they happen to have been constituted by chance so as to conform with their conditions of existence. And those things which did not happen to be constituted in that way, die out, and have always died out, as, according to Empedocles, happened in the case of the oxen with human faces.

A vain explanation, replies Aristotle, for the organs of animals and the majority of the beings with which nature brings us in contact are what they are, to wit, harmonious compounds, either in every case, or in most, at all events. Now, it is never so with things produced by chance; here, fortunate occurrences are never anything but exceptions.

But, we shall be told, there exist monsters. Monsters are but incomplete pieces of work, the results of effort which is incapable of realising the perfect type. Nature, as well as art, may make mistakes, by reason of the obstruction which the very matter, on which it is working, sets up against it.

Finally, will the objection be raised that we do not see the mover deliberating and choosing ? That matters little, for art does not deliberate either ; it acts intelligently, without giving account of what it does.

Nature, then, is a cause, and a cause that acts with a view to an end. It must, however, be recognised that it is not the only cause in the universe. Its action is only possible owing to the co-operation of the material or mechanical cause, which, though yielding to its attraction, never allows itself to submit completely. Along with finality, then, we find everywhere throughout the universe, a certain proportion of brute necessity and chance.

This explains why, on the one hand, the principle

I

of the best may legitimately be employed in explaining the things of nature ; though, on the other hand, the things of nature can never come within the domain of perfect science, wherein everything seems wholly determined from the point of view of the intelligence. The science of nature is always imperfect in some direction ; it admits of degrees, as do the parts of nature itself. In accordance with these principles, the cause of natural things may be found, either in their matter, or in their form or destination. And, as far as possible, the teleological explanation should complete the mechanical one, which, however finished it be, leaves things indeterminate in the sight of reason. Such is the method Aristotle is to pursue in his investigations into natural things.

Motion or change is the realization of a possible. There are four kinds of change : 1st, substantial change, which consists in being born and in perishing. This is motion which proceeds from relative non-being to being, and from the latter to the former. There is no such thing as absolute generation and destruction. Individuals alone are born and die : genera remain. 2nd, quantitative change : increase or diminution ; 3rd, qualitative change, or the transition from one substance to another ; 4th, spatial change, or displacement.

All modes of change are conditioned by motion in space. Aristotle makes a profound study of this motion. He brings against the arguments of the Eleatics, who deny the possibility of motion, the doctrine that the infinite exists only in potency, not in act. The infinite consists only in the possibility of an indefinite increase of numbers and in the indefinite divisibility of dimensions : it cannot be the given.

When, therefore, we reason about the real, we should presuppose only finite quantities.

As regards space, Aristotle investigates the nature of place. The place of a body is not something in itself, it is the interior limit of the surrounding body. It is like a motionless vase which contains the body. Consequently, all bodies are not in a place, but only those enclosed in other bodies. The sky, the universal container, is not itself in a place. Space, or rather the extent of the world, is limited.

Time is the number of motion as regards before and after. It is limitless in both directions.

Continuousness is the characteristic of time and space. It is divisible *ad infinitum*, though in dimensions that are themselves continuous : not, as Zeno supposed, in indivisible points. All dimension is divisible into dimensions. Moreover, continuousness is an imperfect notion, and relates to sensible things, for it is divisible *ad infinitum*, and consequently is indeterminate as regards the number of its elements.

From these principles Aristotle concludes that, outside the world, there is neither space nor time, that the *vacuum* of the atomists is inconceivable, that all motion takes place in the *plenum* by a process of substitution, and that time, which is a number, presupposes, as does every number, a soul which counts its units. Motion in space, the condition of all other motions, is the only one that is continuous. And circular motion is the only kind that is capable of being both one and continuous, without beginning or end.

Aristotle does not regard it as possible to explain all changes by motion in space alone. He looks upon qualities as realities, and admits that qualitative change is incapable of being reduced to motion in space. This theory he sets up in opposition to the mechanism of Democritus and the *mathématisme* of Plato. He raises two objections to the doctrines of these philosophers : 1st, Democritus and Plato reduce dimensions to indivisible points : now, all dimension is divisible *ad infinitum* ; 2nd, however we set about it, it is impossible to extract quality from quantity, pure and simple.

It is for this reason that Aristotle lays down the principle of a qualitative distinction in substances.

And, just as there is a qualitative nature, there is likewise a qualitative transformation. One substance, acted upon by another, becomes modified in its inner nature. This phenomenon is possible when two bodies are partly alike and partly unlike, that is to say, when two substances are opposed to each other within one and the same genus, and it is possible only in this case. The changing of one of these substances into the other is no mere mechanical displacement, in which the elements remain identical throughout the change in the compound substance : it is really the formation of a new substance, fundamentally different from the former. The given substance bears the same relation to the substance resulting from the qualitative change that potency bears to act.

X.—MATHEMATICS

Mathematics considers relations of dimension, quantity, and continuousness, neglecting the other physical qualities. Thus, it deals with things that are immovable without existing apart, essences intermediary between the world and God. By a process of abstraction the mathematician isolates form from matter, in sensible things.

Mathematics is either pure or applied. Geometry and arithmetic constitute pure mathematics. Mathematics may be applied either to the practical arts, geodesy, for instance, or to natural sciences, such as optics, mechanics, harmonics, or astrology. In the latter case the question of fact is the business of the physicist, the why or wherefore is the business of the mathematician.

Mathematics makes use of the notions of the good and the beautiful, because order, symmetry, and determination, all of which are pre-eminently mathematical, are some of the most important elements in the good and the beautiful.

None of Aristotle's mathematical works have come down to us. His principal ones were treatises on mathematics, unity, optics, and astronomy. In the works we possess we frequently come across examples taken from mathematics.

XI.—COSMOLOGY

From the eternity of form and matter follows the perpetuity of motion, as well as that of the existence of the world. Species in themselves are eternal, and there have always been men : individuals alone are born and perish. As the world is eternal, the science of the world is not a cosmogony, but rather a cosmology. Aristotle has not the formation of the universe to explain, but only its system.

The world is one, finite and well regulated. It is a work of art, as beautiful and good as the resistance of the material element permits. It has a perfect form, the spherical, the only one, moreover, that enables the whole to move without causing a vacuum outside itself.

It consists of two unequal halves : 1st, the supra-lunar or celestial world, the vault to which the fixed stars are attached ; 2nd, the infralunar or terrestrial world.

The celestial world is animated with a rotatory motion produced directly by God. The imperishable nature of the stars and the unchangeable regularity of their motions prove that they differ, as regards matter, from terrestrial things, which are subject to continual change. The matter composing the stars is ether, or the fifth element (quint-essence), the body that is without a contrary, and is therefore incorruptible, admitting of no other change than that of place, and no other motion than a circular one. The other elements, on the contrary, being formed of terrestrial bodies, are corruptible and admit of motion from below, upwards, and from above, downwards, that is to say, from centre to circumference and from circumference to centre. The heaven of the fixed stars is the abode of being, of perfect life, and of unchangeable order. The stars are beings which are not subject to old age, beings that live a life of happiness whilst exercising eternal and inde-fatigable activity. They are far more divine than man. Our ancestors had a vague intuition of the truth when they regarded the stars as being gods.

Within the heaven of the fixed stars is the region of the planets, including, says Aristotle, the sun and the moon, as well as the five planets known to the ancients. In the middle of the world is the earth, spherical in form. The heaven of the planets is made of a sub-stance that is less and less pure in inverse ratio to its distance from the heaven of the fixed stars. In contra-distinction to the first heaven, which is a single sphere bearing all the stars, the heaven of the planets consists of a multiplicity of spheres, for the movements of the planets, being relatively irregular, presuppose a multiplicity of movers whose actions combine with one another.

Beings other than the fixed stars are made of the four elements. Each element has a motion of its own, the rectilineal march towards the place natural to it. Hence we obtain weight and lightness. Weight is the tendency of each body to follow its own direction. It is not possible to say, with Democritus, that all motion is simply the result of impacts *ad infinitum*. A halt in retrogression must be made, in the logical order of things, at all events. The motion that results from compulsion presupposes spontaneous motion.

It is the property of the terrestrial element to incline towards the centre, hence the position of the earth, immovable in the centre of the universe. The earth is spherical. Its elements are in double opposition—of weight and quality—to one another. On the one hand, they are heavy or light ; on the other, they are hot or cold, dry or moist. The result of this opposition is that the elements of the earth are constantly changing into one another. Heat and light are generated by the friction to which the air is subjected owing to the extreme velocity of the celestial spheres. By reason of the inclination of the ecliptic, light and heat are produced in different degrees in different regions of the earth and at different times of the year. This is the origin of the circulus of generation and destruction, that image of eternity in perishable nature. Action proceeds from periphery to centre ; the heaven of the fixed stars representing highest form, the earth representing lowest matter. The various mineral and organised bodies are formed by the mutual action of the two active potencies, heat and cold, and of the two passive potencies, moisture and dryness.

Terrestrial beings form a hierarchy, extending from the being which is nearest to brute matter up to the male human being. Each lower form is the basis of the higher ones ; each higher form the relative completion of the lower ones. The principal stages in the hierarchy are represented by lifeless bodies, plants, animals, and man.

XII.—Astronomy

Aristotle made much study of astronomy. Simplicius, so Porphyry tells us, relates that, with a view to investigations in this science, he instructed Callisthenes to collect the astronomical observations made by the Chaldaeans in Babylon, especially those that dated back nineteen hundred years before the time of Alexander. Aristotle himself tells us that he utilised the observations of the Egyptians and Babylonians, dating back to a very distant age. He wrote an 'Αστρονομικόν, which is lost.

All the celestial beings, according to Aristotle, are spherical. The first heaven, that of the fixed stars, is a sphere. The planets are moved by spheres ; the earth is spherical.

All simple motion is rotation round an axis. The heaven of the fixed stars has only one motion. The heaven of the planets (Saturn, Jupiter, Venus, Mercury, Mars, the Sun, the Moon) has several for each planet. The earth is without motion.

Aristotle maintains the doctrine of the sphericity of the earth, and gives the correct explanation of the phases of the moon.

He worked with the astronomer Callipus in completing and rectifying the theory of the spheres formed by Eudoxus, the first astronomer of his day, as well as the theory of Callipus himself. His theory may be summed up as follows :—

We must admit, said Aristotle, along with Plato—who in this matter followed the lead of Eudoxus and Callipus—the number of spheres and their mode of motion, necessary for the explanation of the revolutions of the planets, as they appear under observation, with no other elements than uniform rotatory motions. Presenting the problem in this way, Eudoxus inferred that there were twenty-six spheres, Callipus thirty-three. Aristotle accepts the latter figure. But since, in his philosophy, the exterior spheres are to the interior what form is to matter, he is obliged to add antagonistic spheres, in order that each exterior sphere may not communicate its motion to all the spheres interior to itself, as does the sphere of the fixed stars. For each planet, then, there are as many antagonistic spheres as are needed to counteract the action of the exterior planetary spheres. The supplementary spheres are twenty-two in number, and these, added on to the thirty-three of Callipus, make fifty-five spheres. But if we consider that the sun and the moon, being far away from the rest of the planets, have no need of antagonistic spheres, the total number of the spheres will be reduced to forty-seven. This, says Aristotle, is probable enough.

To each of these spheres motion must be communicated, as it was to the first heaven, by an incorporeal substance, a spirit, or a god. The constellations, the object and end of the motions of the spheres, are moreover, for that reason, their true causes. Conse-

quently the constellations are animated beings, endowed
with reason and superior to man.

XIII.—METEOROLOGY

Meteorology had been much studied since the time
of Thales.   Aristotle profited by the labours of his
predecessors, though he also made original investigations
in this science along the lines of his own philosophy.

Meteorological phenomena are the result, he says, of
the action of the four elements upon one another.   In
accordance with the nature of these elements, the results
of their mutual action are less determined and obey less
strict laws than the phenomena that take place in the first
element : the ether.   It is for this reason that Aristotle,
when considering meteors, seeks after explanations
that are mainly of a mechanical and empirical nature.
He attributes a preponderating influence to heat.   In
this way he explains comets, the Milky Way, clouds,
fogs, winds, the relations between seas and continents
and the formation of the sea.   His explanations often
testify to exact observation and skilful reasoning.
Winds, for instance, are explained by the motion of
vapours, as a result of their differences of temperature.   Earthquakes are due to the action of subterranean
gases.   The rainbow is but a phenomenon caused by
reflection : in the sun's light, the spray composing the
clouds acts as a mirror.

These investigations are purely theoretical : Aristotle
does not dream of using them for the purpose of pre-
dicting phenomena.

XIV.—MINERALOGY

Minerals are homogeneous bodies which remain so,
without becoming organised into individuals consisting

of different parts. These bodies are formed by cold and heat, combining or disintegrating—in so far as they are active properties—the moist and the dry, which play the *rôle* of passive properties.

XV.—GENERAL BIOLOGY

Biology forms a considerable portion of Aristotle's scientific work. He probably utilised many of the works of his predecessors, mainly those of Democritus, but he went so far beyond the rest that he stands out as the true founder of biology in Greece. He works mainly by observation, the determination of phenomena being made to precede the investigation of causes. To simple observation he would appear to have added dissection. He proceeds from anatomy to physiology and, speaking generally, regards biology as the groundwork of physics, basing it on a knowledge of the four elements. He deals not only with every conceivable problem of his own times, but also with almost all the problems that engage the attention of modern scientists. The solutions he offers are, for the most part, carefully set forth ; and, considering the state of knowledge at the time, his reasonings are correct and ingenious. It must be confessed, however, that his explanations are frequently arbitrary or rather metaphysical ; at times, even, he appears to have given demonstrative value to mere legends.

Life is motion. Now, all motion presupposes a form that moves and matter that is moved. The form is the soul ; matter the body. The soul is neither body nor without body. It moves without moving ; it is immovable, not self-moving, as Plato imagined. As being the form of the body, it is its goal ; the body is nothing but the instrument of the soul, and its structure is guided by this destination. Aristotle correctly defines the soul as the first entelechy of an organic physical body. This means that the soul is the permanent force which moves the body and determines its constitution.

It is natural for the finality of nature to appear in living beings more clearly than anywhere else, because everything, in them, at the outset, is calculated with a view to the soul. But just as form only gradually overcomes the resistance of matter, so there are degrees in the psychic life, and these are essentially three in number : nutritiveness, sensibility, and intelligence. Nutritiveness is the fundamental quality of living beings ; from it proceed vital development and death. It exists both in plants and in animals. The latter possess sensibility in addition. Man, a superior animal, possesses all three : nutritiveness, sensibility, and intelligence.

Aristotelian biology deals principally with animals. The body of an animal consists of homoeomerous substances : a mixture of elementary substances. The immediate matter of the soul is breath ($\pi\nu\epsilon\hat{\upsilon}\mu\alpha$), the principle of vital heat, a body akin to ether, along with which the soul is transmitted, in the semen, from father to child. The principal seat of heat is the central organ, that is to say, the heart, in animals endowed with blood. In the heart the blood is cooked, after being formed of the nutritive substances introduced by the veins, and blood, as final, definite nourishment, feeds and sustains the body. It becomes flesh and bone, nail and horn, etc. The nutritive power of foods is not the result of their containing particles of flesh, bone, and marrow, which would go to unite directly with like substances existing in the body, it is rather owing to the food being cooked several times that it reaches a state enabling it to be assimilated by the organism. Though very precise on the matter of assimilation, Aristotle would appear never to have thought of disassimilation.

XVI.—Botany

Aristotle's works on botany are lost, but he certainly gave an impetus to the investigations made on plants in his school ; he seems to have largely contributed to the creation of scientific botany.

XVII.—Animal Anatomy and Physiology

A distinction must be made between general anatomy and physiology and comparative anatomy and physiology.

The parts of the animal organism are of two kinds : the homogeneous, such as the tissues ; and the heterogeneous, such as the organs. Each organ has a function, the tongue, hand, etc. The tissues have properties. Aristotle studies first the homogeneous, then the heterogeneous parts.

The homogeneous parts are : 1st, veins, bones, cartilages, nails, hair, horn, etc. ; 2nd, fat, grease, blood, marrow, flesh, milk, semen, membranes. In many cases, Aristotle's explanations regarding these parts are finalistic, and derive the nature of the part from its function. For instance, he says the incisors appear before the molars, because food must first be cut up or torn to be in a fit state to be ground.

The anatomical study of the heterogeneous parts is not distinct from their physiological study.

The first of all the organs is the heart. Aristotle has no notion of the circulation of the blood, as we understand the word, nor does he say anything of the two kinds of blood ; he acknowledges, however, that it is carried throughout the body by the veins, as by canals. The heart is the centre of the living being, the seat of the formation of the blood, and the source of its heat. All animals possess a heart and blood, or substitutes for these primary conditions of life. Those animals that can be divided or cut up without the parts immediately ceasing to live, are not simple animals, but rather aggregates of animals. The degree of unity is the standard of the perfection of the being. No mutilated animal recovers from its injuries as does the plant, in which the life principle is dispersed throughout the entire being.

The other heterogeneous parts are : the diaphragm, the sense organs, the organs of motion, the encephalon, the lungs, the abdominal viscera, and the sex organs.

Aristotle enlarges on the senses. Sensation consists in being moved, in experiencing some change. There are two kinds of senses : the mediate, which act through the medium of the atmosphere, as sight, hearing, and smell; and the immediate, which act by contact, as touch and taste ; the latter being more important for the preservation of the individual. The mediate senses estimate either differences in the nature of objects, or else distances ; consequently we must make a distinction between their acuteness and their sphere of action.

The eye is not a mere mirror : the presence of an image would not suffice to produce vision : there is required a psychic property, which a mere mirror does not possess. The inmost recesses of the eye not only reflect the image, they have the property of seeing as well.

Indirectly, hearing is the most intellectual of all the senses, for it enables ideas to be communicated by means of language. Speech is nothing but a sequence of sounds that have entered the ear ; it is one and the same motion diffused from ear to throat.

Touch differs from the rest of the senses in that the latter supply us with oppositions or contrasts of a single kind only, whereas touch enables us to distinguish hot and cold, dry and moist, hard and soft.

Aristotle is acquainted with no other organs of motion than the tendons, and these he calls nerves. He tries to discover the principle thereof, not in the limbs themselves, but in a central organ of motion. The principle of motion is the heart, or, in the case of animals that have none, the corresponding organ. Motions are of two kinds, voluntary and involuntary. The beating of the heart, for instance, belongs to the second type of motion.

As the heart is a calorific organ, so the encephalon and the lungs are refrigerant organs.

Of the abdominal organs, Aristotle carefully studies the stomach, giving remarkably correct descriptions as regards ruminants, birds and the organs of sex upon which his observations are frequently very apt and successful. His investigations lead him to discuss the part played by both sexes in the production of the new being.

He also applies himself to the question of heredity. He rejects pangenesis (which states that the parents contribute germs resembling themselves), alleging that there are products which do not resemble their parents : for instance, caterpillars born of butterflies. According to Aristotle, the material that goes to the formation of the new being is made up of substances different from that of the parents themselves. There is a male seminal fluid, the' sperm, and a female one, the menstrua. From the blending of these two elements, as from the union of form with matter, results the germ. Thus, from the man there is born the soul, and from the woman the body, of the child resulting from their union.

The difference in the sexes may be reduced to a difference in degree. In the woman food has not received so complete an elaboration as in man, the creative power has not finished its work.

In like manner Aristotle explains instances of teratology. Monstrosities are only greater or less dissimilarities, the result of excess or defect. They deviate from the ordinary course of events, though having their basis in natural forces.

In the same spirit Aristotle dealt with embryogeny. Interpreting the results of his delicate observations in accordance with the principles of his philosophy, he admits that the development of the germ is an epitome of the general progress of life in nature. First, the life of the germ is comparable to vegetable life ; afterwards, the embryo is in a state that may be compared to sleep : sleep, however, from which there is no awakening. The foetus becomes animal when it acquires feeling ; then only is it capable of genuine sleep. The order in which the organs appear is determined by their utility and by the share they have in the formation of the other organs. Thus, the heart is the first organ to be developed.

In Aristotle we find numerous aphorisms and biological considerations resulting from what we call comparative anatomy and physiology. He makes a careful study of organic resemblances and differences. Organs may resemble one another in form. Organs apparently different may be only more or less complete developments of one and the same type, so that, at bottom,

excess or deficiency really constitutes the whole difference. There may be resemblance by analogy; for
instance, the feather is to the bird what the scale is to
the fish. There is the same relation between the bones
of land animals and those of fishes, between nails and
horns, etc. Different species may have the same organs
diversely situated. Different organs may perform the
same function.

Aristotle determines numerous organic correlations.
For instance, all animals have blood, or its equivalent.
Animals with no feet at all, and those with two and four
feet, possess blood; in those with more than four feet
lymph takes the place of blood. In ruminants there is
a correlation between the possession of horns and the
lack of canine teeth. The lateral movements of the
lower jaw are found only in such animals as grind their
food. All truly viviparous animals breathe in air, etc.

The law regarding division of work is clearly formulated. Nature, says Aristotle, if there is nothing to
hinder, always employs two special and distinct organs
for two different functions. When this cannot be done,
the same instrument is used for several purposes; though
it is preferable that the same organ should not be used
for several functions.

The influences of environment are shown to contribute to the determination of animal forms. In hot
climates, says Aristotle, it is principally animals which
are cold by nature, such as serpents, lizards and
those covered with scales, that grow to considerable
dimensions.

Aristotle also studied physiognomy, or the relation
which the physical bears to the moral. In all probability
the *Physiognomonica* is not an authentic work, though
doubtless it owes its origin to his teaching. In the

K

Historia animalium we find him trying to find out to what moral differences the physical differences in the human face correspond.

According to our philosopher, the species, properly so called, are stable and separated from one another. Along with the absolute, however, Aristotle recognises the existence of the contingent. Consequently, there is a certain freedom of action in nature, and organic forms and faculties admit of restricted variability. An apparently insignificant difference, found in small parts, may suffice to produce considerable differences in the *ensemble* of the animal's body. For instance, only a small portion of an animal's body is removed by castration, and yet this removal changes its nature, bringing it into closer resemblance with the other sex. When the animal is in the embryonic state, a very slight difference will cause it to be either a male or a female. The difference between the terrestrial and the aquatic animal results from the different arrangement of small parts. In a word, says Aristotle, in nature there is unity of composition and progressive continuity. Man himself, who, as far as we know, is at the top of the ladder, is only separated from the animals, physically speaking, by more or less pronounced differences. The transition from one kingdom to another is imperceptible. Thus, in the sea we find beings at a stage intermediate between animals and plants, *e.g.* sponges. The principal types and stages of growth, as it were, are none the less determined and mutually irreducible.

XVIII.—Zoölogy

Aristotle was the first classifying zoölogist. Truth to tell, he does not appear to have had any intention to set up a zoölogical classification, and his attempts in this direction are offered only as examples. Nor did he make any sharply-drawn distinction of animals, distributing them in a hierarchy of genera and species ; he merely assigned limits to the principal groups. He clearly saw, however, that the criterion of species is obtained through reproduction—interfecundity. He regards as of the same species only such animals as spring from common parents. His classification aims at being natural, that is to say, it tends to bring together those animals that have a fundamental resemblance to one another. Here, as elsewhere, his object is to distinguish essence from accident.

The first division is that between animals that have blood (our vertebrates) and those that have no blood (our invertebrates). The divisions between sanguineous animals are mainly based on embryogeny and a consideration of the element in which they live. Sanguineous animals are divided into true vivipara, ovovivipara and ovipara. Animals devoid of blood are divided into mollusks (corresponding to our cephalopoda), crustacea, testacea (corresponding to our mollusks, with the exception of the cephalopoda) and insects.

In his description of the species—he mentions about four hundred of them—Aristotle shows that he possesses extensive knowledge. Amongst other things, he deals with the mental and moral faculties of animals. Bees he calls the wise—the well-behaved—ones.

As regards the first origin of man and of the other sanguineous animals, he is inclined to think that they proceed from a sort of scolex (head of the tapeworm), or else from a perfect egg, in which only a portion becomes the germ, developing at the expense of the rest. He considers the spontaneous production of a perfect egg as not at all likely, since we never meet with an instance of it. Testacea and worms, on the contrary, have spontaneous birth.

XIX.—PSYCHOLOGY

That which differentiates man from the rest of the animal kingdom is the *νοῦς*, which, in him, is united to the animal soul. He possesses faculties common to himself and the animals, and faculties peculiar to himself. In common with the animals, man has sensation and the faculties derived therefrom.

Sensation is the change effected in the mind by a sensible object, as by a contrary, through the agency of the body, and consisting in the form of the object that is sensed being communicated to the subject that senses. Thus, sensation is the common act of a sensible object and a sensing subject.

Each sense gives us exclusive information regarding the properties of those things with which it specially deals ; what it tells us of these properties is always true. General properties are known by the *sensorium commune*, in which all sensible impressions meet. Here, too, sensations are compared and related to objects as causes, and to ourselves as conscious subjects. The organ of the *sensorium commune* is the heart. Its data may be either true or false.

Sensation is the basis of animal psychic life. Both from the theoretical and the practical standpoint it is capable of a development which brings several other faculties into being.

When motion in the sense-organ continues beyond the duration of the sensation, extends to the central organ, and there causes a new appearance of the sensible image, we have *imagination*. The products of this faculty may be either true or false. When an image is recognised as the reproduction of a past perception, we have *memory*. Aristotle adds to the study of these faculties investigations as to the nature of sleep, death and dreams, from the psychological point of view.

Looked upon from the practical standpoint of good and evil, sensation admits of development along the lines just mentioned. From the sole fact that an animal is endowed with sensation, it is capable of *pleasure* and *pain*. When its activity is unchecked, we have pleasure ; in the contrary event, pain. Pleasure and pain, in beings fully susceptible to them, are really judgments upon the true value of things. Consequently, beings capable of pleasure and pain have *desire*, which is nothing but the seeking after what is agreeable. They also have *passions*.

All these functions already appertain to animals, though they are realised to perfection only in man. Man possesses *intelligence* in addition to the rest. Hitherto we have seen that there has been continual development and progress. Between the animal soul and the νοῦς, however, there is a break of continuity. The νοῦς is the knowledge of first principles. It has no birth, but is eternal. Exempt from passivity, it exists in act. Being without organ, it is not the result of the development of sensation, but comes from without, and is separable.

Human intelligence, however, is not merely this complete, immovable νοῦς. It learns, becomes acquainted with perishable things, things capable of being as they are or otherwise. The νοῦς, therefore, in man blends with the soul : there is a lower intellect, intermediary between the absolute νοῦς and the animal soul. This intellect may be called νοῦς παθητικός, passive intellect, in opposition to νοῦς ἀπαθής, or active intellect. This lower νοῦς is the subject, but not the object ; perishable things are its object. Depending on the body, it perishes with the body. There are rudiments of this passive intellect in certain animals, e.g. in bees, but only in man is it fully developed.

The νοῦς παθητικός has two kinds of functions, theoretical and practical.

From the theoretical point of view, the νοῦς παθητικός, at first, is νοῦς only in potency. It is a *tabula rasa* on which nothing has yet been written. The νοῦς παθητικός thinks only by the aid of images, and under the influence of the higher νοῦς. It thus deduces from sensation the general contained therein, and which sensation reaches only by accident : it gradually becomes determined by reason of these general essences. Perfect science, however, belongs only to the νοῦς θεωρητικός, the higher νοῦς, which, starting from causes, proceeds *a priori*.

The νοῦς, as regards its practical use, has no principles of its own : practice consisting only of the application of theoretical ideas. This realisation comes about in two ways : 1st, by production (ποιεῖν) ; 2nd, by action (πράττειν).

With regard to action, Aristotle offers a theory of will, the spring of action. Will is the combination of intellect and desire. As desire, it posits ends to be realised ; as intellect, it determines the means that correspond to these ends. The objects of will are determined with reference to two principal ends : the good and the possible.

Free-will is connected with the existence of will. In beings devoid of reason, desire can only spring from sensation. In man, it may be engendered either by sensation or by reason. Engendered by sensation, it is appetite ; engendered by reason, it is will. Between appetite and will we have free-will : the faculty of self-determination. Virtue and vice depend on ourselves ; each man is the principle of his own actions. The reality of free-will is proved by moral imputability, which legislation, praise and blame, exhortation and prohibition imply. The essence of free-will is spontaneity, in more precise language, that spontaneity which manifests preference ; for children and animals show considerable spontaneity, but man alone is truly free, for he alone is capable of choice.

XX.—Morals

In the case of beings without intelligence, ends are attained immediately and of necessity. Man has a loftier end, which is not only realised by the sole operation of natural forces, but also by using his freedom. The problem is to find out how to organise one's life in order to realise the human idea, to act according to one's own essence, and not from necessity or chance. Hence the idea of practical philosophy : the philosophy of human affairs. The aim of this philosophy is to find out what are the end and the means of that activity which is proper to mankind.

Practical philosophy comprises three parts, corresponding to the three spheres of action that open out to man : 1st, *ethics*, or the rules of individual life ; 2nd, *economics*, or the rules of family life ; and 3rd, *politics*, or the rules of social life. In chronological order, ethics precedes economics which itself precedes politics. In the order of nature and perfection, the relation is inverted. Politics, indeed, is the completion of economics, which itself determines human activity with greater precision than ethics, pure and simple.

We will begin with ethics or morals. Morals may be divided into general and particular morals.

In Aristotle morals does not bear the same relation to physics as in Plato. The good is not transcendent ; nature is not hostile or simply passive when brought in contact with the ideal. As form exists in potency in matter, so nature is inclined to virtue, which is only the normal development of natural tendencies. We may not be born virtuous, but of ourselves we tend to become so : culture and art are the completion of nature. Moreover, we must distinguish between good in itself and good for mankind. The good which is taken into consideration by morals is not good in itself, but only so far as it deals with human nature.

What is moral good ?   Since all action has an object, there must be a supreme object, and this can only be that good which is superior to all other good, the best. What is this best ?   The general impression is that it is happiness, but there is no agreement as to the definition of happiness. We must try to find out in what it really consists.

For every living being, good consists in the perfection or full realisation of the activity peculiar to itself. Such is the distinctive mark of true happiness. This happiness, then, cannot be said to be either in the enjoyment of the senses, which is common to man and animal, nor in pleasure, which is not an end in itself but is pursued only with a view to happiness, nor in honour, which does not lie within our power and comes from without. Perhaps even virtue alone does not afford happiness, for we could not designate as happy a virtuous man, hindered in his activity or suffering acutely. Happiness consists of the constant exercise of our strictly human, *i.e.* intellectual, faculties. Happiness is action guided by reason, in circumstances favourable to that action.

If such be the case, the element that constitutes happiness is doubtless virtue or the self-realisation of the higher part of the soul : virtue plays the part of form and principle as regards happiness. But happiness has also, as material to work upon or condition of existence, the possession of external forms of good : health, beauty, birth, fortune, children and friends ; although it is true that even the greatest of misfortunes cannot make a virtuous man really miserable.

Pleasure, regarded as an end, is not an integral element of happiness ; since, however, it naturally accompanies action, being its complement, it is closely allied to virtue. Pleasure is inherent to action as vigour is inherent to youth. It is the consciousness of activity. The value of pleasure may thus be gauged by that of the activity it accompanies. Virtue carries with it a special kind of satisfaction, necessarily possessed by the virtuous man. Pleasures are admissible in so far as they spring from virtue or can be reconciled therewith. Coarse or violent pleasures, which disturb the soul, ought to be spurned. In a word, pleasure has its place in happiness not as an end, but rather as a result.

Finally, happiness implies leisure, one condition of activity. This latter, indeed, needs relaxation ; it is not, however, leisure that is the end of work, but work that is the end of leisure. Leisure should be devoted to art, science, and above all, philosophy.

And what is virtue, the principle of happiness?
What are the principal virtues? Virtue is a habit
whose characteristic is the complete realisation of the
powers of man. Now, human nature is two-fold, to
wit, intellectual and moral. The intellectual element
has the necessary for its object, and is immovable ; the
moral element, in so far as it is connected with the contingent, desires and acts. Thus there are two kinds of
virtues : the dianoëtic or intellectual, and the ethical or
moral.

The dianoëtic virtues are the higher of the two
kinds ; they can only be acquired by instruction, not
by an effort of the will. The virtue that affords the
greatest felicity is science or contemplation. This is
the noblest of all human occupations, for the νοῦς, its
organ or instrument, is the most divine of all things.
It is the most disinterested activity, the one that causes
least fatigue, and most readily admits of continuity.
And it is the calmest, the one that best suffices unto
itself. It is by science that man draws nearest to divinity.
Therefore we must not follow the advice of those who
maintain that we should have only human feelings
because we are men, and only aspire after the destiny
of a mortal creature because we are mortal. As far
as in us lies, we should do our best to make ourselves
worthy of immortality.

Supreme felicity, however, joined to the possession
of perfect science, falls but seldom to the lot of man.
It is the ethical or moral virtues that are truly congenial
to him and adapted to his condition as spirit joined to
a body. Ethical virtue is a mental habit or disposition which tends, in all things, to choose the golden
mean suitable to our nature, and is determined by the
practical judgment of the intelligent man.

It is a habit, a mode of the will. Socrates, who made a science of it, forgot that, in considering virtue, we have nothing to do with the knowledge of moral rules, but only with their realisation. Moreover, to constitute virtue, there is needed not only a present determination of the will, but rather a habit, a lasting mode thereof.

Again, all virtue is a mean between two vices, and this mean varies in different individuals. Virtue in a man is different from virtue in a woman, a child or a slave. Time and circumstance must likewise be taken into account. Thus, courage is the mean between rashness and cowardice; magnanimity is the mean between insolence and baseness, and so on.

Finally, it is the good man who is the rule and standard of the good in each particular instance. Indeed, abstract rules determine only what is good in a general way. In each instance that offers itself there is something unique which these rules neither could nor must have foreseen. The living, universal judgment of the highly gifted man makes up for their insufficiency.

Aristotle studies in detail the different virtues, both dianoëtic and moral.

The dianoëtic virtues are the perfect habits of the intelligent part of the soul. Now, the intellect is of two kinds : scientific and logistic. The virtues of the scientific intellect are : 1st, the νοῦς, which knows the principles of things ; 2nd, science, which, from these principles, deduces particular truths. The union of the νοῦς and science constitutes wisdom (σοφία). The virtues of the logistic intellect are : the art or capacity of producing with a view to an end ; 2nd, judgment, or practical intelligence.

The moral virtues are as numerous as the different relations in human life. Since the number of these relations is indeterminate, no complete list of the moral virtues is possible ; *a fortiori*, these virtues cannot be reduced to a single principle, as Plato insists upon. Aristotle investigates the most important of the moral virtues. His dissertations are very remarkable, abounding in keen psychological and moral observations. His analyses of justice and friendship are particularly deserving of mention.

Justice, he says, is the restoration of true or proportional equality in social life. Equity is more perfect than justice, for whereas the latter takes actions into consideration only from a general and abstract point of view, equity takes account of the particular element in each separate action. It is the completion of justice, demanded by reason, since the law cannot provide for every individual case. It is concrete, actual justice superposed on abstract, and still indeterminate justice.

Friendship is supreme justice, delicate and perfect, wherein a blind, dead rule is entirely replaced by the living intelligence of the good man. Friendship has three sources : pleasure, interest and virtue. Virtue alone creates firm and lasting friendships.

XXI.—Economics

Man, in family life, attains to a degree of perfection superior to that of which individual life admits. The family is a natural society. It comprises three kinds of relation : that between man and wife, that between parents and children, and that between master and slave.

The family relation between man and wife is a moral one, based on friendship and mutual service. The wife has her own will, her own virtue, different from the man's : she ought to be treated not as a slave, but as a free person. Still, as the wife is less perfect than the man, the latter ought to have authority over her. The family is an aristocracy or community of free beings, to whom different attributions are assigned. The wife, man's free companion, ought to have in the home her own sphere of influence, with which man does not interfere.

The relation between parents and children is that between a king and his subjects. Parents and children form a monarchy. As regards his father, the child has no rights whatsoever, for he is still a part of the father; it is the father's duty, however, to watch over his child's best interests, for the child also has a will and a virtue of his own, imperfect though they be. The father should transmit his own perfection to his son, and the latter appropriate to himself the former's perfection.

Aristotle makes a special study of slavery, showing its necessity and justifiableness, and determining the way in which slaves ought to be treated. Slavery is necessary, for the home has need of living and intelligent workers. And slavery is justifiable. Given, indeed, a being fit only for bodily labour, such a being is the justifiable possession of one who is capable of intellectual activity ; the relation of the former to the latter being that of matter to form. Now, such a relation actually exists between the Barbarians and the Greeks. Thus, the free man is owner of the slave. None the less ought he to look upon the slave as a human being, and treat him as such.

XXII.—POLITICS

Aristotle's politics deals : 1st, with the State in general ; 2nd, with the Constitutions.

Politics is the end and completion of economics, as the latter is the proximate end of morals. The individual, of himself, cannot attain to virtue and happiness. Now, the tendency towards social life lies in the very nature of man. This kind of life, which is one of the conditions of human existence, is likewise a means of moral improvement. Politics, which sets forth the ideal and the rules relating to human communities, is thus intimately linked with morals : it is the whole, whereof morals and economics are but parts ; the act, of which they are the potency. Politics is the true name of all practical science. Philosophy should set forth the ideal of politics ; but just as morals, in its application, takes individuals into account, so applied politics will take circumstances into account.

How is political society formed? In the order of time, the family is the first society to be formed. Then we have the union of several families, or the κώμη. Finally comes the State, or city (πόλις) : the highest society of all. This is the chronological order; from the standpoint of nature and truth, however, the State is before individuals, family and village, as the whole is before its parts : the latter having in the former their final cause and loftiest realisation.

The end of the State is the highest that can be conceived, for the State is the most perfect expression of the social tendency. This end is neither the mere satisfaction of physical needs, the acquisition of wealth commerce, nor even the protection of the citizens by means of laws. It should consist in the happiness of the citizens. It is the mission of the State to see that its citizens possess, first, inner good, or virtue, and afterwards, outer good. The State completes the progress of human nature, rising from potency to act.

Although in agreement with Plato as regards the final good of politics, Aristotle is none the less led to criticise his master in things that concern the rights and duties of the State. He opposes the Platonic doctrine that tends to dower the State with the greatest possible unity, from which doctrine resulted the necessity of sacrificing property and family to the State. Unity belongs only to the individual. Already the family has ceased to be a unit. By nature, the city is a plurality, and a heterogeneous one. The Platonic theories of property and the family cannot be admitted. Not only are they inapplicable; they even misunderstand both the tendency of nature and the interests of the State. Property and the family are by no means artificial products, they are the objects of natural tendencies. Besides, they are useful to the State, procuring for it advantages it could not obtain by any other means. The State, therefore, ought to regulate property and the family, not to do away with them. In practice, of course, Aristotle often agrees with Plato, whom he opposes in theory ; but the conclusion could not therefore be drawn that there is no difference between Platonic and Aristotelian politics. The importance assigned to nature in the latter turns it in quite another direction.

The following, then, is the essential tendency of Aristotle's politics. As supreme good lies in intellectual leisure, the useful professions are incompatible with the title of citizen : farmers, business men, workmen, cannot be members of the city ; of an ideal one, at all events. The *rôle* of the State is to educate its citizens ; its efforts are directed to regulating their actions. The worst of States is that which allows every man to live as he pleases. The State regulates the age and the season for procreation, fixes the number of the population, orders that abortion be practised, in case this number is likely to be exceeded, and likewise the exposing and abandoning of crippled children. Education should be public, ever keeping in view the good of the intellect through the attention bestowed on sensibility, and that of the soul through the attention bestowed on the body. It includes grammar, gymnastics, music and drawing. In all things, its aim is to form the moral habits of the child. It is essentially liberal; such arts and sciences as are of a mechanical and utilitarian nature being eliminated. The essential virtue of the State is justice, *i.e.* the order by virtue of which each member of the State occupies the post and condition of life suitable to him, and is entrusted with the function he is able and worthy to exercise.

The maxim by which the Constitutions ought to be regulated is as follows :—the realisation of the end of the State presupposes two instruments : laws and the magistracy. The true sovereign, the only ruler, is reason, order. As this sovereign or ruler is invisible, reason, in practice, must be represented by laws. But laws are, of necessity, set forth in general formulae. Now, however comprehensive a formula, it necessarily allows of an infinity of particular cases escaping through its toils. Hence the necessity of the magistrate. He is sovereign arbiter whenever the law is unable to solve a difficulty, owing to the impossibility of specifying all the details of the case under general regulations.

Aristotle does not, like Plato, lay down one form of

government as being good, and all others bad. He says that the Constitutions ought to fit in with the character and the needs of the nations for whom they are framed; that the one which is worst in itself may be the best under certain circumstances. He also examines how bad governments may be utilised, when they alone are possible. With these reservations, he classifies the different forms of government.

There are three kinds of government, differing in the number of those who govern : power may be in the hands either of one, of several, or of the majority of the nation. Each of these has two forms, the one just, the other corrupt, according as those who govern have in view the general interest or their own private interest. To the just forms of government, Aristotle gives the names of royalty, aristocracy and polity; the corrupt forms he calls tyranny, oligarchy and democracy.

The best form of government is a republic which combines order with freedom. This is an aristocracy. All the citizens are allowed to participate in public functions ; only those, however, are citizens, whose position and culture enable them to fulfil civic duties. All corporal, toil, especially agriculture and the various industrial arts, must be done by slaves or half-breeds.

Lower than this ideal form of government we have forms less perfect, though justifiable according to circumstances. The most practical of these, under ordinary conditions, is a temperate republic, a mean between democracy and oligarchy. Democracy is characterised by freedom and equality, as well as by the fact that the government is in the hands of the majority of free men and of the poor. In an oligarchy the government is carried on by a minority of the wealthy and the noble.

A temperate republic bestows power on the middle classes. It is the political equivalent of moral virtue, which is the mean between two extremes.

Evidently Aristotle's political ideas are often only the putting into theory of the facts that fall under his observation ; still, it would be an exaggeration to see in them nothing else. Though the means he advocates are frequently the result of a necessarily restricted experience, the ends he has in view are determined by reason and philosophy, and even nowadays Aristotle's politics is a mine of information for statesmen and historians.

XXIII.—RHETORIC

In rhetoric, Aristotle tells us, he had nothing to create, for this science had been developed before his time by Tisias, Thrasymachus, Theodorus and many others. These authors, however, confined themselves to the particular, never going beyond the empirical point of view. To Aristotle belongs the idea of scientific rhetoric, and more particularly the determination of a close connection between rhetoric and logic. Plato had unsuccessfully endeavoured to base rhetoric on science. Aristotle, thanks to his logical theories, finds in dialectic, as distinguished from apodeictic, the very basis of rhetoric. Rhetoric is the application of dialectic to politics, *i.e.* to certain practical ends. Logically, dialectic is anterior to rhetoric ; it is the whole of which rhetoric is only a part. In the order of time, rhetoric is anterior to dialectic ; but in the order of science, it is the contrary that holds good.

Rhetoric teaches persuasion by likely reasons. Thus, the essential part of rhetoric is the doctrine of oratorical

means.   These are of three kinds : 1st, those referring
to the object ; 2nd, those referring to the speaker ;
3rd, those referring to the listener.

The first consist in making affirmations appear true.
They are based on proof.   Proof is thus the main
element in rhetoric ; it is also the one on which Aristotle
insists most.   As dialectic proves by means of syllogism
and induction, so rhetoric proves by means of enthymeme or imperfect demonstration, and by example or
imperfect induction.   There is no kind of proof, it
would appear, that cannot be reduced to these two
arguments.   The enthymeme is a syllogism in which
reasoning is carried on by probabilities or signs.   Example, like induction, consists in judging of a thing by
other particular things similar to the one in question,
but example does not proceed from the part to the
whole, it proceeds only from the part to the part.
Rhetoric determines the points of view that give rise
to enthymemes and examples : this determination is the
object of oratorical *topic*.

Aristotle distinguishes three kinds of speech : the
deliberative, the legal and the epideictic ; he also lays
down the rules governing each.

Such are the oratorical means relating to the object.
The speaker's *rôle* is to have himself regarded as
intelligent, upright, and benevolent.

Finally, the means relating to the listener consist in
being able to rouse passion and to lull it to sleep.
Aristotle dwells at length on this part of his subject,
giving proof of a very shrewd psychological sense.
He makes an interesting study of the influence of
age and environment on character and disposition.

Following on these theories, which constitute the
basis of rhetoric, come studies on elocution and dis-

position, denoting a considerable degree of truth and sagacity in judgment, along with a profound knowledge of the matter in hand.

XXIV.—Esthetics

Aristotle divided philosophy into three parts : the theoretical, the practical and the poetical, or the one relating to art.   Though he made no attempt to develop this latter, the proofs and examples he gives show him to be the founder of esthetics.

Aristotelian esthetics does not proceed so much from the concept of the beautiful as from that of art ; all the same, a theory of the beautiful is therein outlined. According to Aristotle, coördination, symmetry and precision form the essential characteristics of the beautiful.   Sensible manifestation is not an essential element of the beautiful, which shows forth as being realised more especially in the mathematical sciences. The beautiful dwells in the general.   Poetry, which bears upon the general, is more beautiful, more serious and philosophical than history, which is contained in the particular.

Aristotle, like Plato, regards imitation as the essence of art.   Art results from man's tendency to imitate and the pleasure he thereby obtains.   What man imitates is nature, that is to say, according to the Aristotelian philosophy, not only the outer appearance, but the inner, the ideal essence of natural things.   Art is capable of representing things as they are or as they should be.   The representation is all the more beautiful in proportion as the artist proves himself able to complete, in the way in which nature herself was going, the work she necessarily leaves unfinished.   All art tends to represent the general and the necessary. This is true even of comic poetry, the real aim of which is the representation of characters.

The arts include more than one kind of utility, or service. They produce distraction, moral culture, intellectual enjoyment, and that particular effect which Aristotle calls cleansing, or purification (κάθαρσις). Purification is the proprium of the highest arts, more especially of serious poetry.

What is this famous purification ? It is not exactly moral improvement, but rather the suppression, by homeopathic treatment, of some passion that troubled and domineered over the soul. Moreover, it is important to note that not all excitation to passion is capable of producing this curative effect. Excitation of a salutary nature is that which comes from art, it is subject to law and propriety, and, by magnifying the object of the passions, detaches them from the circumstances of individual life in order to apply them to the destiny common to all men.

Aristotle gives no systematic classification of the arts, the highest of which, according to him, are music and poetry.

XXV.—Poetics

Almost all that is left of Aristotle's *Poetics* deals with the study of tragedy, though he is known to have dealt fully with poetics.

Poetry arises from the tendency to imitation. A tragedy is the imitation of a serious and complete action, of a certain extent, in noble language and a dramatic form devoid of narrative : an imitation that excites terror and pity, thereby cleansing the soul of these passions.   In the persons and destinies of his heroes, the tragic poet offers us general types of nature and human life.   He shows us immutable laws which dominate and control apparently accidental events. Hence the efficacy of tragedy in cleansing the soul of all its inordinate affections.

The most important part of tragedy is action. Action ought to be natural.   Not that the author should simply set forth what has happened, he ought also to show what might have happened, what is possible either according to the laws of probability or according to those of necessity.   Action ought to be one and complete.   It should be impossible to disturb or curtail any part of the work without disuniting and spoiling the *ensemble*.   For, in any whole, that which can be added or taken away, without the change being noticed, forms no part of that whole.

The only unity on which Aristotle insists is that of action.   He does not mention unity of place, and, as regards unity of time, merely states that, speaking generally, in tragedy an effort is made to confine the action within a single day or to go beyond that limit but slightly.

He determines the rules that refer to the parts of the action, to the characters, which ought to be more finished and beautiful than they are in real life, and also to composition and elocution.

He regards tragedy as superior to epic poetry because its unity is more strict and confined, whereas an epic poem includes parts, each one of which would suffice to form material for a tragedy.

XXVI.—Grammar

In ancient times Aristotle was looked upon as the founder of grammar and criticism, for he had written works—now lost—on the subject of poetical explanation and the criticism of poets. Such indications with reference to grammar as we possess are not given for themselves, but only as they affect something else. None the less are they important in the formation of the science of grammar. Aristotle applied his usual powers of observation to the subject of grammar ; but the theory of language was then in its infancy : hence the vagueness and obscurity frequently met with in his assertions.

He recognises three parts of speech : noun, verb and conjunction. The two former are subject to inflection. Nouns are divided into masculine, feminine, and neuter.

Words are based rather on mutual agreement amongst men than on nature. Subsequently, in their formation, it is less the principle of analogy than the arbitrary that dominates.

XXVII.—Speeches and Poems

Several speeches of Aristotle are mentioned, including a λόγος δικανικός or *Apology*, in which he defends himself against the accusation of impiety, a *Eulogy of Plato*, a *Eulogy of Alexander* ; but the authenticity of these works—now lost—has been much disputed.

He also composed poems, a few authentic lines of which remain, though many fragments are of very doubtful authenticity. The most important of these is a portion of a scolion in honour of Hermias of

Atarnea, his friend. Aristotle here sings of virtue, to which, like the ancient heroes of Greece, Hermias has sacrificed his life. Mention may also be made of a few distachs of an elegy to Eudemus, composed in honour of Plato, "a man whom the wicked may not even praise."

The following is the fragment of the *Scolion to Hermias* :—

Virtue, object of effort on the part of the race of mankind, supreme reward of life ! For thee, O virgin, for thy beauty, the Greeks are ready to brave death, to endure terrible, never-ending toil. So beautiful is the fruit thou dost engender in the heart, immortal fruit more precious than gold, nobility or soft-eyed slumber ! For thee, Hercules, the son of Zeus, and the sons of Leda bore many a trial, for they were noble hunters in pursuit of the power thou bestowest. Through love of thee, Achilles and Ajax entered the abode of Hades. Thou, too, wert ever the object of the love of Atarnes' son ; for the sake of thy beauty he deprived his eyes of the glorious light of the sun. That is why he is praised in song for his noble deeds ; the Muses shall magnify his name and make it immortal, the Muses, Mnemosyne's daughters, who honour the majesty of Jupiter the protector of hospitality, and who likewise honour the glory of faithful friendship.

XXVIII.—LETTERS

Aristotle's letters have been celebrated by Demetrius and other authors as being models of epistolary style. Simplicius states that the style of these letters combined clearness with charm of diction to a degree attained by no other known writer. Diogenes mentions letters to Philip, the letters of the Selymbrians, four letters to Alexander, nine to Antipater, and others to Mentor, Ariston, Philoxenes, Democritus, &c. As the fragments that have come down to us are for the most part unauthenticated, we are unable to judge for ourselves of either the contents or the form of Aristotle's letters.

XXIX.—Aristotle as a Writer

Aristotle wrote in the Attic language of his age. The multitude of new ideas he undertook to express, however, had a considerable influence upon the instrument he used. The consideration of things in their individuality, the clear delimitation of scientific domain, the effort to form concepts exempt from every sensible element, are all reflected in his language and style. As Aristotle's logical analysis only ceases when it has grasped the final, specific differences, so also, in Aristotelian language, apparent synonyms are distinguished from each other and defined with great preciseness.

Aristotle had two ways of defining terms : the scientific determination of the meanings of traditional words, and the creation of new terms. He used both methods, especially the former. He mainly starts with an ordinary term ; and then, sometimes restricting, sometimes extending its meaning, he makes it the exact expression of a logical concept. Traditional language, however, was full of gaps. To fill them up, Aristotle coined words, always, as far as possible, seeking a basis to work upon in tradition itself. Owing to the perfection of the terminology thus constituted, he proved himself the true founder of the language of science throughout the world.

The following are instances of expressions coined by Aristotle : ἀδιαίρετος (individual) ; αἰτεῖσθαι τὸ ἐν ἀρχῇ (*petitio principii*, begging of the question) ; ἄμεσος (immediate) ; ἀνάλυσις (analysis) ; ἀνομοιομέρης (heterogeneous) ; ἀντίφασις (contradiction) ; ἀποδεικτικός (demonstrative) ; ἀπόφασις (affirmation) ; γενικός (generic) ; διχοτομία (dichotomy) ; ἐμπειρικός (empiric) ; ἐναντιότης (opposition) ; ἐνέργεια (energy) ; ἑνότης (unity) ; ἐντελέχεια (entelechy) ; ἐξωτερικός (exoteric) ; ἐπακτικός (inductive) ; ἑτερότης (alterity or otherness) ; ἠθικός (morals) ; θεολογική (theology) ; κατηγορικός (categorical) ; λογικός (logical) ; ὀργανικός (organic), &c.

The following instances may be quoted in which Aristotle confined himself to a scientific determination of the meaning of the term: ἀντίθεσις (antithesis) ; ἀξίωμα (axiom) ; ἐναντίος (contrary) ; ἐνυπάρχειν (to be immanent) ; ἐπαγωγή (induction) ; ἔσχατον (last) ; ἴδιον (characteristic property of a species) ; συμβεβηκός (accident) ; συλλογίζεσθαι (to reason) ; συνεχής (continuous) ; συνέχεια (continuity) ; σύνολον (whole) ; ὕλη (matter) ; ὑποκείμενον (substratum).

Finally we will take a few instances of the distinctions he draws between concepts, by means of analysis and opposition : γένος (genus) ; εἶδος (species) ; κίνησις (movement) ; ἐνέργεια (act) ; ἀντίφασις (contradiction) and ἐναντίον (opposition) ; ποιεῖν (to make) and πράττειν (to do) ; δύναμις (potency) and ἐνέργεια (act) ; ἐπαγωγή (induction) and συλλογισμός (deduction) ; οὐσία (essence) and συμβεβηκότα (accidents) ; διαλεκτικός (dialectic) and ἀποδεικτικός (demonstrative) ; πρότερον τῇ φύσει (anterior per se) and πρότερον πρὸς ἡμᾶς (anterior from our standpoint).

Aristotle's style is no less personal than his language. The ancients extolled his fluency and charm ; the words flowed from his lips, said Cicero, in a golden stream. Such praise evidently applies to his dialogues, his published works. In his didactic works (πραγματεῖαι) which alone have come down to us, we note the exactness of his definitions, inimitable clearness, precision and brevity, a strictness and exactness in the meaning of words, suggestive of the language of mathematics. In a word, Aristotle's style is distinguished by an exact appropriation of form to content. Frequently, however, especially in such of his works as are incomplete, Aristotle writes with a certain degree of aridity and carelessness. Not only are the sentences not arranged in periods, but there are numerous anacolutha and parentheses, which, in no small measure, militate against clearness. At times, too, in these abstract dissertations, we come across passages that are not lacking in fire and eloquence. Of such a character is the end of chapter 7, book 10, of the *Nicomachean Ethics* :

The life of the statesman and of the soldier, then, though they surpass all other virtuous exercises in nobility and grandeur, are not leisurely occupations, but aim at some ulterior end, and are not desired merely for themselves.

But the exercise of the reason seems to be superior in seriousness (since it contemplates truth), and to aim at no end beside itself, and to have its proper pleasure (which also helps to increase the exercise) ; and its exercise seems further to be self-sufficient, and leisurely, and inexhaustible (as far as anything human can be), and to have all the other characteristics that are ascribed to happiness.

This, then, will be the complete happiness of man, *i.e.* when a complete term of days is added ; for nothing incomplete can be admitted into our idea of happiness.

But a life which realised this idea would be something more than human ; for it would not be the expression of man's nature, but of some divine element in that nature—the exercise of which is so far superior to the exercise of the other kind of virtue (*i.e.* practical or moral virtue), as this divine element is superior to our compound human nature.[1]

[1] *I.e.* our nature as moral agents, as compounds of reason and desire.

If, then, reason be divine as compared with man, the life
which consists in the exercise of reason will also be divine in
comparison with human life.   Nevertheless, instead of listening
to those who advise us as men and mortals not to lift our
thoughts above what is human and mortal, we ought rather,
as far as possible, to put off our mortality and make every
effort to live in the exercise of the highest of our faculties ;
for though it be but a small part of us, yet in power and value
it far surpasses all the rest.[1]

XXX.—Aristotle's Influence

The first effect of Aristotle's teaching was to bring
into being the Peripatetic school, which flourished for
a period of from two to three centuries, and whose
principal representatives are : Theophrastus of Lesbos
(372?-287? B.C.), Eudemus of Rhodes (fourth century),
Aristoxenus of Tarentum (born about 350 B.C.), surnamed the Musician, Decearchus of Messena (flourished
320 B.C.) and Strato of Lampsacus (flourished 287 B.C.).
Critolaüs, a member of the embassy sent to Rome
in 156 B.C., by which philosophy was introduced into
the Roman world, was a Peripatetic philosopher.   The
school was distinguished for its minute investigations in
logic, morals and natural science, but the naturalistic
tendency gradually prevailed over the metaphysical.
Strato even went so far as to identify divinity with the
φύσις which acts unconsciously throughout the world,
and to substitute for the Aristotelian teleology an
altogether mechanical explanation of things, based on
the properties of heat and cold.

With the publication of Aristotle's works by
Andronicus of Rhodes, about 70 B.C., began the long
list of interpreters and commentators of the Stageirite,

---

[1] F. H. Peter's translation.

including Boethus of Sidon, Nicolas of Damascus, Alexander of Aphrodisias in Cilicia, surnamed the Exegete *par excellence* (κατ' ἐξοχήν), Porphyry of Batanaea, the Neoplatonist, Themistius of Paphlagonia, Philopon of Alexandria and Simplicius of Cilicia.

Though the Peripatetic school consists mainly of disciples not very advanced in metaphysics or of purely erudite commentators, still, the master's doctrines are very vigorous and instinct with life in philosophies which did not originate with him but were largely inspired by his influence. The principle of the Stoics, intermediary between potency and act, and limited by tension, immanent in all things, the intelligent and supreme final cause, would indeed appear to be nothing else than the φύσις of Aristotle, into which the νοῦς would seem to be absorbed. Through the precise distinction he made between mechanism and finality, between the physical and the metaphysical order of things, between chance and intelligent action, Aristotle rendered possible Epicureanism, which seems largely to be made up of the doctrines which Aristotle defined or created for the purpose of refuting them. Neoplatonism itself, in the matter of its doctrine regarding the νοῦς, is greatly indebted to Aristotle. The Neoplatonists endeavoured to reconcile Plato and Aristotle ; and Plotinus maintained that his doctrine of the transcendent one from which the νοῦς emanates, was the inevitable consequence of Aristotelian teaching.

After defending ancient philosophy to the very end, Aristotelianism, becoming embodied in the beliefs of the Middle Ages, transformed them into philosophical doctrines. It was mainly owing to the influence of Aristotle that there developed, in that period of religious mysticism, the spirit of logic and of rational speculation.

Tardily and indirectly did Aristotle's writings penetrate into the western world.   Even in the middle of
the twelfth century, only small portions of the *Organon*
were known, to wit, the *Categories* and the *Hermeneia*,
in the Latin translation of Boetius.   These, along with
the Εἰσαγωγή of Porphyry and the *Timaeus* of Plato,
formed almost the entire possessions of philosophical
antiquity.   From A.D. 1150 to 1210, the other works
of Aristotle appeared in the form of a Latin version of
Arabic translations, which in their turn had been translated by Christian Syrians, from Syriac translations, in
the ninth century.   Shortly afterwards (thirteenth century), the Greek text was communicated to the scholars
of the West, mainly by Greeks from Constantinople ;
and a translation direct from the Latin was substituted
for the indirect translations.   Robert Greathead, Albert
le Grand and Saint Thomas were the principal persons
engaged in this refining process of translating into Latin.

As showing how dependent on his will is man's
intelligence, people of the most diverse opinions,
strangely enough, found in Aristotle a rational basis
for their beliefs and aspirations.   There could be
nothing apparently more one than the Middle Ages,
for Aristotle was invoked by everybody, though, as a
matter of fact, there were as many Aristotles as
philosophers.   There were even Aristotles who had
only the name in common with the Stageirite.

It was Aristotle's *Organon* that gave rise to the
famous quarrel between the universities, which lasted
from the ninth to the end of the eleventh century.
About this time, complete systems of Aristotelian
philosophy grew up amongst the Arabs and Jews, who
had possession of all the master's writings.   The Arabs,
who were naturalists and monotheists, were captivated

by Aristotle's teachings about God and by his investigations into natural history. Averroës, of Cordova (A.D. 1126-1198), regards himself as a true Aristotelian when maintaining that active understanding is an emanation from God, that it is one for all men and alone is immortal. Moses Maimonides, a Jew of Cordova (A.D. 1135-1204), finds no difficulty in reconciling miracles and the creation of matter with Aristotelianism.

The most brilliant period of Christian scholasticism is also that during which Aristotle's authority is at its highest. Though his doctrines on physics, which are regarded as advocating the eternity of the world and of time, are for a certain period regarded with suspicion, from the year A.D. 1230, the whole of his works begin to be used as text-books for lessons in philosophy. Just as the truths of faith are the expression of supernatural illumination, so the Aristotelian doctrine is the expression of natural illumination. Reason does not coincide with faith, but it is moving towards it. Aristotle, as representing reason, is the forerunner of Christ in the things of nature, as Saint John the Baptist is his forerunner in those of grace. Thus defined, circumscribed and subordinated, Aristotelianism becomes the origin of what has since been called deism and natural religion. At that time there was found in it all that theology required. Naturally it cannot demonstrate the truth of the dogmas, for that would be contradictory; still, it refutes objections brought against them and establishes their probability. In particular, it sets up a theory of substantial form and of real and separable accidents, which makes transubstantiation conceivable in the persistence of the same sensible elements in the Eucharist.

And, indeed, Aristotelianism is as favourable to dissent as it is to orthodoxy. Amaury of Chartres and David of Dinant (thirteenth and fourteenth centuries) claim that it upholds pantheism, for the one identifies the God of the Stageirite with form, the other with universal matter. The German mystics, too, Theodoric of Freiburg and "Meister Eckhart" (thirteenth and fourteenth centuries), present their doctrine of the substantial union of the soul with divinity, as the development of the Aristotelian theory of the νοῦς ποιητικός.

And lastly, Aristotle is not only the master of philosophers in the Middle Ages ; he is even regarded as the patron of those who, in opposition to the Church and the philosophy of the times, claim to harness and control the mysterious forces of nature. These reprobates look upon Aristotle as a magician. He is credited with having written alchemical treatises on the occult philosophy of the Egyptians, and is placed, with Plato, at the head of the list of oecumenical alchemists. Alchemists called themselves the new commentators of Plato and Aristotle.

Thus we find Aristotle, in the Middle Ages, everywhere stirring up the minds of men and regarded as an authority : his main work, however, was undoubtedly the organisation of that Christian philosophy which was so complete and detailed, so logical and firmly based throughout, that it seemed destined to last for ever. This philosophy held sway in the colleges of the University of France up to the eighteenth century. In the Sorbonne, in 1624, it was forbidden, under penalty of death, to propound doctrines opposed to those held by the ancients. Even in 1671, the professors were called upon to respect Peripateticism under penalty of exclusion. Only at the beginning of the eighteenth century did scholastic Aristotelianism make way for new ideas.

It was from faith, not from reason, that the first really savage attack came. Not only did Luther note how important were the differences that divided Aristotelian philosophy from Christianity, he even regarded it as impious to seek for a reconciliation between God-given faith and sin-stained reason. Aristotelian philosophy, the work of man, with its claim to deal with things divine, could be nothing else than error and sacrilege ; religion, once reconciled thereto, could only become distorted and misrepresented. Aristotle was an arch-heretic : religion would only be safe on condition his doctrines were utterly abolished.

Opposed in the name of the Christian religion, Aristotelianism, in spite of its glorious revival by the scholars of the Renaissance, Pomponatius, Scaliger, Vanini, Gennadius, and George of Trebizond, speedily became an object of attack by science and philosophy. Bacon saw in the Aristotelian method nothing but deduction applied to the data of opinion and language ; in his eyes, Aristotelian metaphysic was only the claim to explain things, exclusive of mechanical causes, by supernatural and divine actions. He therefore condemned the philosophy of Aristotle, as being contrary to the conditions of science, which latter seeks mechanical explanations and proceeds by induction. Descartes looked upon Aristotelianism as the doctrine that realised sensible qualities, and explained phenomena by these chimerical entities. Barren and obscure ideas, these abstractions could not possibly be the principles of things. In direct opposition to Aristotle, Descartes restores quality to quantity, not quantity to quality.

It appeared as though the Aristotelian doctrine would

M

have definitely lived, when Leibnitz triumphantly restored it to philosophy, declaring that in the theory of
substantial forms and entelechy, when rightly understood, there was more truth than in the entire philosophy of the moderns. Following in the steps of
Aristotle, Leibnitz placed substance in a principle of
action, relegated extent and matter from the class of
substance to that of phenomenon, and reconciled final
with efficient causes by making mechanism dependent on
finality. Aristotelianism, since the time of Leibnitz,
has maintained a place of its own in philosophy, more
particularly playing an important part in the formation
of the Hegelian system.

However great his place in history, can it be said
that Aristotle, even at the present time, is one of the
masters of human thought ?

As regards philosophy strictly so called, there can
be no question as to the answer that must be given.
It appears as though Aristotelianism responds particularly to the preoccupations of modern times. The
two doctrines that until recently, have occupied the
largest place in the world of philosophy were Kantian
idealism and evolutionism. Now, Aristotle's system
may without disadvantage be set up against these two
systems.

It is opposed to Kantism. As a matter of fact,
Kant rejects the dependence of the mind in respect of
being, the ontological value attributed to the laws of
the mind, the theoretical unconditioned and the subordination of practice to theory ; all of which belong to
the very essence of Aristotelianism. The philosophy of
Kant has been set up in direct opposition to dogmatic
philosophy, of which Aristotle is the representative

par excellence. But if Kant discovered a new conception of things, a conception which must henceforth be examined by all interested in philosophy, it cannot be affirmed that he fully succeeded in getting his hypothesis accepted universally. If this hypothesis has on its side the testimony of conscience, which, by the way, it undertakes to satisfy, it cannot obtain the frank, complete approval of the intellect. This latter persists in saying, with Aristotle : " Everything has a reason of its own, and the first principle must be the final reason of things. Now, explanation implies determination, and the final reason cannot be anything else than fully determined being. When we consider the infinite and the finite, it is the finite, in so far as it is intelligible, that is the principle ; the infinite, in so far as it is unintelligible, can only be phenomenon." As regards Aristotle and Kant, what we have to do is to find out whether the supremacy must be attributed to the will or to the intellect ; now, even at the present time, this question does not appear to have been answered once for all.

The position of Aristotelianism as compared with evolutionism is quite different. Not only does it not oppose the latter, it even recognises and includes it, at the same time affording the means of going beyond it. Historically, it is one of the most direct antecedents of evolutionism. Whether in nature or in man, Aristotle shows that everywhere we have continuity—a process of development from the lower to the higher. Plants imply minerals, animals imply plants, man implies animals, and man is nothing but the completion of the being roughly outlined in the lower productions of nature. Even in man, imagination springs from sensation, memory from imagination, and the intellect cannot think without images. We can find no scientific thesis of evolutionism that would be incompatible with the natural philosophy of Aristotle. But is this mechanical order of things the absolute order? Do these explanations fully satisfy the intelligence? This is the question Aristotle asks, a question he finds it impossible to answer along the lines of spiritualistic metaphysics.

To our philosopher, the order which proceeds from the indeterminate to the determinate, from genus to species, cannot be regarded by the intellect as the absolute order of the generation of things, for the indeterminate always admits of other determinations than those it receives in the real world. Though man is the completion of the animal, still, the animal admitted of other determinations than those that made it into a man. Why do genera find their realisation in certain species rather than in others? The reason of this choice from amongst all possible developments can be found only in the very being which is the term of the development. The perfection of this being must be a force controlling the evolution of the matter from which it is to be born. In this way, the order which proceeds from the indeterminate to the determinate does not exclude; it calls for a symmetrically contrary order, the hidden principle of its direction and realisation. And so Aristotle reconciles the evolutionistic mechanism with finality by making a distinction between the order of things in time and that of things in the absolute. Evolutionism is truth from the standpoint of the senses; from that of the intellect, however, the imperfect exists and is determined only with a view to the more perfect. The finalistic explanation is the justifiable and indispensable complement of the mechanistic one.

Thus Aristotelianism still has a place of its own in philosophy. But has it not become, for the future, banned and barred from science ?

Here a distinction must be made between the moral sciences, on the one hand, and the mathematical and physical sciences on the other. Aristotle's ethics, and even, in many important respects, his politics, far from being forgotten, are in greater vogue than ever nowadays. The recommendation to live as a man when one is born a man, and to attribute real sovereignty in politics to reason and law, are by no means on the point of sinking into oblivion. But the sciences dealing with nature, all henceforth positive, seem to have little in common with the natural philosophy of the great metaphysician.

In order to express a fair judgment on this subject, it should at once be stated that a man may have exercised great influence on the development of the sciences without any of his ideas being recognised in present-day teachings. The sciences are built up stage by stage ; and though some particular ancient theory may not be recognised in modern theories, it may well have played its part in paving the way for their reception. Now, merit of this kind may certainly be attributed to Aristotle. He advanced theories and concepts which may be vastly different from modern methods and principles, and yet have none the less controlled the formation of these very principles. For instance, we have the Aristotelian theory of induction which doubtless determines rather the end to be attained than the means to be employed, and prefers to regard this end as being the discovery of types and not that of laws, but which is none the less very important because of the precision with which, in induction, it shows how we have to set free the necessary from the contingent, the universal from the particular. Such also are the ideas of genus and species, potency and act, mechanical blending and qualitative combination, chance, in reference to the conjunction of causes independent of one another, continuity in the scale of beings, classification of the sciences, etc.

But the simple acknowledgment that Aristotle has supplied science with many starting-points is not sufficient. Many of his principles may still quite well be recognised in the spirit of contemporary science itself. His great principle that there are laws in nature and that they can be discovered only by deducing them from experience by the aid of reflection, his constant wish to investigate things in their details, to understand them not by means of vague formulae, but in themselves with their own characteristics, his definition of cause as existing in that element which makes production known as necessary, his doctrine of biological continuity and of the solidarity of the higher with respect to the lower ; all these essential features of Aristotelian philosophy may be met with in modern science. Though an authority belonging to the past, Aristotle has not ceased to be a master, even in these days.

The objection, however, will be urged that Aristotle is finalistic and that science does not now trouble itself with the consideration of ends.

Perhaps there is some misunderstanding here. Aristotelian finality is not the building up of the world, as though it were a watch, by an artisan who sets before him an idea and calculates how to realise it. It consists, we may say, of the three following principles : 1st, throughout the world, order is the rule, disorder the exception ; this is equivalent to saying that the combinations of phenomena which result immediately from the laws of nature, harmoniously united in types, and consequently normal in their development, are far more numerous than the combinations due to the fortuitous conjunction of laws independent of one another ; 2nd, in every individual there is an organising force or φύσις by virtue of which it tends to be and to realise a certain form ; 3rd, the specific types are strictly determined, separated from one another, and immutable. Is it quite certain that finality, thus interpreted, is altogether absent from modern science ?

The first of these three principles signifies that it is possible to obtain knowledge of fundamental laws by means of observation and induction. In contrast with this theory we have the mathematical theory of Descartes, according to which there are really no qualitative and multiple laws of nature, but only various determinations of homogeneous and mathematical quantity. But though we have the Cartesian conception as an ideal representing complete science, the Aristotelian method of advance is still the one best suited to our means of knowledge. The only thing in which Aristotle erred was in imagining that by the process of induction we could arrive at simple and absolute laws which presuppose nothing anterior to themselves.

The second principle bears a striking resemblance to that of the struggle for life. Here, too, we presuppose in every individual a tendency to exist and develop along fixed lines. It is true that modern science would like to reduce life itself to a mechanism ; all the same, it acknowledges that life, as we find it, plays the part and possesses the characteristics that Aristotle attributed to it. The entire difference consists in regarding as derived what Aristotle looked upon as primitive ; but until this reduction is effected, we do not think we are wrong in saying: everything takes place as though there were in each living being a tendency to exist, and that in some determinate manner.

Finally, the third principle, which still counts adherents amongst scientists themselves, is not, as Aristotle understood it, in absolute contradiction to the teachings of the evolutionists, from the physical point of view. What is it that Aristotle means ? He does not wish to affirm that the history of the beings of nature began in time, with the creation of separate species : he means that the realisation of a certain number of types, both distinct from and in harmony with each other, is the end and rule of the productions of nature. He admits that nature, for the most part, succeeds in realising this end ; but, apart from the perfectly regular productions of nature, he acknowledges productions partly regular, partly irregular. Now, if we leave the past out of account, and also any beginning in time, about which Aristotle did not trouble himself, we shall find no very great divergence between this point of view and that of evolutionism. In contradistinction to materialism and the doctrine of chance, evolutionism recognises that species exist, at the present time, at all events. It also recognises the tendency in nature towards an increasingly complete specification. The principle of Aristotle, then, subsists, even in these days, in the hypothetical form at any rate, the only form a principle can admit of in science ; everything takes place as though there were a hierarchy of ideal forms, distinct from one another, and which the beings of nature tend to realise.

JACOB BOEHME, THE GERMAN PHILOSOPHER

"Gott ist von der Natur frei, und die Natur ist doch seines Wesens."—J. BOEHME (*Vom dreifachen Leben des Menschens*).

I

IT is not the custom, even in Germany, to assign a place of importance in the history of philosophy to Jacob Boehme, the shoemaker theosophist of the *Renaissance*. Along with Hegel, he is recognised as a man of powerful mind ; but whilst it is admitted that from the whole of his obscure, involved writings a certain number of doctrines capable of being understood to some extent by the intellect can be evolved, these doctrines are regarded as coming under the category of theology and Christian edification rather than as monuments of profane and rational science. Such appreciation is natural in France where philosophy, in the spirit of Descartes, mostly depends on the understanding, and is suspicious of anything resembling mysticism. In Germany, however, philosophy has not adopted the rationalistic form in so constant a fashion. Alongside of Leibnitz, Kant, Fichte, and Hegel, the Schoolmen, so to speak, of modern Germany, we find philosophers of belief, religion, or feeling, such as Hamann, Herder, Jacobi, Schelling the theosophist, and the famous Christian philosopher Franz von Baader. These latter, as against the former, are mystical dissidents, just as, in former times, Eckhart and Tauler were opposed to Thomist rationalism. Even the German philosophers of concept and reflection, the followers of Kant and Hegel, if we consider the basis and spirit of their teaching, and not the form in which they set it forth, are not so free from mysticism and theosophy as would seem to be the case, or even as they state. For they too look upon the veritable absolute as being not in space or thought, but rather in spirit, which is regarded as superior to the categories of the understanding ; they too endeavour to base nature on this absolute. Now, taking into consideration this element of mysticism and theosophy, set forth in Germany not merely by a whole series of important philosophical systems, but even by the preëminently classical systems, if we inquire into the origins of German philosophy, we can hardly fail to bestow considerable attention upon the shoemaker theosophist. We will seriously ask ourselves whether he did not deserve the name of *German philosopher* given him during his lifetime by his admirer and friend, Dr. Walther.

True, at first sight, the name scarcely seems to suit him. Boehme is neither a scientist, a dialectician, nor even a disinterested investigator. The son of peasants, his first occupation was that of a cowherd. Then he became a shoemaker at Görlitz, the town adjoining his birthplace, and here he conscientiously practised his trade in the fear of the Lord. He married the daughter of a worthy butcher living in the town, Catharina Kuntzschmann, by whom he had four sons, and, it is said, two daughters. He brought up his sons in his own station of life and made workmen of them. He lived in piety, simplicity, and Christian meekness, and was ever engaged in meditation on religious things. But it was his continual desire, he tells us, to seek in the heart of God for a refuge from divine wrath and the wickedness of the devil. He wrote a considerable number of books. But what was the source of his inspiration? He had read neither the classic authors nor the Schoolmen, and was acquainted only with mystical and theosophical writings. And even for what he knows he is indebted to personal and supernatural revelations. Four times the heavenly light was revealed to him, when he saw either Christ or the eternal Virgin; during the few moments these visions lasted he learned more than he would have done had he attended classes for years. At the beginning of each of his books we find the words *geschrieben nach göttlicher Erleuchtung*, written by divine enlightenment.

The work corresponds with the conditions under which it was composed. It is a mixture of abstruse theology, alchemy, speculations on the undiscernible, and the incomprehensible, fantastic poetry and mystic effusions; in fact, a dazzling chaos. His first book is entitled, *The dawn at its rise, or the root and mother of philosophy, astrology, and theology considered in their true principle: a description of nature, in which is seen how all things were in the beginning, etc.* Boehme herein sets forth the genesis of the holy Trinity, the creation and fall of the Angels, the creation and fall of man, the redemption and the end of the world. He sees, and would have others see, far more than he demonstrates; his science is a metaphysical hallucination. Accordingly he is constantly doing violence to language, requiring it to express the inexpressible. He uses the terms of ancient mysticism, of alchemy and philosophy; he imposes on them meanings of extraordinary subtilty, and insists on there being the infinite and the mysterious at the base of all thought. Is it possible that from such a work anything can be gleaned by the historian of philosophy, unless by an arbitrary interpretation he transforms into concepts what, on the part of the author, is pure intuition and imagination ?

In forming an opinion of this man, whose sole aim was to set the spirit free from the letter, it would be unbecoming to judge by appearances. In reality, Boehme is not the simple, ignorant man he tells us he is. He was open-minded and possessed of a keen intellect, as his first teachers immediately recognised. He lived in a country and at an epoch in which the greatest of all problems were being discussed. The mysticism of old was still flourishing in Germany during the times of Schwenckfeld and Sébastien Franck. At the same time, ever since Nicolas de Cusa, there had been developing, beneath the influence of Italian naturalism, a profound and brilliant theosophy represented by Agrippa von Nettesheim and Paracelsus, the rehabilitation and deification of that nature which the mystics of the Middle Ages were destroying. In another direction, over against the moral optimism of Eckhart and his disciples, Luther had recently set up the doctrine of a positive, radical evil, rising up to oppose God and incapable of being brought within the compass of mere diminution or deprivation. The new principles had early entered either into connection or into conflict with the principle of ancient mysticism. Protestantism was already attempting that reconciliation of its mystical with its Pauline origins, its spiritualistic monism with its moral dualism, and its principle of liberty with that of discipline, which she is still following. Theosophy was united with mysticism in Valentin Weigel, who submitted as matter for the subjective reflection of Eckhart, the man of

Paracelsus, a *résumé* and perfection of the three natures, the terrestrial, sidereal, and the divine, of which the created universe consists.

From his youth onwards, Boehme eagerly took an active part in this movement of ideas. In his wanderings to and fro as a journeyman before becoming a master-shoemaker, he conversed of things religious and theosophical ; he observed, read, and reflected. Though he read but little, what he did read was important and full of profound thought. The Bible was for him the book of books, that thrilling, deep word which, especially since the days of Luther, has ever been the most powerful incentive to reflection. But Boehme read the writings of many other masters besides. He read Schwenckfeld, noting his objections to that doctrine of vicarious atonement which tends to replace by external and accidental action the internal working of grace, the only possible source of essential conversion. He read Paracelsus, and was delighted to find in him an enthusiastic apostle of life, a revealer of the magic power of imagination, a seer who finds, in the world and in natural man, that image of God which mystics had ceased to find therein. He studied alchemy, trying to discover its true, its spiritual meaning. To him, transmutation was the symbol of the new birth to which man is called ; the philosopher's stone found its realisation for him in the power of faith and of surrender to God. He read Valentin Weigel, and became imbued with the spiritual mysticism this pious pastor inherited from Tauler, from German theology, from Schwenckfeld, and from Sébastien Franck ; thanks to him, also, he conceived the idea of combining mysticism with theosophy.

Boehme read not only books of written characters, he also read the book of nature. Every manifestation of nature is instruction for him ; matter is not a being apart, foreign to spirit ; it is spirit itself, revealed and visible. The stars, the sun, the elements of the earth, life everywhere, in its origin and in every one of its phases, the growing tree, the animal with its desires and disinterested instincts, man with his inner life, his struggle with evil, his defeats and triumphs—all these things Boehme contemplates and meditates upon, and in this immediate and religious communion with nature, waits for her to infuse into him her own spirit and reveal the mysteries of being.

It is eternal, interior, and living being that he seeks everywhere and in all things. Thus, the phenomena of nature, like the teachings set forth in books, are signs for him to decipher, not the object about which knowledge is sought. The reason why he reads and observes is to have matter on which his spirit may dwell for reflection. It is Boehme's endeavour to set the spirit free from the letter, to find out the force which works at the heart of inert phenomena, and to penetrate to the very source of all reality. Therefore inner experience and reflection are, once for all, his true means of investigation. True, he was an illuminate ; his meditation was a prayer ; his discoveries, divine revelations. Still, what matters the explanation the individual himself gives of the channel along which his ideas entered his consciousness ? Is Descartes' analytical geometry any the less true because he claimed that he owed its invention to the assistance of the holy Virgin ? It may be because of the way in which the human mind is constituted that he at first attributed to supernatural revelation the new ideas that arose within him, impressing him by their beauty and illuminating power, and that he regarded them as entering his mind from without.   Plato's essences, the νοῦς of Aristotle, the Christian ideal, the supreme principles of knowledge and action, were looked upon as beings and things in themselves, before they came to be explained by the laws of the human mind.   The natural has first been supernatural ; for the genius does not know how he arises ; to himself he appears as a god visiting his creature.   Boehme, indeed, is not content to receive into his own intelligence the revelations of divine intelligence ; he is a seer of visions.   Increate wisdom, the eternal Virgin, appeared to him several times. But enthusiasm, even when of a somewhat sickly nature, is just as likely to strengthen as it is to weaken the powers of the human mind, and a shock to the organism is nothing but the result of the excessive tension to which the mind has had to subject the body for the realisation of its creations.   The thinking reed[1] bends beneath the effort of thought, even more than beneath the weight of matter.   After all, there is only one interpretation, only one standard of either a thinker's or an artist's work, and that is the work itself.   The author is the mould which is broken that the statue may be made visible.

II

What is it, then, that we find in the work of Boehme when considered in itself, both in its spirit and inner meaning, as the author would have it studied, and in its real and objective content, as history would have it studied ?

First of all, what is the motive of the theosophist shoemaker's reflections ?

---

[1] Pascal in his *Pensées* (*édition Havet*, i. 6) says : " L'homme n'est qu'un roseau le plus faible de la nature, mais c'est un *roseau pensant*." (Translator's note.)

"From my youth up," he tells us, "I have sought only one thing : the salvation of my soul, the means of gaining possession of the kingdom of God." Here, apparently, is nothing more than an altogether practical and religious object ; but in Boehme's mind, this object is destined to raise the most profound, metaphysical speculations.

He learnt from the mystics what it means to possess God. One must take care, so these masters teach, not to liken the possession of God to the possession of anything material. God is spirit, *i.e.* for the man who understands the meaning of the term, a generating power previous to all essence, even the divine. God is spirit, *i.e.* pure will, both infinite and free, with the realisation of its own personality as its object. Henceforward, God cannot be accepted by any passive operation. We possess him only if he is created within us. To possess God is to live the life of God.

On the other hand, Boehme learnt from Luther that the natural man is not simply a son separated from his father, that between God and his creature there is something more than inert space, unresisting non-being. The natural man has rebelled against his creator : between him and God, sin raises its head, like a real, positive power, endeavouring to defeat the divine action. Evil is not non-being, it is a real being that combats the principle of good. Everywhere in nature Boehme finds that effective warfare being waged, which Luther enabled him to see in the human conscience. Whether he beholds sun and stars, clouds or rain or snow, creatures with reason or creatures without reason, such as wood, stones, earth, or elements ; no matter in which direction he turns, he sees everywhere evil over against good, anger opposing love, affirmation opposed to negation. Even justice, here below, is at grips with its contrary. For the godless are as prosperous as the god-fearing, barbarous nations possess the richest lands and enjoy the good things of earth more than do the servants of God. Observing these things, Boehme tells us, I fell into a state of deep melancholy and my spirit was troubled. Not a single book, of all those with which I was acquainted, brought me any consolation. And the devil was there, watching for me, and filling my mind with heathenish thoughts such as I should be ashamed to express here. Is it true that God is love, as Christianity teaches, that God is omnipotent, that there is nothing which has reality in his presence ? Such, doubtless, are the questions Boehme felt starting to life, deep in his consciousness. Gladly would the devil have seen him give up all hope of fathoming the mystery and sink to sleep in indifference. Boehme, however, guessed his designs and determined to foil them.

How was he to reconcile the end of human activity, of which mystics had so noble a conception, with the reality of things, so concisely stated by the founder of Protestantism ? If mankind and the whole of nature have radically rebelled against God, how can one maintain the possibility of the birth of God within the human soul ? If man, like a decayed tree, can will and do nothing but evil,[1] there is no middle course to adopt, it would appear, between leaving the tree to rot, and, after uprooting it, flinging it into the fire. If nature is absolutely opposed to God, either God has no power over her, or he ought to destroy her.

To maintain the spiritual and optimistic ideal of the

---

[1] According to Luther's expression.

N

mystics, whilst at the same time regarding nature from
the pessimistic standpoint of Luther, and, in a more
general way, from a realistic standpoint : such is the
task Boehme sets himself. This task determines itself
in his mind as follows. Whereas the mystics wished to
know how God can be born in that which is not himself,
Boehme asks himself how God can be reborn in that which
has violently separated from him. Now, he imagines
he can solve this problem if he is able to discover both
the source of divine existence and the origin of the
world and of sin. This science will be regeneration
itself. For knowledge, when it penetrates to its source
and origin, blends and unites with action and reality.
To see things from the standpoint of God is to be
reborn to divine life.

The following, therefore, is to be the fundamental
division of Boehme's system : 1st, How does God
engender himself ? 2nd, Why and how did God
create the world and how did evil enter therein ?
3rd, How can God be reborn in the heart of the
corrupt creature, and what is the final end of all
beings ?

As we see, this is the question of the beginning and
the end, stated in all its generality and dominating all
others. Whereas the ancients tried to discover *a
posteriori* what stable, determinate principles lie hidden
beneath the movement and indetermination of phenomena, and knew no mean between an altogether
illusory, indeterminate absolute such as chance, and a
full and perfected absolute such as intelligence, our
philosopher, for whom the whole of nature is the result
of an action, tries to find out how the absolute itself
came into being, in so far as it is this and not that ;
even as regards God, he descends from infinite power

to the production of determinate being. The philosophy
of the ancients was a classification, more than anything
else, that of Boehme is to be a construction. The
problem of the genesis of things has been substituted for
that of their essence. And as the being whose genesis is
here sought and whose internal movement should explain
nature is distinctly the conscious, free and acting person,
the system we are about to study appears before us as
the dawn of a new philosophy, which may be called the
philosophy of personality, considered in itself and in its
connection with nature.

What method does Boehme recommend in this
enquiry ?

The problem now before us, we must remember, is
to see being proceed from its primary source, that is,
to apprehend the transition from nothing to something.
Now, the means at the disposal of ordinary philosophy
are powerless for such a task. What will erudition
give us, except opinions, abstract ideas ? The Bible
itself, if we seek enlightenment therein without going
farther back in time, is nothing but a dead letter, a
symbol that cannot be explained. It is the same with
the senses and the reason as it is with erudition. The
senses enable us to know only the cut-and-dry appearances of things and their products, not their real nature
and inner life. Exterior reason, or the natural elaboration
of the data of experience, is as dead as the materials it
brings together. It analyses and separates ; and the
objects it considers, thus snatched from the living
whole of which they formed part, are no more than
fictitious beings, incapable of telling us anything of
their origin and true nature. It is this exterior reason,
which, seeing the wicked in this world of ours prosper
equally with the good, insinuates to man that evil is the

equal of good, and consequently that the existence of the God of religion is problematical.

All these methods have the same flaw : they are passive and dead. They presuppose a given, realised object, and set the mind, like a motionless mirror, opposite that object. A living method, alone, enables us to penetrate into the mysteries of life. Being, alone, knows being ; we must generate with God in order to understand generation. Therefore the true method consists in witnessing, or rather taking part in the divine operation whose end is the blossoming and dominion the rule of the personality ; it is knowledge as consciousness of action: a method, indeed, which proceeds from cause to effect, whereas any purely logical method, limited to the working out of the data of experience, is and can be nothing more than a vain effort to rise from effect to cause.

But then, how can man thus place himself at the standpoint of God ? It is impossible for him to ascend to God : there is no transmutation of creature into creator. Still, though man cannot ascend into God, God can descend into man. Not that God can be evoked and materially constrained, as it were, by the practices of false magic or outward devotion, but rather that God descends into man, when man dies to his corrupt, inborn nature, to give himself up to divine action. Christ said that you " must be born again," if you would see " the kingdom of God." The conversion of the heart opens the eye of the intelligence. Just as the exterior man sees the exterior world, so the new man sees the divine world in which he is living. And this return to God is possible for man, since man was created in the image of God. He has only to go down to the deepest recesses of himself and set free the interior man from the exterior man in order to participate in divine life. " Reflect on thyself, search thyself, find thyself : this is the key of wisdom. Thou art the image and child of God. Such is the development of thy being ; eternal birth in God. For God is spirit, and likewise in thee that which commands is spirit and is the creation of divine sovereignty."

Once man thus adopts the eternal standpoint of universal genesis, everything which at the outset was only veil and mist interposed between himself and the light, becomes a transparent symbol, a faithful expression. Erudition, the Bible, tradition, concepts, the phenomena of nature, all these things, though dead in themselves, become animated and living when regarded with the eye of the spirit. The eternal word, speaking within ourselves, tells us the true meaning of the written, the sensible word. Nor is this all, for between the within and the without there is reciprocity of action. Of a surety, the sight of exterior things, in itself alone, would never have revealed to us the principle which these things manifest, this principle wills to be understood in itself. Primary being, however, is to us nothing but empty form ; it is by the correct interpretation of phenomena that it assumes body and is determined. All the same, it could never find adequate expression in phenomena. Being infinite, spirit could not be wholly manifested, for all manifestation takes place by means of the finite. Spirit is eternal mystery in its essence. Therefore not only should we make use of phenomena in order to catch a faint glimpse of the details of divine perfection, but we should also remember that phenomena are never anything else than an imperfect manifestation of this perfection. And when we speak of the origin of God and of things, we ought to appeal to all the images with which our senses and reason supply us, and always look upon these images as but clumsy metaphors which should be understood in spirit and in truth. The wisdom of God is beyond all description.

III

This maxim meets with its application at the very first step theosophy attempts to take. To begin with, we have to set forth the birth of God, the way in which God generates himself. To speak of the birth of God, however, taking these words literally, is to speak the devil's language ; it is saying that eternal light flashed out of darkness, that God had a beginning. Still, I am compelled to employ this term : the birth of God ; otherwise, thou couldst not understand me. Restricted as we are, we speak only by parcelling things out, by breaking the unity of the whole. In God there is neither Alpha nor Omega, neither birth nor development. I, however, am compelled to place things one after the other. The reader must by no means read me with the eyes of flesh.

Eternal nature generates itself without any beginning. How does this generation come about ?

Boehme here sets himself the famous problem of self-originated existence—of *aseity*. Whereas, however, by this term the Schoolmen understand a mere property of perfect being, a property, too, that is, above all, negative ; Boehme insists that the strange expression, " God self-caused," shall have a precise, concrete and positive meaning. To fathom the mystery it contains is, to him, the first and main question, the solution of which will throw light on all other questions. Nor does he think he ought to abandon the search until he has reconstructed in thought the logical sequence of the operations by which God rises from a state of nothingness to one of fulness of existence.

What, then, was there in the beginning ? From what germ did God generate himself?

In the beginning was being which presupposes nothing anterior to itself ; in which, consequently, nothing is essence, or nature, or finite, determinate form : for everything that exists as a determinate thing demands a cause and a reason. We, for our part, can conceive of this being only as the eternal no-thing, the infinite, the abyss, the mystery. Boehme uses the word *Ungrund* to designate this first source of things, meaning thereby that, beneath God, there is nothing to serve him as a foundation, and also that in the first being the ground or reason of things is not yet manifested. Thus, the primordial infinite in itself is nothing but silence, rest without beginning or end, absolute peace and eternity, unity and identity. In it is neither goal, nor place, nor even the impulse to seek and find. It is free from suffering, that companion of desire and quality. It is neither light nor darkness. It is an unfathomable mystery unto itself.

Such is the initial condition of divinity. Is it also its fulfilment? If the answer is in the affirmative, God is reduced to being nothing more than an abstract property, wanting in force, intelligence and science ; he is rendered incapable of creating the world in which the very perfections he lacks are to be found. But it is impossible that God should be an inert being, dwelling somewhere beyond the skies. The Father is omnipotent and omniscient ; he is the essence of gentleness and love, pity and blessing. The world, too, derives from him all the perfections to be found therein. Then how is the transition to be brought about from God, who is nothingness, to God the person and creator?

Here we come to the main point in Boehme's system. The solution of the problem of eternal generation, given by our theosophist, is the distinctive task he set himself; it opens up a new path along which many philosophers were subsequently to proceed.

Of course, the mystics of old had already taken up this line of research. Eckhart asked himself how merely potential, motionless and inactive divinity, which is the first being, becomes the living and personal God, who alone is true God. He explained the transition from the one to the other, by considering the part played by the image or idea of God, which emanates spontaneously from primordial power, just as from each of our tendencies there goes forth an idea that makes it objective and manifest. Beholding itself in its own image, absolute substance became conscious of itself and was constituted a person.

Boehme is inspired by this doctrine, but he does more than return to and continue it; with that sense of concrete existence, of life and nature, which characterises him, he can find no satisfaction in the abstract God of the mystics of old. Eckhart had almost explained how God becomes conscious of himself; consciousness of self, however, is no more than the shadow of existence. In order then that God may really be a person and that nature may find in him the elements of a positive existence, divine generation must be something different from what Eckhart teaches.

Boehme starts with the principle that God, who is mystery, wills to reveal himself in all the fulness of his being, i.e. to manifest himself as a living person, capable of creating. In so far as he pursues the revelation of himself, God wills and posits all the conditions of this revelation. Now, according to Boehme, there is one supreme law which governs all things, both divine and human : that all revelation calls for opposition. As light is visible only when reflected by a dark body, so anything whatsoever is posited or constituted only by being set over against its opposite. That which meets with no obstacle always goes forward and never returns within itself, never manifestly exists, either for itself or for another. Two moments may be distinguished in the relation of the given principle to its contrary. The mere presence of the negative principle over against the positive principle manifests the latter only as a potency or a possibility. If it is desired that this potency become reality, it must act upon the negative principle, discipline it and make thereof its instrument and expression. This law of opposition and reconciliation governs divine genesis. If the divine spirit is to be revealed, it will not remain within itself, it will create its contrary. Nor is this all ; for, acting on this contrary, it will assimilate it to itself and spiritualise it. And so we find that Boehme is to involve God in a series of oppositions. In proportion as contradictions and reconciliations come about, in like proportion will divine personality be realised. The contrary essence or nature on which God will rely in order to personify himself, will constitute, within God himself, the eternal basis of our created nature.

Such are the ideas that govern Boehme's system and give it its distinctive character. They have their centre in a principle which may be formulated as follows : being is constituted as potency by opposing itself and as reality by reconciling to itself that which is opposed to it. These general ideas, however, are not so much formulated in one special place, as employed in the development of the system.

In the beginning was no-thing. This no-thing is not absolute nothingness. On the contrary, it is being itself, eternal Good, eternal gentleness and eternal love, but still, being in itself, *i.e.* non-manifested. And so in this no-thing there dwells an internal opposition. It is nothing, and it is all; it is indifference and it is excellence. That is the reason this no-thing must appear to us as unstable and living. It will move itself, in order to become reconciled with itself.

The first result of the opposition just noticed is the scission of the primordial infinite into two contraries : desire (*Sucht*) and will (*Wille*). No-thing is desire, because it is mystery, and mystery tends to manifest itself; no-thing is the desire to become some-thing. But the object to which it tends is not an indeterminate one : it is the manifestation and possession of oneself. And so the infinite is desire on the one hand, and what is called will on the other. Unconscious and un-assuaged desire generates will; but will, to which belong knowledge and understanding, regulates and determines desire. The one possesses motion and life ; the other, independence and power of command. Will is greater than the power which gave it birth. This duality is the origin of all the oppositions which the march of divine revelation will arouse. Will is the germ of divine personality and the basis of all personality ; desire, the essence and body of will, is the germ of eternal nature and the basis of sensible nature.

And so will is manifested because of the presence of desire, with which it is contrasted. Yes and no, however, are not two things outside of each other ; they are one and the same thing, divided only to allow the yes to reveal itself. That is why separation, in its turn, is an unstable condition. The yes which, in this separation, is *per se* devoid of essence and looked upon as no-thing, endeavours to make itself concrete by absorbing the no and reconstituting unity to its own advantage. On to the two opposite terms, desire and will, there is now added a third, the idea of a reconciliation of the first with the second. The production of this third term is the work of imagination. Speaking generally, this faculty of imagination is desire, applied to an image and tending to absorb it—as hunger absorbs food—and then to produce it in the outer world, transformed into a living reality by the action of the subject itself. Now, the will which is mind, and whose object is the revelation of itself, unites with desire, in order to imagine this revelation ; and, in doing so, become capable of realising it. Imagination makes the will into a magician. What the will wills is determined in the very effort it makes to represent it to itself. It wills to find and lay hold upon itself ; consequently, to form an interior mirror of itself ; and as desire is the matter on which it works, it wills that infinite desire, fixing itself on the Good, shall become this mirror.

The task, then, before God or the will is the following : the regulating of desire according to the law of the Good, and hence, the forming of an object which is a mirror of the will, and wherein the latter can contemplate and recognise itself. In accomplishing this task, divine will is to issue from a state of nothingness and attain to reality.

God wills to manifest himself, to form a mirror of

himself. He can do this only in a threefold manner.
First, he must posit himself as indeterminate will,
capable of willing good or evil. Such a will, however,
is neither good nor bad : God must come out of this
indifference. He does this by generating within himself the one, eternal Good, or determinate will. This
good, which is God, is not an object or a thing ; it
remains will, though strong, infallible will. With the
generation of this will, a beginning has been constituted
in the infinite, a foundation has been formed in the
abyss, and a reason for things has been superposed upon
the eternal mystery. Nevertheless, the first will has
not exhausted itself in the generation of determinate
will : it retains its infinite fecundity. Thus, from the
conjuncture of infinite will and determinate will springs
a third will, to wit, will that goes forth of itself to
produce an object. The object resulting from this
threefold action is none other than the mirror of will
itself, eternal wisdom. This image is not God, it is
only the image of God. Still, by it, God is henceforth
self-revealed, he sees himself as a will that is threefold
and one at the same time. These three moments of
divine activity may be characterised by the names of
will, strictly so called, *reason* and *force*. They may
also be named Father, Son and Spirit. These are not
three gods, for each of the three is a spiritual being,
and separation of substances exists only in the material
world. Nor are they even three persons ; for will, as
against its image or idea, is only knowledge and
consciousness of itself, it does not yet exercise that
empire over a thing-being, which is the condition of
personality. In truth, God is person only in Christ.
In the generation that has just been considered, there is
nothing else than a threefold action of the one will.

Eternal wisdom, whose production is the result of this action, in which, too, the Trinity sees and finds itself acting, is not a fourth will, but is set over against the Trinity as its representation or object. It is this reconciliation of desire with will that the latter had undertaken to effect. Like every mirror, it is passive and does not generate at all. It is the eternal virgin. In it are all the divine perfections, though rather as ideas and paradigms than forces and living beings. For these perfections are objects of will, not wills themselves : and life could not exist without will, on which it is founded. Life and fruitfulness belong not to ideas or generalities, but to persons only, in so far as they act in accordance with ideas.

Such is the divine genesis following the appearance of desire and will in the heart of the primordial infinite. Here, indeed, we have God far removed from a state of nothingness. He knows himself as will, and even good will. But is he God the Father, omnipotent and omniscient, love and pity, light and joy, of whom we try to catch a glimpse and whom we seek ?

This God, if we note well, by no means realises personality yet. He is intelligence ; he knows himself. But intelligence, such as we see it within ourselves, is not something concrete, something we can grasp. It is not an essence, but rather the potency or germ of an essence. The God, whose action, altogether interior, has no other object than himself, is still a hidden, an incompletely revealed God. He is God as far as possibility will allow : the divine ideal. In order that this ideal may be realised and God be the living person, will must continue the work of eternal generation, which, so far, has only been begun. God must have a second birth.

Here, more especially, the law of contraries will find

its application.   If we consider all the things that really
exist in this world, we find they are made up of yes and
no : *In Ja und Nein bestehen alle Dinge.*   Day could
not be without night, nor night without day ; cold is
the condition of heat, and heat of cold.   Do away with
opposition and struggle, and everything will return to
silence and immobility, everything will revert to a state
of nothingness.   The one, in so far as it is one, has
nothing that it can will.   For it to will and live, it must
divide into two.   In the same way, unity cannot sense
itself, but in duality sensation is possible.   For a being,
then, to be posited as real, it must be opposed against its
contrary, and the degree of opposition is the measure ot
the degree of realisation.

Now, in the development of the divine activity just
considered, God was not opposed against anything which
might rightly be called his contrary.   The power of
objectivation in whose presence he has found himself and
which he determined and limited so as to form his true
image of it, differed from him only as idea differs from
intelligence.   In this passive principle, there is nothing
to oppose divine action : a mirror reflects—without
resisting—the rays that fall upon it.   In this altogether
ideal opposition, God could acquire only an ideal
existence.   In order that he may assume bodily form,
as a person, he must be engaged in strife with a real
contrary, *i.e.* with a positive power whose action is
opposed to his own.   Therefore God must raise up
such a contrary, become connected with it, oppose it
and finally discipline and permeate it ; only thus will
the work of divine generation be accomplished.   How
is this new development to be effected ?

The will that has realised itself in the evolution
through which we have just passed, and which may be

called reason, is still pure spirit, infinitude, a mystery.
But mystery, whilst it continues such, calls for revelation which alone determines it as mystery. Like all
contraries, mystery and revelation imply each other.
Therefore, the will could not remain the obscure dark
potency it still is (*Finsterniss*). Within its murky gloom
is kindled a new desire, the desire to exist in a real,
concrete, that is to say, corporeal fashion. But it is not
of itself that darkness glows and becomes fire, or that
motionless reason is changed into the desire to live. The
term or goal to which divine will tends is the realisation
of the personality, the excellent form of life. At the basis
of reason, then, there was light as well as darkness, the
dawn of perfect life as well as the dim desire of
life in general ; and it was by contact with the new-
born light that the dark was kindled and became fire.
The desire to live is, at bottom, the will to live well.
And so the possible God divides himself into desire
of life in general and will to realise perfect life.
These are no longer two abstract, ideal entities, but
rather two forces, alike positive and living. And these
forces first appear as two rival energies, ready to enter
upon a struggle with each other. For the love of life,
when left to itself, impels the being to exist in every
possible manner : it makes no distinction between good
and evil, the beautiful and the ugly, the divine and the
diabolical. On the contrary, the will to live well and
be a person requires a choice from amongst all possible
forms of life, and excludes those that do not conform
with the ideal. The dividing of the eternal no-thing
into passivity and activity, desire and will, had produced
only the logical opposition of subject and object. The
dividing of will into negative and affirmative will,
fire and light, force and love, results in a real opposition

and the beginning of internal warfare within the heart of divinity. The first of the two rival powers, force or life in general, is the principle and the mother ; the second, love or enlightenment, is the law and the end. The one is the substratum of real nature, the other that of divine personality.

In this second opposition, God awakes to personal life ; set over against nature, however, as against some inimical power, he is at first nothing more than latent energy, mere capacity for love and light. In order that this energy may be displayed and realised, love must enter into relation with force, imposing its law on this latter. And so the progress of divine revelation demands a reconciliation of the two contraries that have sprung up in the heart of will. Now, that this recon-ciliation may come about, it must in the first place be posited as both idea and goal : afterwards, the divine will must work to realise this idea. But the reconciliation of force with love, or of fire with light, is nothing else than the realisation of that eternal wisdom, which divinity has formed as a mirror wherein to contemplate and know itself. Thus, what has to be done is to bring down the idea from the empty heights of a transcendent heaven, in order to blend it with living forces and manifest it in a corporeal nature. Ideal wisdom as an object to be realised : that is the third term superposed on the two contraries into which divine will has divided itself.

How will the new task resulting from the position of these three terms be accomplished ? Here we are on the plane of life : matter, agent and end are, each of them, beings endowed with force and activity. It is by the coöperation of these three principles that reconcilia-tion will be brought about. If love is an action that tends to temper force, force is an unconscious impulse towards love ; and the idea itself, ideal wisdom, seized with the desire to live, tends to its own realisation : the virgin, God's companion, aspires after the manifestation of the divine wonders slumbering within her. From these elements, eternal magic forms God in person. Will is linked in imagination to the idea it purposes to realise ; contemplating, it becomes enamoured of it ; and, eagerly desiring union, seizes upon and absorbs it. It absorbs it in order to generate it within itself and produce it in the form of a reality. On its side, too, the idea is active and desires existence : it is a soul seeking for itself a body. It goes to meet the will that is calling to it. The idea is accordingly realised, beneath the generating action of imagination and desire : spirit, by a wholly interior operation, devoid of any preëxistent corporeal reality, takes to itself a nature, an essence and a body.

This realisation of divine wisdom is a wonderful and complex work which it is important to consider in detail.

God effects it by means of seven organising spirits which he generates with a view to this task. These spirits are the forces born in the heart of the dark element beneath the influence of the light element, forces whose mission it is to transform the will which says "no" into the will which says "yes" ; to discipline and deify nature. Boehme here resumes and adapts to his system the ancient kabbalistic doctrine of the seven natural essences, the last of which is the divine kingdom. According to Boehme, the seven spirits are born in succession from one another, and their succession marks the progress of nature in the direction of God. The first three bring nature or the dark element to the point at which contact will be possible between itself and the light element. The fourth realises this contact, and the last three cause light and love to reign over nature, now prevailed upon and induced to follow spontaneously.

First, there springs up in the will, *desire* properly so called, or the egoïstic tendency. The will wills to be something. Now, there is nothing over against it, the possession of which is capable of determining it. Therefore it takes itself as object and wills everything for itself. It then imagines itself to be something, though it is still nothing but hunger and emptiness. This first essence is the dark, the solid, the force of contraction, the salt of the alchemists.

Then there comes about *motion*, as the second essence or second natural spirit. For, as it is infinite and void, the will cannot find any satisfaction in taking itself as object. Therefore it turns without and becomes the acute, the bitter ; pain : that spur of sensibility, the force of expansion, the mercury of the philosophers.

Meanwhile the two forces thus produced are in conflict with each other. The first directs being towards itself, the second directs it towards something else. The result of this opposition is the third essence, *restlessness*, the incessant motion of a soul that cannot find its good within itself and knows not where to look for it. The two forces in the soul, the forces of contraction and expansion, are contradictory, and yet they cannot be separated from each other. The soul, void in itself, cannot remain fixed in egoïsm : moved by egoïsm even when it goes forth from itself and seeks its good without, it cannot attain to abnegation and love. It is continually fleeing from and seeking itself. This restless motion is that of a wheel, a motion which reaches no goal and yet is in perpetual pursuit of itself. Thus, the third essence has for its expression : rotation, or the combination of the centripetal and the centrifugal forces.   It forms the base of the sulphur of the alchemists.

Nature rises to this point of herself, but here her power stops.   She has shaken off the dull slumber and ignoble ease of egoïsm, and sought without for the thing she could not find within.   To the eye of the body, however, the exterior infinite is just as void as the interior infinite ; and the soul has done no more than abandon itself to two contradictory impulses and bring itself into a state of embarrassment, placing itself before a spinning-wheel, as it were.   This interior contradiction in a being which seeks for rest by means of agitation, is an intolerable torture ; but nature, of herself, cannot put an end to it.   She has exhausted all her resources : nothing within will extricate her from the state in which she is.   Salvation can come only from what is above nature, *i.e.* from God or eternal freedom.   But how will these two contrary powers succeed in reuniting with each other ?

The restlessness with which nature is tortured has this advantage, that it manifests her weakness and cries out to her that she cannot suffice unto herself and form a whole.   The man who knows his wretchedness is not so wretched as he who is ignorant of it.   Under the influence of the spirit hovering above nature, the latter soon feels an anxious desire for freedom.   Something tells the soul that it must give itself to that which is superior to it, that in self-sacrifice it will find itself, that in dying unto itself it will be born in very truth.   On the other hand, spirit and freedom need nature in order to manifest and realise themselves.   If nature has a dim consciousness of her own law and harmony in spirit, the latter seeks in nature his own reality and body.

Spirit wills to exist, as nature tends to free herself from suffering. Thus impelled in the direction of each other, spirit and nature approach each other. Nature, however, has her own distinctive motion, and her force of inertia. The new desire she feels only just shows itself, it does not modify her wonted course. And so nature comes into collision with spirit whom she is seeking and who now comes down to her ; from the impact a new phenomenon is born : *the lightning flash.* This is the fourth moment in the march of existence, the fourth essence. This moment is the manifestation of the contact of nature and spirit. In the flash of the lightning, the dark, the coarse and the violent, all that makes up the egoïstic tendency of nature, is swallowed up and reduced to nothingness. The darkness is illumined and becomes living, manifest fire, the centre of light. Henceforth, nature is subject to and capable of realising spirit. There has come to pass a divine law which will henceforth apply to all beings. All life, according to this law, implies a dual birth. Suffering is the condition of joy, only through fire or by way of the cross do we attain to light. *Per crucem ad lucem.* Both in the intellectual and the physical order of things, parturition is preceded by a state of unrest and anxiety. Nature labours and suffers, feeling she has not the strength necessary to bring forth the fruit she has conceived. Suddenly, however, a supernatural effort, as it were, takes place ; suffering and joy clash together in one indivisible instant, the lightning flashes forth and the new being passes out of darkness into light. Henceforth the child of flesh is in possession of his own form and will develop by himself in accordance with his controlling idea ; the fruit of intelligence is no longer a chaos of vague, incoherent ideas, it is a conscious thought, sure of itself, entering unhesitatingly into the expression which manifests it.

With the appearance of the lightning flash, the first existence of divine nature, the development of the negative triad, comes to an end. At the same time there begins the development of a positive triad, representing the second and definitive existence of nature. Contraction, expansion and rotation, will be found in the march of this regenerate nature, though in a new, a supernatural sense.

The new concentration is the work of *love* : the unifying power of the spirit. Beneath its influence, forces abandon all their violence and take delight in each other. Egoïstic passions die away, and in place of the unity of individuals, each one of whom claims to exist alone, there is substituted a unity of penetration where each seeks, in its accord with the whole, a participation in true unity. Thus, love is the fifth spirit, the fifth essence. Its symbol is water, which extinguishes the fire of desire and confers second birth, birth according to the spirit.

Still, beings ought to do more than simply melt into each other. Their unification cannot be absorption and annihilation. The march of revelation ought to make multiplicity perceptible, even to that profound spiritual unity conferred by love. And so there appears a sixth spirit, which releases the elements of the divine symphony and causes them to be heard in their individuality as well as in their relation to the general effect. This sixth spirit is the intelligent *word*, or sound, by means of which voices cease to be indistinct noises, for they acquire that determination which makes them discernible and comprehensible in themselves. As love was the unification of the multiple, so the sixth essence is the perception of the multiple in the heart of unity itself.

All that now remains to be done, in the completion of the task of realising God, is to collect and coördinate all the forces that have successively created each other. If the higher is to govern the lower, it is not to substitute itself therefor and annihilate it, for the lower is its reality and its very existence ; deprived of this support, the higher element would be dissipated in the void of transcendent space. Light can only exist with darkness as its background. Therefore there appears a seventh spirit which, winning over the lower to the higher by persuasion, and bringing down the higher into the lower by grace, summons the whole of nature, great and small, first and last, to the manifestation of the divine will. This essence is *body* or the spirit of harmony. By its action the revelation of the Eternal is finally accomplished. Wisdom is no longer an idea. It is a kingdom of living beings, the kingdom of God or of Glory.

Thus Boehme regards as a reality and an essential condition of divine life, this uncreated heaven, the kingdom of the Father, the glory of God, of which the Scriptures speak in so many places though the language used is often interpreted metaphorically. The lily is clad in beauty, a beauty surpassing the splendour of Solomon. Man has his vesture of glory : his wealth and his home, power and honours, all that manifests his invisible personality. God, too, reveals himself in a phenomenon that has no other content than himself, and yet is distinct from him. The Glory of God is his vesture, his outer form, his body and reality : it is God seen from without.

To describe the harmony and beauty of this kingdom

of Glory is impossible. It sums up all we see on earth, though in a state of perfection and spirituality to which the creature cannot attain. Its colours are more brilliant, its fruits more savoury, its sounds more melodious, and its whole life more happy. Along with purity of spirit, divine beings possess the full reality of body. Their life is not an imperfectly satisfied desire : it is being in all its fulness and completion. Above all else it is harmony, reconciled with the free and perfect growth of all individuals. Consider the birds in our forests : each praises God in its own fashion, in all keys and modes. Do we find God offended by this diversity, does he impose silence on the discordant voices? All forms of being are precious in the sight of Infinite Being. But if divine gentleness is manifested in our world, *a fortiori*, beings in the kingdom of Glory are free from all restraint, since all in that kingdom, each according to its nature, not only seek God but also possess and manifest him.

Such, in its completion, is eternal nature, the revelation of the divine mystery. She carries within herself three principles, the three reasons, as it were, or bases of determination, born of primordial no-thing. The first principle is the substratum of the first three qualities, or of nature left to herself. It is darkness, or latent fire, waiting for the spark in order to become manifest. Boehme generally calls it *fire*. The second principle is the substratum of the last three qualities, *i.e.* of the form or expression of ideal wisdom. This is the principle of *light*. Each of these principles is eternal ; and, in a sense, they exclude each other. Fire admits of no limit, it devours everything with which it is brought into contact. Light is the absolute of sweetness and joy, the negation of darkness, the goal of all aspiration. The former is the life of the all or of the inde-

terminate infinite : the latter is the life of God or of
the excellent, the determinate one.   Still, neither of these
two principles can suffice unto itself.   In vain does fire
will to be the whole, it is only a part.   In vain does
light scorn darkness : it is realised only when reflected
from the dark.   That is why a third principle is necessary, which will unite the first to the second, in such a
manner as to produce real existence.   This third principle
is *body*.   By it, spirit incarnates in matter and becomes
real and living.   This union of the first principle with
the second is, after all, not a complete absorption, and
the three principles remain irreducible.   Indeed, the
operation which places fire under the laws of light does
not annihilate even the basis of fire.   Infinitude of life
subsists beneath the form of perfection that determines
it.   The divine command is not addressed to slaves ;
it wills to have free beings and finds them.   Fire, light,
body, *i.e.* life, good and their union in one real being ;
such are the three principles of divine nature.

We must now take care not to identify this nature
with the true God.   However excellent she be,
divine nature exists neither in herself nor for her
own benefit.   She is the realisation of the perfections
comprised in the idea of wisdom.   She is the eternal
virgin, who, at the voice of God, has come down from
the limbo of the possible into the paradise of actual
existence.   Nature will now return thanks to her
creator, handing over to him her life and her bodily
existence.   The eternal virgin, fecundated by spirit,
henceforth brings to birth, and the fruit of her womb
is God the person, *i.e.* the God who not only knows
and possesses himself, but also projects himself without, in love and action.   Whereas the latter, God the
person, set before himself, as a mirror of his infinite

will, eternal wisdom or the idea of divinity, God constituted himself only as ideal trinity, a possible personality. By giving himself in nature a living contrary, and bending this contrary to the laws of his good will, God enters upon a differentiation which is real and no longer ideal, and hence attains to effective personality, that of the Christian trinity. Self-knowledge confers only existence for self; action alone generates absolute existence and completes personality.

Now, this action is threefold: it posits three persons corresponding to the three principles of nature. In the first place, God is the will that presides over life in general, or over eternal fire. In this sense he is the Father, power, justice, divine wrath: he is, as it were, the consciousness of infinite vital activity. God, however, does not desire life for life itself. His will is to have life as a realisation of idea, to generate the living word. This is why the Father gives birth to the Son, who is the consciousness of the second principle or of light, and wills the subordination of life to good, its *raison d'être*. By the Son, the God of love and compassion, the fire of wrath is for ever appeased. Accordingly, the Son is greater than the Father. Still, the existence of the good will as against the universal will to live is not sufficient to realise the good ; these two wills must come together and become reconciled, and this is what takes place in a third consciousness and a third person, whence proceeds the third principle called the Holy Ghost.

Thus, whilst forming eternal nature, and by reason of the very activity expended in forming it, God truly constitutes himself Father, Son, and Spirit, without on that account abdicating his unity. Because the three realisations of God are indeed persons and not things,

they do not come under that law of time and space
which insists that unity is incompatible with multiplicity. Personality admits of mutual penetration :
further than that, it implies it. Only in its union
with other persons can a personal being be constituted
as such. In so far as a being is conceived as external
to other beings it is constituted in space and attributes
to itself individuality, that enemy of true personality.
Egoïsm is the basis of individuality : it is the gift of
oneself that makes the person.

The generation of God is now accomplished. God
is perfect personality realised in three persons, each of
which is the part and the whole, at one and the same
time. These three persons are the Father, or the consciousness of force ; the Son, or the consciousness of
good ; and the Spirit, or the consciousness of the
harmony set up in God between force and good. And
over against God, as being his work and his glory,
stands arrayed eternal nature, in whom all possibilities
are realised, in proportion as they express divine perfection.

Such is the teaching of Boehme regarding the birth
of God. Through the theological and alchemical
symbols in which this teaching is clothed for the purpose of self-manifestation is it not clear that it possesses a philosophical meaning and import? The main
idea of the teaching is that the person is the perfect
being and must exist ; consequently, that all the conditions of the person's existence must themselves be
realised. From this principle all else follows. Personality, says Boehme, implies thought and action ;
now, in order to think and act, one must be in rapport
with something opposed to oneself. Thought must
have some object to consider and resolve into itself ;

action must have matter which it may subdue and spiritualise. This law is universal; absolute personality itself could not escape from it without contradiction. On the other hand, absolute being must be self-caused, must depend on nothing foreign to itself. Thus if absolute being wills to become person, it must draw from itself an object opposed to itself, to which its intelligence applies, and which its activity modifies. It is necessary that the one infinite divinity be transformed of itself into a duality, one of whose terms will be the true God, and the other will be nature, of whom this God has need. Thus conceived of as being subject and agent as against object and matter springing from his own inmost being, God has a task to perform : the solution of the antinomy he has created within himself; and by the accomplishment of this task he realises himself *qua* person. His action and thought, life and existence, are henceforward something else than the shadow of human life and activity : they are perfect types of which the existence of creatures affords us nothing but feeble images.

Now, what is this system wherein God generates himself by positing and rising above his contrary? Is it not that ancient doctrine of Night as a first principle which Aristotle had already repudiated in his predecessors? The first being, said Aristotle, is not the imperfect, but the perfect; in the order of phenomena, the perfect is subsequent to the imperfect; but in the order of being, it is the perfect that is first and absolute. Boehme's doctrine, like that of the old theologians, appears to be only an anthropomorphism or a naturalism. He noticed, we may say, that in the case of man, indetermination precedes determination; that struggle is the condition of life and progress;

that an image is necessary for the understanding, and matter for the will ; that the action of our faculties consists in assimilating to oneself external objects ; and he transferred to God this condition of human existence.

Even were this judgment well founded we could not regard it as a condemnation of the doctrine, purely and simply. Though Boehme's system were, in reality, to apply only to finite beings, it would not, on that account, be without importance. We must forgive our theosophist for his imperfect teaching as to the history of the divine trinity, if, when thinking he is speaking to us of God, he is really speaking of ourselves, and that with much sagacity. The great principle that will is the basis of life and existence, and that, in its turn, life finds in freedom its end and *raison d'être*, will lose none of its interest by being concerned only with the created world instead of being applied to the Creator as well. This strange system, whose very opulence is utter confusion, and whose glory is dazzling lightning, contains many a delicate, modest, and psychological observation, many a wise, practical, and moral reflection. As Boehme tells us, it is in the depths of his consciousness that he seeks after divinity ; it is because God generates himself in man that man can be made acquainted with divine generation. What wonder if his knowledge of God is, above all, knowledge of ourselves ?

Moreover, it does not follow that Boehme, from the metaphysical point of view, is a mere naturalist. Without delighting, as he does, in speculations that we cannot possibly verify regarding the birth and development of God, at all events we can see the difference between his teaching and that rejected by Aristotle. According to the ancient philosophy of chaos and the

infinite, the generation of the perfect by the imperfect
was the absolute reality of things. To Boehme there is
no before or after in God, the absolute. It is our condition as finite and belonging to nature that forces us
to regard God from the standpoint of nature, and to
picture to ourselves his life as being progressive.

This is not all, however. The chaos of the ancients
was a given nature, a thing, and that the most confused
and indeterminate conceivable ; and from this thing, by
a necessary process of development, determinate and
perfect being was brought forth. The standpoint of
the ancients was an objective one. Aristotle, under the
name of pure action, contrasts the thing that is wholly
determinate with the thing that is wholly indeterminate ; whereas Neo-Platonism, returning to the idea
of progress, posits, as first being, a unity which, superior
or inferior to intelligence and life, unnamable and
unintelligible, still seems to be only the thing, stripped
of the last of its qualities by the final effort of abstraction. The principle of our theosophical mystic is
something quite different. A Christian and a spiritualist, he assigns the first place to personality in its
most perfect form. From the point of view at which
he is placed, indetermination, infinitude, no-thing have
quite different meanings from those contained in ancient
philosophy. No longer is no-thing the lack of quality
and perfection in a thing that can exist only if it is
determinate ; it is the infinite fecundity of a spirit
which *is* by its very potency, and is exhausted by none
of its productions. Negative, from the outer standpoint of objectivity, Boehme's principle is altogether
positive from the inner standpoint of life and generation. In itself this principle is not the imperfect, it is
the perfect ; and the progress admitted by Boehme,

though in a way relative to the human mind, is progress in manifestation, not in the intrinsic perfection of God. The system of the metaphysical world has been inverted ; no longer is it intelligence that depends on the intelligible, it is the intelligible that depends on intelligence. It is no longer the subject that derives its existence from the object, it is the object that exists by the subject. The reason this substitution has come about is that man has discovered in that which constitutes the foundation of the subject, in mind and will, something irreducible that baffles description, and which he regards as more real in its indetermination and nothingness than all the tangible realities of given substance.

Thus, Boehme's course is by no means that of the Pythagoreans or even of the Neo-Platonists. The progress which proceeds from will to its workings cannot be assimilated to the progress which proceeds from the indeterminate thing to the determinate. The theology of Boehme is not an evolutionistic monism.

Nor, on the other hand, is it a system of dualism : Does it not, indeed, appear as though Boehme escapes one danger only to fall into an opposite one ? How does Boehme maintain the perfection of the divine principle unless it be by positing, outside of God, as a subject of evil, a hostile and coeternal principle ? And, according to him, God himself is one with and responsible for this latter principle. *Per crucem ad lucem* : this is both the divine and the human law. No light without darkness, no action without matter, no subject without object, no God without nature. Is it not just this universal and necessary coexistence of two principles, the one positive, the other negative, that is called dualism ?

It cannot, indeed, be denied that Boehme sees in matter the condition of the manifestation of spirit ; this is even an essential part of his system. But Boehme does not regard himself as a dualist on that account. In his eyes it is monstrous to make evil the equal of good, and nature the equal of God. The negative principle does not exist in itself, but only by the action of the positive principle, which creates it in order to manifest therein. God alone is sovereign ruler, and it is the internal motion of divine will that posits matter, outside of God, as the condition of this very motion. Matter is the exterior aspect, the phenomenon of the invisible action of spirit. It fixes in dead forms the continuous flashing forth of living light. Dependent on spirit as regards her origin, nature is subject to spirit as regards her final purpose. Her end is to supply spirit, by manifesting it, with the object it needs in order to lay hold of and personify itself. She resists spirit only in order to afford it an opportunity to display its might, her instinct is an intelligence that is ignorant of itself ; her passion, an unconscious desire for freedom. Far from nature being the equal of God, it is at God's summons that she begins to exist, and the limit of her development is her exact adaptation to the will of spirit.

Thus Boehme's theology borders on dualism as it did on evolutionism without running counter to it or foundering therein. At bottom, Boehme purposes to find a middle term between these two doctrines. In his opinion, the mystics of old were in the wrong when they rejected dualism altogether. This was the reason they could not realise the philosophy of personality that they had conceived. Their God lacks the conditions of real existence, he does not outstep the limits of ideal

existence.   It is only by borrowing from dualism
the idea of the eternal existence of matter as contrary
to spirit and giving this matter as a body to divine
spirit, that divine personality can be conceived of as
really existing.   But, on the other hand, God the
person must remain infinite being outside of which
nothing exists in itself.   Dualism is repugnant to
religious thought which would have God not only a
form and an ideal, but also omnipotent and independent
being.   Thus, matter must not be a first being for the
same reason that God is, its very existence must result
from the working of divine power.   How can matter
issue from God and yet, at the same time, be the contrary of God ?   Boehme solves the difficulty by saying
that God, in order to reveal himself, makes himself
objective and real, and that this object and this exterior
reality, though posited by God, are not confounded
with him, because will, which is the basis of his being,
is infinite ; its efforts cannot possibly be wasted.   Thus
God has a nature or body that is not himself and that
forms his real existence ; but this body is posited by
God and is none other than his will itself, seen from
without.   In this phenomenon of God, the eternal
mystery is revealed, without the revelation ever dispelling
the mystery.   Nature is of the essence of God but God
is independent of nature.   This system is a kind of
concrete or naturalistic spiritualism.

IV

The knowledge of divine genesis is the first we need,
in order to attain to the possession of God.   But this
knowledge is not enough.   It was a mistake on the
part of the mystics to believe that all science was com-

prised in the science of God. Nature and man cannot be explained by a mere diminution of perfect essence. In creatures there is something peculiar to themselves that distinguishes them from God and even allows them to rebel against him. Evil, the work of creatures, is not a non-being, it is a being that says no ; hatred that would destroy love ; violence that would break the law. Accordingly, there is a science of nature, apart from the science of God. The difficulty consists in accounting for this distinction whilst maintaining that relation of dependence which should link all science with that of absolute being.

The first problem raised by the existence of nature is that of creation. On this point Boehme cannot adopt the doctrine usually called theism. According to this doctrine, it would appear that God made the world from absolute no-thing, i.e. created it by his infinite will alone, without using any matter at all, either sensible or suprasensible. But such a world would have no true reality, for its reality would not be founded in God. It would be simply a possible and ideal world, like the very principle to which it would owe its birth : intelligence without matter creates only ideas. Therefore there is no true personality in creatures. The reason some are good and others bad, some predestined to happiness and the rest given up to damnation, is not because there are living and opposite energies in the souls of creatures, it is because it has so been willed by the God who transcends all arbitrary wills. Idealism and fatalism are the consequences of the doctrine of theism.

Still, if Boehme rejects theism, will he not, as a consequence, sink into pantheism? We know that he recognises in God the existence of a nature. Is it not this nature that is to constitute the substratum of visible nature ?　Can the latter be anything else than a development of the former ; and must we not say, with the pantheists, that the world is, if not God himself, at all events the body and manifestation of God ?

Certainly such an interpretation would be contrary to Boehme's plan, which is even more energetically opposed to pantheism than to theism.　Surely, he says, in one sense God is everything, heaven and earth, spirit and world ; for everything has its origin in him.　But then, what becomes of his glorious immensity if the world is the standard of his perfection ?　Doubtless he created the world by his wisdom and might : but he did not form it so that he himself might become more perfect.　His perfection is complete independently of all creation.　God formed the world so as to be manifested in a manner that would be sensible.　Let not sophists tell me that, in my doctrine of the divine nature, I am confounding God with the world.　I am not confounding exterior with interior nature.　The latter is truly living and is perfect.　The other has nothing but a derived life, and remains imperfect.　No, the exterior world is not God, nor could it without blasphemy be called God.　To say that God is all, that God is himself and heaven and earth and the outer world, is to speak as the heathen, to make profession of the devil's religion.

Boehme's problem, therefore, is to derive matter from spirit and yet not sink into theism, and to base sensible nature on divine nature without falling into pantheism.　How does he solve the problem ?

Whereas the birth of God was a mere generation, *i.e.* a magical production accomplished by spirit through its two powers at once homogeneous and contrary, and without any pre-existing matter, the birth of the world is a creation, or production brought about by a spiritual agent through matter. The spiritual agent is the one God in three persons. Matter is eternal nature. Neither of these two principles is the world, or contains it. God the person, as such, is pure spirit. Eternal nature is perfect harmony, in which beings, although distinct, interpenetrate : it is a multiplicity each part of which, in its own way, expresses the unity of the whole. These perfections radically distinguish God and the divine nature from the sensible and created world, which, on the one hand, is material, and on the other consists of parts and fragments exterior to one another. But though God the person and eternal nature are not the world, they contain its elements ; the world has its own mobility and reality so far as there is in it something of the divine perfection. And first ,God, seeing, from all eternity, in wisdom, the ideas of things, formed the design of creating the world, *i.e.* of causing to exist in corporeal fashion what existed in him in essential fashion, or rather of causing to appear separate what, in him, was together. He formed this design from love alone, without being constrained or forced thereto in any way. There is not the slightest reason for creation. Its wherefore is a mystery and admits of no revelation whatsoever. If creation had its first origin in the manifested God and not in the primordial abyss, it would be explained, it would be necessary, and would force itself upon God. But God wills to have children, not masters. Though the world depends on God, God has no need of the world.

The world was not made from some thing, *i.e.* brute matter, the absolute contrary of a person. It was made of the divine nature, in the sense that the seven spirits constituting this nature realised in the form of bodies the ideas contained in wisdom. The productions of these spirits in the world of Glory were figures with floating contours, instinct with life and spirituality: the infinite visible in the finite. The same spirits now fix the idea in hard compact matter which conceals the infinite that it realises. In the world of Glory the real and the ideal balance each other : in the created world, it is the real that predominates.

Such is the portion of God the person, such the portion of the divine nature in creation. A third worker, however, intervenes in order to realise the world, this worker is the creature itself. Just as when the artist is working, the work itself, that wills to be, furthers by its distinctive life the efforts of will and intelligence ; so the creature, when brought to the threshold of existence by the union of spirit and increate nature, endeavours to cross this threshold and display itself in fulness of light. All spirit is a soul which desires a body. Now, the creative word had the effect of breaking the bond that held together the spiritual forces in union and harmony. Each of them, thenceforward, wills to exist for itself, to become manifest in accordance with its distinctive tendency.

What, then, is creation ? It is the introduction of space and time into the world of particular wills. Deep in the heart of eternity, wills, individual in themselves, were universal in their object. Realised in bodies separated from one another by time and space, wills are thereby detached from the all and thrown back upon themselves. Thus, space and time are the special foundation of the reality of the sensible world. Here, there is nothing that does not come from God, but nothing that was in God could produce this form of existence by mere development : it is by a free, original act, a veritable creation, that God causes the world of discontinuity and exteriority to appear.

God, then, is by no means swallowed up in his creation, any more than the intelligence of man is exhausted by being manifested. The divine will is as tenuous as a no-thing. No given solid being is capable of enclosing it within itself and making it immovable. Besides, the world does not issue from God himself, but from his glory, *i.e.* his exterior form. And this very glory, the periphery of divinity, remains after creation what it was before. For if the less is included in the more, the more is not included in the less ; *a fortiori*, the different cannot be included in the different. Neither as subject nor as object is divinity absorbed in its sensible manifestation. Creation is not at all a transformation of force.

Thus God creates, at the same time, from nothing and from matter. God the person creates with the divine nature as matter, but personality and the divine nature alike have their root in the primordial no-thing, in the mystery of infinite will.

Now what is it that God creates, what are the essential parts of the world system ? The model and instruments of creation are found, under the form of eternity, in the divine wisdom and nature. Creation is to be the realisation of this wisdom and nature under the form of time and separation. And so there is a relation between created things and eternal things, and it is to a certain extent possible to deduce from the latter the knowledge of the former, by placing oneself at the standpoint of God. This deduction is what is called the philosophy of nature, a speculation destined later on to assume a considerable degree of development in Germany, and rudiments of which we find in Boehme's theosophy.

The construction of the exterior world is brought about in a manner similar to that of the interior, divine world. In sensible bodies as in eternal nature, it is personality that seeks manifestation for itself : the only difference is that this manifestation, which is fully effected in eternal nature, remains of necessity incomplete in sensible nature. In the world there will then be three principles corresponding to the three divine principles : fire, light, and the union of these two principles in corporeity. Of the first and second, without appealing to the third, God forms the angels, who are still as near to divine perfection as the created condition permits of. The angels are spirits only. They do not exist of themselves, however, and their body, though spiritual, is harder and more compact than the glorious body of divinity. The angels are not yet placed in time ; they enjoy a derivative eternity intermediary between absolute eternity and the succession of parts independent of one another. At the same time that God formed the angels from the first two principles, he formed from the third a terrestrial nature, more concrete and material than the divine though still subject to spirit and relatively harmonious. This nature is governed by the angels. All these beings were created in order that divine light, reflected from harder surfaces, might appear more shining, that sound might have a clearer ring, and the kingdom of joy extend beyond the circle of divine glory. Not that the manifestation of God might thereby become more perfect, for it is at the cost of a diminution of harmony that any particular quality thus becomes more vivid, but rather that it was expedient for infinite power and love to realise possibilities which, though they had no place in the divine nature, still showed forth the signs of perfection.

To fulfil their destiny, the angels must proceed from Father to Son, from wrath to love, after the fashion of God himself. Besides, they were created free, and, like God, determine themselves, without compulsion from without. They are masters of their determinations. Now, whereas one portion of the angels made their own freedom of will conformable with the divine will, another portion rebelled against God. Lucifer was the chief of these rebel angels and the first author of evil : he sinned freely in accordance with his own will and without compulsion.

Sin came about in the following manner. A compound of nature and spirit, Lucifer, employing his own free will, fixed his imagination on nature. Beneath the gaze of this magician, nature was transformed ; from being dark she became shining ; full of defects, she decked herself with all simple perfections ; from being a part she became so puffed up as to appear like the all. The soul of the angel became enamoured of this idol, desiring it exclusively. In doing so, it rejected God and separated from him.

Then hell was created. Lucifer obtained what he wished for : separation. This result he obtained not by the transcendent intervention of God, but by the immediate effect of wrath or nature to whom he had devoted himself. Hell is the principle of darkness, nature, force, life pure and simple, given up to itself and henceforth contradictorily opposed to love and light, and so deprived of all direction, control, and harmony. Hell is life that has no other end than to live. Thanks to Lucifer, it was now let loose.

Nor was this all ; Lucifer was created eternal. The

desire for life and the desire for good, which God had implanted within him, had not as their common support a sensible body subject to succession and consequently capable of breaking with its past habits. The free will of a mere spirit is exhausted in a single act. Lucifer's fault, therefore, is irremediable. No conversion is possible for him, for he is nothing more now than fire and wrath, and light has no longer any hold upon him. The hell he has created is as eternal as his own will itself.

And yet, the terrestrial nature ruled by the angels suffers from the effects of their wrongdoing. Confusion finds its way into this nature. Love, being exiled therefrom, the bond uniting the forces is broken, and each of these latter escapes and goes wherever it pleases. We no longer have personal unity, in which the parts are the organs of a whole ; but individual multiplicity, in which each part regards itself as the whole to the exclusion of the rest.

Such now is nature : the earth is formless and void, darkness covers the face of the deep. The spirit of God, however, hovers above his shattered work, and the Father resolves to effect a new creation by drawing nature out of the darkness into which she has fallen. This creation is the one related by Moses. God said, " Let there be light ! " and the light was separated from the darkness. In seven days, in accordance with the number of divine spirits, God restored nature to a state of harmony. He did not, purely and simply, destroy Lucifer's work ; he gave nature a weapon against evil and an instrument of regeneration, to wit, time. Thanks to succession in time, to conceive is no longer to act ; will may halt at the very brink of the precipice. Even when accomplished, the act no longer exhausts activity. Henceforth, the good are neither fixed in good nor the evil in evil. To time is attached space, which makes individuals relatively independent of one another. Life in space and time has for its object sensible matter, *i.e.* matter properly so called.

The term and perfection of creation is man, the excellent and harmonious concentration of the three principles. There are in man three parts : soul or the infinite power of good and evil ; mind or intelligence and sound will ; and body, or concrete reality. The first of these three parts corresponds to the principle of fire, the second to that of light, and the third to that of essence or reality. The three principles are manifested in man with all the perfection that existence in time and space implies.

Man's duty is to subordinate within himself two of these principles to the third, *i.e.* will and action to the law of good, and his end is to generate the king of nature, whom God has resolved to create in order to dethrone Lucifer. As God the Father eternally wills to generate his heart and his Son, so the soul ought to fix its will in the heart of God. Adam is to be the seed of the Christ. The task that has fallen to man, however, is by no means a purely spiritual one. The paradise in which he is placed and which he must cause to blossom forth is a sensible nature. It is by working to draw out of this nature all the treasures she contains, and bring them to light, that man prepares for the coming of the Son. The world, developing in time and space, consists of individuals separated from one another : these individuals have to be united in one common homage paid to the Eternal, and, without their distinctive characteristics being effaced, these latter must be raised to participation in absolute personality.

This is the destiny prescribed for man, though not imposed upon him. His will is free. In him there is fire and light, violence and gentleness, egöism and self-denial. In addition, as the result of his terrestrial nature, there is a temporal will, set between these two principles and capable of being turned in the direction of the one or the other. Man, therefore, possesses all the conditions of freedom, and is able, as he pleases, either to be lost himself or to find himself effectively by self-renunciation.

How has he used this power ? That is a question of fact, it finds an answer in tradition and experience. Now, we know that man, following the example of Lucifer, disobeyed God and fell from his original state of nobility. The fall of man, according to the Mosaic account, when interpreted in the light of the spirit, was brought about in the following manner.

Giving reins to his imagination, man began to contemplate and admire nature, in preference to God. By degrees, he attributed to his idol every imaginable perfection, making her the all, including even divinity itself. Then he grew enamoured of her and ardently longed to engender her as he saw her in his imagination. Forgetful of the rights of spirit, he wished nature, untrammelled, to be all she was capable of being. Soon afterwards, in accordance with the law of being, the idea of image and desire became a body ; nature proclaimed her autonomy, and man fell beneath the sway of the violent, egöistic forces he had let loose. Such, abridged, is the story of the fall. The sacred text, however, enables us to distinguish its different phases and note its various stages.

The starting-point was the desire to know things, no longer in their union and harmony, as God had made them, but by separating and analysing them, attributing to them a fictitious individuality. Man was determined to know what hot and cold, moist and dry, hard and soft, and all the other qualities, taken separately, were in themselves. In death, the congealer and disperser, he was determined to discover the secret of life, the organiser. No longer had that divine fruit, concrete knowledge, any savour or attraction for him : he was determined to taste of abstract knowledge, parcelled out, the fruit of terrestrial nature. Nature, thereupon, responded to his desire by making this latter objective in the form of the tree of the knowledge of good and evil. This tree of temptation is none other than the sensible realisation of the will to know good and evil separately, in so far as they are opposite and contradictory. Through it, man sees good and evil as two things exterior to each other, according to the condition of objects set in space : he is able to choose the latter to the exclusion of the former. The fact of having raised up the tree of analytical science is the first sin, that of understanding. This is a dangerous declivity, for man now conceives evil, and, consequently, is capable of willing it; still, this does not yet constitute the fall, since he possesses the power to choose between good and evil.

A second temptation follows the first. Hitherto, Adam has had the eternal virgin for his companion ; hitherto, the ideal or the image of God has been the object of his thought. Having begun to look upon things from the view-point of analysis, in their terrestrial form, he became enamoured of the world of forces and instincts which henceforth appeared before his gaze. He wished to live an animal life, to reproduce himself after the fashion of the beasts. The image of

God was effaced, the virgin fled before the passion kindled within him. Then Adam fell asleep : for the image of the world is not of like nature to the image of God. The latter, which slumbers not, constantly keeps awake the spirit contemplating it. But the image of the world, being subject to succession in time, tires the sight and engenders sleep. A change of condition was then brought about. Man had fallen to sleep in the world of angels, the world of eternity : he awoke in time, in the exterior world. Before him he saw the human objectivation of his earthly desire in the form of a woman created by God during his sleep. Aware that the woman came from himself, man sought to unite with her, to unite with her in body. This is the second sin, the sin of sensibility. Man has taken another step towards perdition. Still, he is not fallen, for carnal desires, in themselves, do not deprive man of self-possession ; his will still remains his own.

The fall, that neither the perversion of the intelligence nor that of sensibility has brought about, is to be effected by the perversion of the will. The devil breathed into man the desire to live by his own distinctive will, to suffice unto himself, to make himself God. Man consented to the temptation, and, by disobedience, set himself over against God as his equal. From that time he was not only inclined towards evil, he plunged therein. He became what he had willed to be, though in a way contrary to what he had imagined. He became god, not the god of love, light, and life, the only true God, but the god of wrath, darkness, and death, who is nothing more than the sacrilegious and diabolical personification of the mysterious substratum of divinity.

Thereupon, man was cursed ; or rather, he declared

himself to be the child of the devil. His will, evil in itself, separated him from God, and dedicated him to wrath. Following on this curse, the world, of which man was both the *résumé* and the mover, passed from a condition of harmony to one of individual dispersion. Each human being claimed to live in the world for himself alone, and to effect his own development without any thought for his neighbours. The struggle for life became the world's only law.

Still, man was not condemned by God for all eternity as Lucifer had been ; the conditions of the fall were different. The devil, of himself alone, was the entire cause of the sin he had committed. Before him, indeed, evil was non-existent, there was only the possibility of evil. Of this possibility, Lucifer had formed evil with all that it comprises, its matter as well as its form : he was the author of the motives that had tempted him, as well as of the determination he had arrived at in accordance with these motives. The position of man was quite different. Before him, evil was already in existence as a given reality, and, along with evil, a downward tendency to new falls. It was at Satan's solicitation that man sinned. Though the decision he came to was his own, the motives of this decision were not at work. They were within him as instincts, a pre-existing nature. Man is thus responsible for his own determination alone, not for the motives to which he has yielded. This is the reason why the fall of Adam, which indeed would be a mortal one were man left to himself, is not irremediable. It is possible, if not for justice, at all events for divine mercy, to set the tendency towards good, deep in the human soul, in opposition to evil solicitations, and to give man's will, which is temporal in its nature, the

power to retract its resolution. Will God now come
to the aid of man, who has rebelled against him?
Will he send man a redeemer and saviour? This is
what no necessity either commands or excludes, it is
something to be decided in the mysterious depths of
infinite will.

V

God, having already restored harmony to the world,
harmony that had been disturbed by Lucifer, resolved
to summon man to regeneration. Good and evil were
now in the presence of each other, not only in eternity
but also in time : God decided to bring about, as far as
possible, the reconciliation of these two principles. In
accordance with the divine decrees anterior to the fall
of man, the Son was some day to be born in human
form, so that the word might be manifested in time.
As man was given up to wrath and the devil, God
decreed that the coming of the Christ should be not
only the coming of one who would compass human
perfection, but also that of a redeemer and saviour.
He prepared for this coming by the series of events
related in the Old Testament, and finally gave up his
Son to the world to be crowned with thorns and
crucified. *Per crucem ad lucem!* The Christ is a
human creature, and he is the Son of the eternal Virgin.
In him death is overcome. He who suffers with him
is also glorified with him.

Still, we must examine more closely and see how
man's salvation is realised by Jesus Christ.

When the reason hears mention of God, of his
nature and will, it imagines that God is something
foreign and far away, living outside this world and
above the stars, ordaining things mechanically after the

manner of a force situated in space. Hence reason, assimilating God to his creatures, attributes to him a mode of thought and action analogous to that of man. It believes that God, before creation, deliberated within himself as to the place he should assign to each creature. It also implies that God decided to summon a portion of mankind to heavenly joy, in order to manifest his grace, and condemned the rest to damnation, in order to manifest his wrath. Thus, God would appear to have made a difference, for all eternity, between men, for the purpose of manifesting his power in the direction both of wrath and of love.

Most certainly there is an election of grace, though it could not come about in the way reason imagines. Were God to deliberate and come to a decision as we do, were he to govern things from without, he would be divided against himself, he would be changeable, not eternal. Besides, how could God will to condemn a portion of his creatures? God is love ; he wills the good of all beings. Election and damnation are not the act of a will exterior to man. Man is free, absolutely free ; for the root of his being is plunged in the eternal, infinite substratum of things. There is nothing behind the human will capable of constraining it. Itself is the first beginning of its own actions. Election or damnation is the result of this very freedom. By it, man can turn, as he pleases, towards light or towards darkness, towards love or towards egoism : man can make either an angel or a devil of himself. Within himself he bears his own paradise and hell : the exterior paradise and hell are nothing but symbols of good and evil will. Not that man is sufficient unto himself and can do without divine grace. His good will is but a prayer, unavailing without the help of

God ; God has foreseen from all eternity that he either would or would not offer up this prayer. Free actions, however, remain free in divine foreknowledge, which, sunk in the primordial deep, cannot be distinguished from the common substratum of all wills.

The first sign and the first effect of election is faith. Like election, faith is often misunderstood. Every one boasts of having faith. Where is it in reality ? Present-day faith is nothing but a story learnt by heart. Where is the man with a child-like faith in the birth of Jesus ? Did he really believe it, he would draw nigh to the Infant Jesus whom he would welcome and tenderly nurture within himself. No : he is acquainted only with the historic child, deceiving his conscience with vain erudition. Never has there been so much talk of faith, and never was real faith more lacking. Would you have a proof of this ? Never before has there been so much disputing, so much judging and condemning of one another. Does God judge and condemn the birds of the forests because each of them praises him in his own way, and in a different tone from the rest ? Does not the infinite might of God admit of an infinite variety of expressions of homage ? You, who persecute your brothers, are more useless than the flowers of the fields, more foolish than beasts lacking in intelligence. You are the birds of prey that affright the other birds, preventing them from chanting the praises of God. To believe in Jesus Christ from an historical point of view is no more helpful than believing a fable. How many Jews and Turks are more Christian than those sham Christians who know what Jesus did and yet do what the devil does ! But, the answer will come, we believe in the word. Then we must try to understand what the true word is. The Scriptures are helpful, but they are not the word, they are only its mute, obliterated signs. The word is living, for it is the vehicle of the spirit. No formula can define it, for it is infinite as God himself. That is why true faith is, in fine, a righteous will, freely subject to the law of the spirit. It consists in renewing within oneself the birth and life of Christ, his baptism and temptations, sufferings and death. The imitation of Christ is the distinctive mark of the children of God. Consequently, the true Christian is of no sect ; he may live in one, but he does not belong to it. His religion is interior, it cannot be confined within any form.

Faith, when thus understood, is the beginning of regeneration. What is to be thought of the exterior means and methods that the Churches add on to it? Speaking generally, works are nothing in themselves, and the Roman Catholic Church, which attributes value thereto, is the Babel of the Christian world. Erroneous also is it to believe that faith saves us because through it the merits of Christ would be attributed to us from without, just as a new form may be given to passive matter. Such an operation would not change the root nature of the soul, it would not be a second birth. Faith could not save us by some theurgic operation that compelled divine justice to benefit us : it saves us only by the sanctifying grace it bears within itself, and which, from without, engenders within us both penitence and the redeeming Christ. Justification is sanctification. It is not the object of faith that regenerates us, it is faith itself.

For this reason no particular means of regeneration is efficacious if faith be not the soul thereof. True prayer is not a passive request for divine assistance, it is the humble action of the will that recognises its

Q

need and goes to God as for food ; it is the soul beseeching and receiving sanctifying grace. True preaching is not the teaching specially given by the priest or even by the Bible. The faithful who see and hear with the spirit learn from all creatures. Sacraments are not aids granted to man without himself contributing thereto. The true sacrament consists of divine grace descending upon the soul, which can appropriate it only by faith. And regeneration, the object of prayer, of sermons and sacraments alike, is not a new nature grafted on to the old : it is the spirit, awakening and expanding, deep within the nature ; it is the person creating himself by renunciation of the individual I, the interior man who is substituted for the exterior man.

Now, of what nature is the life of the regenerate man ? Is it only apathy and indifference, mere reflection of the spirit upon itself, annihilation deep in primordial no-thing ? Spirit, we know, is not this inert no-thing at the conception of which, by suppressing differences, human logic arrives. All interior being tends to become exterior, all infinitude is the desire to take form, all mystery is an effort to reveal itself, all spirit is the will to become a body. So also is it with the Christian virtues. They do not remain abstractions ; they develop and become manifest. They become manifest by complete renunciation of self, by total abandonment to the will of God, by meekness, by human love, by communion of souls in spite of all outer differences, by mastery over nature, i.e. over earthly desires, and by joy, that foretaste of eternity. The new man does not destroy the old, the outer man, though he takes care not to forget himself therein. Thou art in the world, Christian ! Thou art engaged in an honourable trade. Remain in it, work, act, earn the money thou need'st, make the elements produce all they are capable of producing, dig in the ground for silver and gold, make them into works of art, build and plant. All this is well and good. Listen, however, to the A B C of wisdom : Put not thy soul into this exterior life. Chain not thy free spirit down in this prison. If thou retainest thy freedom, all that thou do'st in the world will prosper. For everything sings forth the praises of God to him who has ears to hear. Even the backslidings of thy earthly companion shall not harm thy soul, but they will be beneficial to him. A single action is not a habit ; a powerful tree stands erect before the raging storm. When thou see'st the exterior man offend, thou wilt the better understand the frailty of nature, the greatness and might of divine mercy. Let not man, however, imagine that in his life on earth he can ever dispense with prayer and effort. Man is and remains free; consequently, he is never established in good. Time cannot hold eternity. However strong be our link with God, we remain in the devil's power. Resistance to evil is our condition in this world, right on to the end. If we grow remiss, nature once more lays hold upon us : the form in which the spirit is manifested binds and imprisons this latter as soon as it ceases to act. Each moment we must correct ourselves, revive our new birth, create God anew within ourselves. Only when life comes to an end does the tree of faith, hope and love, nurtured by our own unremitting efforts, stand erect and incapable of being uprooted.

And so, in the world of time, there is being prepared the *rapprochement* of the good and the evil principle, and the conscious, definitive reconstitution of primordial unity. All end has a tendency to rejoin its beginning,

though on a higher plane, ascending right to the fixed
point on which this beginning depends. As long as man is
a terrestrial body, he can and ought to choose. Along
with his temporal nature, however, disappears the contingency of his actions. Death introduces him to eternity.
The fruit of his free determinations is now ripe : he
detaches himself ; that which he is, he is once for all.
Man, then, according to the nature he has created
within himself, henceforward belongs either to God or
to the devil. His free will has become changed either
into freedom and love or into caprice and violence.

And so the final end of things is the definitive
dualism of good and evil, so far as they are the products
of a will that is free. In the beginning, God engendered
good and evil considered as possibilities, *i.e.* he created
the conditions and materials of good and evil actions.
From the way in which free beings acted, there resulted,
in fact, the realisation of the two possibilities God had
formed. On both sides, being has passed through
three phases : possibility, the contingent fact, definitive
determination. It was by thwarting conscious will that
idea became thing ; and possibility, necessary. The
kingdom of God is the harmony, henceforth inde-
structible, between spirit and nature. Individuals subsist
therein, and continue to be distinguished from one
another, otherwise there would be no more nature ; but
they live without strife, each according to his character :
they subsist by love alone and have nothing to do with
hatred. They have attained true unity which is not
an exterior *rapprochement* practised with a view to the
satisfaction of egoïstic interests, but rather the common
participation of individual souls in divine personality.
In the kingdom of the devil, on the other hand, the
will to live has definitively thrown off all law and

direction. It has what it willed: life as the sole end of life. Henceforward, there is no harmony, goodness or love. Egoïsm and anarchy reign without a rival. The individual is his own master ; and this sovereignty, which rests on rebellion, not on obedience, is the endless struggle, infinite torment.

VI

Boehme's doctrine concludes with an exposition of the final ends of all things. This doctrine presents itself to us as the metaphysical history of Being, apperceived by intuition deep within its physical history. Starting from the eternal, we have come back, through time, to the eternal. The circle is closed again : revelation is accomplished.

Now, what is this doctrine which is called by its author *Aurora* or the *Morning Redness*, the explanation of the celestial and terrestrial mystery, the setting forth of the genesis of God and of all things, and, speaking generally, Christianity interpreted after the spirit?

There can be no doubt but that it is, first of all, a religious doctrine, and it is only natural that Boehme's disciples should mainly be found amongst theologians. But would it be legitimate to abide by the letter of the doctrine in judging one who ever affirmed that truth is in the spirit, not in the letter, and that it is the characteristic of the spirit to be for ever impossible of expression? Evidently, by this theory alone, Boehme relegates to a second place, religion properly so called, religion that is inconceivable without some given revelation, some positive fact, and puts in the first place philosophy, or rather, religion so far as it is allied with philosophy. Indeed, whoever reads Boehme's works in the way he himself recommends us to read them, trying to discover the spiritual meaning in sensible and intellectual images, finds that doctrines of a philosophical character appear at each step beneath his religious outpourings.

The theological mysteries of the Trinity, the Fall and the Redemption are, of a certainty, the promptings that cause him to reflect.   But beneath these mysteries he sees the problem of the reconciliation of evil and the finite, as positive realities, with infinite personality as the first and only source of being.   And the way in which he solves this problem is certainly metaphysics under the cloak of theology.   From the finite and evil, to whose existence our senses testify, the suprasensible conditions of finite nature and evil action are distinguished, and these conditions are deduced from the divine will, in so far as that will wills to be manifested and posited as a person.   No manifestation without opposition.   And so God posits his contrary in order to lay hold upon himself, by distinguishing himself from this contrary and imposing on it his law.   This contrary, or eternal nature bound to the very existence of God, without itself being the finite and evil, is the foundation of their reality.   The finite is the dissemination—freely effected by God, by means of time—of the essences contained in the divine nature.   Evil is nature, which is only a part, posited as the all by the untrammelled will of created beings.   The finite and evil, after all, as regards their matter, are deduced from the conditions of existence of the personality, whereas in their sensible form and realisation they result from the free initiative of the will.   Consequently the world is something quite different from mere non-being or the unstable effect of an act of arbitrary will : it possesses reality, a true, internal existence : though founded on God it is not God : it is based upon the very nature God needs in order to become manifest.

It cannot be denied that in these ideas, clearly expressed by Boehme in all his metaphors, are the germs of a philosophic system. But what is the value and signification of this system ? Is it not an isolated work, without any important relation to the general history of philosophy ?

It must be confessed that—with the exception of Louis Claude de Saint-Martin (the "Unknown Philosopher"), Baader the Catholic theologian, and Schelling in the final phase of his philosophy—the philosophers by profession, after reading and forming an opinion on Boehme, are rather inclined to bestow on him vague encomium than to attempt to assimilate his doctrines. Saint-Martin's ideas have scarcely been mentioned in France except by historians ; and the Germans have developed more especially the intellectualist philosophy born of Leibnitz, Kant and Spinoza, which rejects the absolute reality of nature and the freedom of the will, those essential elements in Boehme's system.

On this point, nevertheless, we must guard against judging by appearances or details. Two traits, in a word, mainly characterise the speculations of our theosophist : spiritualism, posited as a fundamental truth ; and realism, admitted on the faith of experience and connected by way of deduction with the spiritualist principle. On the one hand, Boehme holds that spirit alone is the first and true being : spirit, *i.e.* infinite freedom, that creates for itself objects and forms, and remains infinitely superior to all its creations, imperceptible being that is everywhere in action and itself incapable of being realised and becoming an object of experience ; the perfect person, in word, living and truly metaphysical existence, of which all given, determinate existence can be nothing but an imperfect·manifestation. But, on the other hand, Boehme is a realist. He does not admit that the multiple and the diverse may be a vain image of the imagination, or the purely phenomenal effect of a transcendent cause ; he does not acknowledge that evil may only be a lesser good. Nature has her own principle of existence, contrary to that of spiritual existence. Evil is a living force that tends to destroy good. To posit spiritualism as a thesis and realism as an antithesis, and, in a synthesis, to reconcile the reality of the objects of experience with the supremacy of spirit : such is Boehme's task.

Such, too, in fine, is the ground of the principal German systems. With Leibnitz, Kant, Fichte, Schelling and Hegel it is spirit that is being, and spirit is the living infinite that no form can contain. For all these philosophers, however, the world has a reality of its own, a reality that is a stumbling-block to spirit and yet must be deduced from the nature of spirit. It is in this antinomy of spirit as principle, and matter as reality, that German philosophy flounders ; and monadology, transcendental idealism, the philosophy of the absolute, and absolute idealism are only different solutions of one and the same problem. Nor is this all. Idealism, realism, and the search after the reconciliation of the latter with the former, are traits of German philosophy that are, it would seem, to be met with in the nation itself ; so, at all events, historians have observed. Thus, whatever may have been the exterior link between the German philosophers and Jacob Boehme, they are united to him by a stronger and closer bond than mere influence, they are his brothers, at least, if

not his sons, children of one and the same genius,
expressions of one and the same aspect of the human
mind. Was he, then, a false prophet, who, in 1620,
after reading the *Psychologia vera* of Jacob Boehme,
greeted its author by the unexpected name of "*Philosophus teutonicus*"?[1]

---

[1] "He is known," says Hegel, "as the Philosophus Teutonicus, and
in reality through him for the first time did philosophy in Germany come
forward with a characteristic stamp. The kernel of his philosophizing is
purely German" (*Gesch. Ph*. iii. 1836, p. 300) (Translator's note).

DESCARTES

REGARDING things only from the historical standpoint, Cartesianism dominates the entire development of modern philosophy. Amongst others, the German savants, intent on finding the internal principles of historical developments, took delight in discovering, in Cartesian problems, the starting-point of all the great questions that have stirred the minds of modern philosophers. More particularly, they saw, in the *Cogito*, the living germ from which, by immanent dialectic, all the great systems that have so far appeared were to blossom forth. Thus, Kuno Fischer distinctly regarded Cartesianism, and the antinomies into which it enters as it develops, as the origin or necessary condition of the occasionalism of Malebranche, the monism of Spinoza, the monadology of Leibnitz, the sensualism of Locke, the materialism of La Mettrie, the idealism of Berkeley and the criticism of Kant. In most of the German historians of philosophy similar deductions may be found.

Speaking generally, it may be said that the central problem of Cartesian metaphysics was the transition from thought to existence. Thought alone is indissolubly inherent in itself: how, then, by what right and in what way, can we, in our judgments, affirm existences? There is one case, and only one, wherein existence is immediately connected with thought in the intuition of the understanding : and that is when we say : " Cogito, ergo sum."   How and in what way can we extend to other existences the certainty we directly attribute to that of thought?   This is the knotty point in the Cartesian philosophy.   Now, this problem of existence controlled the investigations of Locke, Hume, Reid and Kant, as it did those of Malebranche, Spinoza and Leibnitz.   Existence, which, to the ancients, was a thing given and immediately apprehensible, and that had only to be analysed, is here something far away, which has to be attained to, if that be possible.   There we find the distinctive characteristic of modern as compared with ancient philosophy, and this characteristic is the mark of Cartesianism itself.

Not only does Cartesianism thus control the progress of modern philosophy, it is also of considerable importance in the general history of the human mind. Doubtless, our seventeenth century in France largely drew upon Christian and classic sources, but science developed alongside of literature ; and science, in those days, was the Cartesian conception of the world : it was the control of the mathematical mechanism over all that was not thought strictly so called, the condition of this very mechanism.   As Huyghens wrote on the occasion of the death of Descartes :

> Nature, prends le deuil, et pleure la première
> Le grand Descartes ! . . .
> Quand il perdit le jour, tu perdis la lumière :
> Ce n'est qu'à sa clarté que nous t'avons su voir.

And when Newton reformed Cartesianism, did he not do so by adopting this very basis of natural philosophy, treated mathematically, which Descartes had discovered and assured?

Nor is this all : as Descartes is a dualist and looks

upon all blending of philosophy with religion, corporeal with spiritual philosophy, as spurious, so too the seventeenth century is simultaneously religious and rationalistic, partaking both of the moralist and of the scientist, without these various disciplines interpenetrating or being weakened by one another. Pascal the mystic does no harm to Pascal the physicist, and *vice versa*.

In a word, Descartes regards thought as without an equal ; he sees in it alone the principle of certainty. The seventeenth century, likewise, considers that in thought lies human dignity, that by it, and not by material greatness, can we rise to our true stature. The conviction of the power of reason creeps into the minds of men to such a degree that the obstacles, both provisional and even definitive, which Descartes had set up, are speedily overthrown. Social and political questions which could not, for a long time, in his opinion, be accessible to science ; religious questions which went altogether beyond it, were submitted to the examination of reason. The eighteenth century dedicated itself to this work ; it has even been said that the French Revolution had its origin in the *Discours de la Méthode*. A false statement, if it means that Cartesianism contained such a consequence ; and yet an assertion capable of being upheld, if the statement is taken as signifying that it was in the name of the Cartesian principle of rational evidence that society was revived in 1789.

And so we see that Cartesianism is an essential element in the philosophical and moral history of modern times. But does it belong only to history ? Has it no longer anything to teach us ?

Huxley, the English philosopher and scientist, affirmed that Descartes' system, far from being a subject of scholarly curiosity, was the very soul both of contemporary philosophy and science. Our philosophy is idealistic, and it is the *Cogito* of Descartes that is the principle of this idealism. Our science is mechanistic, and it is the Cartesian reduction to extent of all that is not spirit, which has founded this mechanism.

Independently of these general tendencies, many questions more especially connected with contemporary speculation have been bequeathed to us by Descartes' philosophy.

Such, in metaphysics, are the problem of existence, that of the relations between will and understanding, that of certainty, that of the relations between science and metaphysics, and that of the relations between spirit and matter. The philosophy of science is specially concerned nowadays with the question of the relation between mathematics and experience. How and in what sense can that which is proved by demonstration agree with that which is known by perception? How comes it to pass that physics can be treated mathematically? Now, this is the very question Descartes first asked himself, and he may be said to have constructed his system of metaphysics for the purpose of answering it.

As regards science, the alliance between geometry and analysis, the mechanical interpretation of phenomena, the exclusion of final causes, mathematical mechanism applied not only to the systematisation of phenomena but also to the explanation of the genesis of the world ; not only to the study of inorganic bodies but also to that of life itself, are all to be found, as so many essential elements, in the Cartesian philosophy. It is also the Cartesian spirit that has brought into existence certain special modern sciences, such as experimental psychology and positive sociology, which attempt to examine psychical or social facts in their elements or mathematically measurable equivalents.

Moreover, let it not be said that, in order to possess these leading ideas, it is enough to receive them from present-day savants in the form they have assumed as the result of two centuries of discussion. It is not the same with ideas as with facts, the knowledge of which almost inevitably becomes more and more perfect. What advantage is it for a man to acquire a rough measurement of some phenomenon when he can become acquainted with an exact one thereof? An idea, however, is a mysterious plant which does not always develop in another in the same way as it does in its originator, without counting the fact that it may have long to wait before encountering soil favourable for its perfect fruition. This is the reason it is so important to consider ideas as they appeared to the genius who gave birth to them. How often have they thus shown themselves to be greater and more fertile than they had seemed as interpreted by disciples incapable of thoroughly understanding them! " *Philosophia duce regredimur* " was a profound motto of the *Renaissance*.

Is it necessary to call to mind Descartes' excellence as a writer? From this standpoint, too, his importance could not be exaggerated. As regards the part he played in history, Désiré Nisard has shown that he was the first to offer a perfect model of French prose. The language of Descartes is the fabric on which the style of our great writers is woven. Considered in itself, this language, stamped with the philosopher's method, possesses in the highest degree the noblest qualities of every language : propriety of terms, and the expression of order in ideas. Cartesian intuition and deduction have left their impress on the style of the *Discours de la Méthode*. Not that this language is abstract or impersonal. Descartes' reason is a living, enthusiastic reason ; it does not merely put acquired truths in the form of syllogisms, but rather endeavours to discover and create, to communicate its creative activity to men's intellects. This life of thought animates the style itself, which, in a surprising way, unites to precision and demonstrative order, motion, accent, originality, colour, wit, and even charm, or irony or pride, according to the intellectual passion which is pouring into the soul of this lover of truth. Whatever impression may at first be felt, when one at times becomes bewildered with those long sentences which demand an alert reader, capable of making his own deductions, one speedily comes under the charm and power of this masterly style. Even nowadays, if an author's manner merely suggests that of Descartes in some respect or other, people vie with each other in praising its superiority and austere seductiveness.

In a word, why should we not call to mind the special motives which cause us to desire that the works of Descartes should be read by as large a circle of readers as possible, both in France and abroad ?

Descartes is one of the purest and finest expressions of the genius of our race : the diffusion of his thoughts represents our life and influence.

We love reason, a middle path between the spirit of positivism, which contents itself with facts, properly so called, and the spirit of mysticism, which tends to believe without demanding proof. Of all intellectual qualities, the one we most prize is the faculty of judgment, in whose sight even experience and reasoning are sources of truth only on condition they have been submitted to the control of the mind. It is in this direction that we seek after clarity and order in ideas. For a system to be well constructed and consistent is not sufficient for us, we want every part of it, taken separately, to be intelligible and true, and we would rather hold separately the two ends of the chain of reasoning without apperceiving the intermediary links, than let slip the truths we have won in order to grasp the hypothetical connection between them. One of the sciences in which we excel is mathematics. Our sense of clarity and logic is here afforded unrestrained activity. In the moral order of things, we love reason with an ardent, enthusiastic love, that has at times gone astray or formed a striking contrast with the very object of that love ; but through all our fluctuations the goal of our endeavours is clearly a harmonious blending of individual freedom and rational law, in which neither would be sacrificed. And whilst seeking, in a practical spirit, for what suits our own nation, it is impossible for us to separate in thought the happiness of others from our own, or to desire good in any other than the universal form which reason ordains.

Now, we find in Descartes these different traits, which are amongst the principal ones in our nature. A clear-headed and profound philosopher and mathematician, excelling in finesse and in geometrical precision alike, jealous of independence though obedient to reason, solicitous of the practical ends of life and ambitious to work for the happiness of all mankind, he offers us, preeminently, the model, and, as it were, the archetype of the qualities we aspire to show forth.

To study Descartes and make him better known is to work for the fulfilment of the scientific and civilising mission of France.

ON THE CONNECTION BETWEEN MORALS AND SCIENCE IN THE PHILOSOPHY OF DESCARTES

Mirum mihi videtur, plerosque homines plantarum vires, siderum motus, metallorum transmutationes, similiumque disciplinarum objecta diligentissime perscrutari, atque interim fere nullos de bona mente . . . cogitare, quum tamen alia omnia non tam propter se quam quia ad hanc aliquid conferunt, sint aestimanda.—DESCARTES, *Reg. ad dir. ing.* Reg. 1.

That portion of Descartes' writings referring to morals is not insignificant, though neither in form nor content does it, at first glance, appear to belong to his philosophical work, properly so called. It consists mainly of the letters to the Princess Elizabeth and the Queen of Sweden ; in them Descartes visibly adapts himself to the needs and desires of his illustrious correspondents. True, a sketch of practical morals forms part of the *Discours de la Méthode*. According to a document published in 1896, by Ch. Adam, it would appear that Descartes added these rules somewhat against his will, because of the pedagogues and others of the same type who were quite ready to accuse him of having neither religion nor faith, and of wishing to destroy both the one and the other by his method. As regards the contents of these writings on morals, they are certainly very dignified and lofty in thought and admirable in form, though evidently possessed of little in common with the philosopher's doctrine itself. Borrowed from St. Thomas, as Baillet says, and intended, according to Descartes himself, to reconcile the teachings of Aristotle, Zeno and Epicurus [1] with one another, they seem to have been particularly

[1] *Œuvres philos. de Descartes*, édit. Garnier, iii. 184-5.

R

stamped with the impress of stoicism.   Now, stoicism
was then a well-known and popular philosophy.   Descartes is a stoic, as the heroes of Corneille are stoics.
His mathematics has nothing to do with his stoicism.
It would therefore seem either that Descartes, so far as
he personally was concerned, had no interest in moral
research, or that, if he did make profession of moral
maxims, they resulted rather from individual feelings or
outer influences than from the logical development of
his philosophy.

I

It is worthy of note that this appreciation, which the
first rapid examination of Descartes' moral writings
induces us to make, by no means conforms with the
continually repeated declarations of the philosopher
concerning the object of philosophy.

What, according to the *Regulae*,[1] is the earnest way
of seeking after truth ?   It is to think solely of increasing
the natural light of reason, not for the solving of any
particular scholastic difficulty, but rather, at every
conjuncture in life, for the purpose of making the
understanding capable of prescribing to the will the line
of action it ought to choose.   The reason Descartes is
keenly desirous of learning to distinguish the true from
the false is, as he tells us in the *Discours de la Méthode*,[2]
because he knows this to be the means of seeing clearly
into his own actions and going through life with calm
assurance.   Again, in the Preface to the *Principes*,[3] he
defines philosophy as the study of wisdom, which, he
says, consists of a perfect knowledge of everything a
man is capable of knowing, both in the conduct in life,
the preservation of health and the invention of all the

[1] i. 1.   [2] i. 14.   [3] Baillet, *La Vie de M. Descartes*, i. 115.

arts. This study, he adds, is more necessary for the regulation of our morality than the use of our eyes for the guidance of our steps.

And indeed, according to Clerselier, who appears to have known him most intimately, morals was the object of his most frequent meditation.[1] True, he did not like writing about such matters, but that is from a feeling of prudence, as he himself explains.[2] In physics, also, he more than once preferred silence to the risk of persecution.

All the same, we may ask ourselves whether, in the work he has left us, the moral ideas and the physical doctrines really form part of one and the same system, or whether they are not like two streams which flow parallel to each other, without their waters ever mingling. Certainly Descartes offers us the rules of his provisional system of morals as being deduced from his method. But then, of what use is it to affirm this, if he introduced these rules only to throw pedagogues off the scent ? In themselves, they appear anything but part and parcel of his philosophy. It is also true that, in the Preface to the *Principes* [3] he speaks of a definitive system of morals which presupposes a complete knowledge of all other sciences. Many, however, consider that he did not even outline this system of morals, and that it is his provisional system which is in reality his final one.[4]

The question is a puzzling one. It would be unfair to judge Descartes solely by those portions of his work which his prematurely curtailed life enabled him to complete. In creations of thought the inner tendency and the living principle of development are frequently

[1] Baillet, *La Vie de M. Descartes,* i. 115.   [2] ii. 282.
[3] Édition Garnier, i. 592.   [4] Cf. éd. Garnier, iii. 179.

more important than the immediately observable results. The reality of a Cartesian system of morals would be satisfactorily proved if it were shown that the philosophy of Descartes contained within itself the germs of such a system.

II

There can be no doubt but that this philosophy, speaking generally, deals with practical experience. Although fond of withdrawing into solitude and seclusion for the purpose of meditation, Descartes is anything but an armchair philosopher. He possesses in the highest degree the sense of reality, interests himself in the doings of his times, converses with men of divers stations and temperaments, and listens attentively to the remarks of each on his own particular subject. He considers that our highest duty is to bring about the general good of all men, to the best of our ability. Consequently his chief grievance against the scholastic philosophy is that it is purely speculative and gives no results. Instead of this philosophy of arguers and disputants, he seeks after a practical system of philosophy calculated to place at man's disposal the power and action of fire, water, air and all the other bodies around us, and which will make him, as it were, master and owner of nature.[1] It is his dream to preserve mankind from illness and disease, perhaps even from the debility of old age. His death was announced in the *Gazette d'Anvers* in the following terms:[2] "In Sweden there has just died a fool, who said that he could live as long as he wished."

Descartes, like Bacon, following the traditions of

[1] *Méth.* vi. 2.

[2] Adam, Göttingen MS. (*Revue bourguignonne de l'Enseignement supérieur*, 1896).

the magicians and alchemists, was inspired with the ambition to dominate that nature which the ancients had contented themselves with gazing upon.

The alchemists, however, believed that in order to make nature act as they pleased, all that was needed was to set it going by an altogether external and empirical imitation of its processes. The magicians regarded nature as a mysterious, perhaps diabolical, power, whose will had to be chained down by means of formulas. Bacon himself, in his immediate search after an active philosophy, can find no reason for admitting that nature will respond to human promptings, except that such response is necessary in order that man may be able to act upon her. His science remains blind because, confounding the means with the end, it recognises no other principles than the rules that admit of being applied, just as they stand, to practice.[1]

Descartes' originality consisted in regarding the legitimacy of the problem of man's rule over nature as uncertain, and its solution doubtful, as long as no attempt was made to discover by what internal mode of working, nature really brings about any particular effect from any particular cause. He considered that practice implied theory in the real sense of the word ; the knowledge of the interior of things. To his mind it was from this standpoint that nature must be considered, if we would succeed in becoming master of her. So, too, in the past, dealing with the moral order of things, Socrates had taught that the practical skill, quite legitimately sought after by the Sophists, could only be attained in a roundabout way, viz. by a rational knowledge of the essence of virtue. And since, to Descartes, the very type of theory, the king of sciences, was

[1] *Nov. Org.* i. 4; ii. 1-5.

mathematics, he made it his object to demonstrate that everything in nature is brought about mathematically ; hence his metaphysical speculations. He proves, both by the perfections of God and by the clear, distinct nature of the idea of extent, that we are entitled to consider mathematical qualities as the essence of material things.

Consequently, he studies mathematics, and his whole work is dominated by this science ; only, however, because, according to him, it is by considering things from this point of view that we can really make them our own.[1] And it is this practical end, ever present in his mind, that determines the general line of his investigations. He does not dwell upon the developments of science, which would be merely of speculative interest. He is content with setting up, in mathematics, the few general principles which will enable him to base mechanics and physics on this discipline. These two sciences, in turn, need to be developed only in the direction and degree necessary to make possible the science of life. His object is to prove that life itself is nothing but a mechanism, and is, consequently, subject to our control. Whilst studying one science, Descartes is thinking of the science which, in the nature of things, is to come after, and bring him nearer to practice. The idea of the goal in view, which never leaves him, controls and restrains his efforts. *Semper ad eventum festinat.*

This method enabled him to conceive the possibility of carrying through, alone, his project of instituting a universal science. In 1637 he came to the conclusion that the truths he had found in the various sciences were nothing but the consequences of five or six main difficulties he had overcome, on which they depended ;

[1] Baillet, ii. 227.

and he imagined he needed only to win two or three other like battles to bring his plans to a successful issue.[1]

Here, too, is the explanation of his apparently capricious passing from one science to another. From 1623 he began to neglect geometry,[2] and six years afterwards plunged into metaphysical meditation, to which, however, he devoted only nine months. A year afterwards he reminds Mersenne that he has long ago abandoned the study of mathematics, anxious not to waste his time any longer in unproductive effort. From 1629 to 1633 he is mainly occupied with physics. At the end of the *Discours de la Méthode* he announces his intention to spend the rest of his life in wresting from physics a more certain medicine, or art of curing disease, than the one in vogue.

This, in short, is the explanation of that particularity of his system for which Newton reproached him so strongly, viz. hypothesis, regarded in certain cases as a sufficient explanation of phenomena. A strict adherent of the principle of following the line of least resistance in his own method of work, Descartes contents himself, in his theories, with what is indispensable for practice. Now, from this point of view, provided it be possible to make a forecast of the result, it matters little that the mechanism of nature, in detail, should be in every respect what it has been conceived to be. Well aware that in mathematics several solutions are often possible, Descartes comes to regard it as sufficient, even in physics, if he obtains one. He believes he has done everything necessary if the causes he has explained are such that all the effects they are capable of producing are similar to those we find in the manifested world. He considers it useless to inquire whether the effects are really brought

[1] *Méth.* iv. 4.   [2] Baillet, i. 111.

about by these causes or by others.   He thinks it is as
useful in life to know causes thus imagined as to know
the real ones.[1]   On this point he is satisfied with moral
certainty.[2]

In the progress of knowledge, as thus understood,
morals cannot fail to find a place, all the more so
because, according to Descartes, the root and trunk of
a tree are mainly held in esteem on account of the fruit
they should produce, and it is mostly on the sciences
which should come last, medicine, mechanics and morals,
that the primary utility of philosophy depends.[3]   And
Descartes does not despair of satisfying himself as
regards these ultimate objects, in spite of the shortness
of human life and the limits of our intelligence, for the
very reason that he is able to economise his strength
and demand of each science only what it can and should
give him for the carrying out of his plans.   The productiveness of knowledge lies not in its extent, but
rather in its clearness and precision.

III

But now, what is the nature of the morals to which
this progress will lead ?   Does it not merely tend to
enable us to dispose of human nature, by means of the
science of man, just as we dispose of the corporal nature,
by means of the science of the body ?   Is not psychical
mechanics all that Descartes has in view?

As a matter of fact, Descartes laid the foundations
of some such morals in his *Traité des Passions*, in which,
expounding the principle governing these mental
activities, he teaches us to modify and control them.

---

[1] *Principes*, iv. 204.   [2] Baillet, ii. 227-8.
[3] Pref. of the *Prin.* Garnier, i. 192.

As, moreover, this study shows us how far the mind
depends on the temperament and arrangement of the
organs of the body, Descartes distinctly concludes that,
if it is possible to find any means whereby men, generally, may be made wiser and more skilful, this means
must be sought for in medicine.

Thus would appear to be completed the edifice
planned by our philosopher. Its culminating point is
a system of morals, though how different from that
indicated in the *Discours de la Méthode* and the *Lettres*!
This latter, instinct with the spirit of antiquity or
with Christian influences, was either an exhortation,
a metaphysic or a religion. That of the *Principes* and
the *Traité des Passions* was only the final and most
immediately practical application of modern science.
According to the *Lettres*, man ought to seek outside
of the world, in those perfections that depend solely
on free-will, resignation, constancy, and the mystical
love of God and men, for those things to which he is
to bend his will. According to the *Traité des Passions*,
man, a mere part of nature, could aim at nothing
else than maintaining the integrity of his existence
by utilising the mechanism of the universe for his
own advantage. Now, it is easy to see how these
scientific morals are the fruit of the Cartesian philosophy, whereas the former seem to remain outside the
logical development of this philosophy.

And yet, is it right to content oneself with this
result, and declare that Descartes, as a philosopher,
knows no other morals than applied science?

It is unnecessary to have recourse to such of
Descartes' writings as deal specially with morals in
order to see how narrow and incomplete such an interpretation would be. Speaking generally, it is not

science that is the centre of the Cartesian philosophy ;
it is man, or rather the reason within man. Even when
studying the sciences of nature, it is not science itself
that our philosopher has in view, it is the formation
of the judgment by science. Judgment is the power
to distinguish the true from the false in all things
without hesitation or uncertainty. To do this we
must develop within ourselves a kind of sense of truth.
Mathematics, especially algebra, is a wonderful help in
this respect.[1] By accustoming the mind to feed upon
truth and never be satisfied with false reasons, mathematics compels it to quit its natural indifference and
leads it in the direction of its own perfection. It is
this mental culture, not the knowledge of particular
truths, that forms the real utility of the sciences.[2]
They cannot be detached from reason, as the fruit is
detached from the tree, for it is in reason that they
have both their principle and their end.

Descartes, however, does more than train his reason
mechanically by exercise and habit ; he uses the intellectual force thus gained in studying the nature of
reason itself, analysing its content, gauging its power
and trying to discover its purpose. He rises above
science to metaphysics. Not that this makes it necessary that he should free himself from the requirements
of science. Rather is it science which, properly interpreted, opens up the path leading to this higher knowledge. He remarks that the mathematical method,
however perfect it be, is nothing but the outer cover
of the true method.[3] The latter, apart from the particular form given to it by geometricians, is of universal
import, and allows of the truths contained in any subject being obtained. By the use of this method, then,

---

[1] *Regulae*, i.   [2] *Méth*. iii. 5.   [3] *Regulae*, iv. 20.

one may succeed in strictly demonstrating the truths of metaphysics as well as those of geometry. To attempt thus to know God, oneself and the first principles of the science of nature, is the main use man ought to make of his reason.[1]

If, therefore, it is conceived that a purely natural philosophy has for its ultimate object the supremacy of man over nature, a more complete philosophy sees in this very supremacy only a means at the service of a loftier end. No longer is it merely a question of governing, but of doing so in the name of, and with a view to, reason. To moderate the influence of the body by medicine is indeed the most practical external means of helping men to become wise ; but medicine is not wisdom, any more than the tool is the work upon which it is used.[2] In the same way, to control one's passions, owing to our knowledge of their mechanism, is not the same as directing them to their true use. Not any thought we please should we attempt to substitute for those which passion suggests, but rather the thoughts which really free the soul, those of which the reason approves. For it is the duty of reason to examine the correct value of the various benefits, the attaining of which depends on ourselves.[3] And even above the right use of the passions, which concerns the soul from the standpoint of its union with the body, Descartes places the benefits of the soul itself from the standpoint of its own life. There is a joy that is purely intellectual.[4] The soul can have its own pleasures apart from all else.[5] The practice of virtue, to which

---

[1] Letter to Mersenne, 15th April 1630, Garn. iv. 303.

[2] Baillet, ii. 11-12.

[3] *Passions*, art. 144. Cf. Letter to the Princess Elizabeth, 1st June 1645, Garnier, iii. 189.

[4] *Passions*, art. 91.   [5] *Ibid.* art. 212.

these pleasures are linked, is not only a sovereign remedy against the passions,[1] it is also the greatest perfection to which one can lay claim, for it is the genuine action of a will that is free.[2]

Above the morals of means, then, which is hardly anything but applied physics, Descartes conceives of a morals of ends which is founded directly on the loftiest elements of metaphysics. Both of these morals are based on science, if this word is taken in its Cartesian sense, i.e. as signifying the clear, distinct knowledge both of corporeal and of spiritual things. The second, however, cannot be derived solely from the science of nature, whose domain does not include reason and will.

Now, when Descartes undertakes to define this superior morals, it is only natural that he should again come into touch with the Stoics and other philosophers of antiquity, to whom the culture of reason formed the main interest in life. Human reason has not changed its nature, from the time of Aristotle to that of Descartes. The most perfect expressions it has met with, ever since men have been able to reflect, thus find their place in the Cartesian system, and that not as mere patchwork, but as integral parts thereof.

They have not, however, been transferred into that system just as they were. Stoic morals, in particular, is for Descartes nothing but a provisional system of morals. To try to conquer oneself rather than fortune is surely the wisest decision to arrive at, as long as we are powerless to modify the outer world. But it is this very power that the Cartesian philosophy confers upon us ; therefore, in place of morals inculcating abstention it substitutes positive and active morals. Likewise, to endeavour to find the rules of conduct in the outer

---

[1] *Passions*, art. 148.   [2] *Ibid.* art. 17-18.

order of things themselves is the best course to follow, as long as we are ignorant of the first principles of which this order is a continuation. But when, as the result of a methodical culture of reason, man has come to know the principal truths from which the laws of nature are derived, he substitutes—and that in a precise and positive sense of which the ancients knew nothing—for the maxim : " Follow nature," that other maxim : " Follow true reason." [1]

The doctrine of a proper content of reason, and of man's possibility to conform things thereto, gives an original stamp to Cartesian morals. When brought in contact with a mysterious, inflexible nature, the ancients could only contemplate and acquiesce in it, or else retire within themselves. In the case of Descartes, reason, grounded on a science which opens out things for its consideration, becomes an efficient power, a natural force ; it assumes the task of employing in its own perfecting the mechanism of external things. And so, whereas Socrates regarded the claim to investigate the causes of physical phenomena as vain and sacrilegious, and the Stoics looked upon resignation and detachment from the world as the principle and the goal of all felicity, Descartes can see no limit to the conquests that science—and by means of science, human reason—will achieve over the world. Whereas the Stoics only condemned passion,—in which they recognised the violence and indiscipline of brute nature,—Descartes, by the aid of a science which penetrates to the causes of passion, subjugates and converts it into an auxiliary of reason. Man is no longer crushed by nature, he makes use of her. The soul, no longer a

---

[1] Letters to the Princess Elizabeth, 1st and 15th May 1645, Garnier, iii. 181, 183.

prisoner of the body, guides and controls it. Morals
is no longer the art of retiring from the world and
being sufficient unto oneself; it is the command to
make of reason—which is our very essence—a living,
sovereign reality, the queen of nature.

And this very sovereignty of reason over things is,
to Descartes, nothing but the means it has for pursuing
the ends proper to itself, such as the love of God,
and interest in the all, of which one forms part.[1] Cartesian metaphysics, by its method, enables us to know,
with certainty these ultimate truths which are the
indispensable illumination of the will. This gives
us another originality of Descartes' morals. Most
certainly the ancients raised the virtues to a lofty pitch ;
but as they were ignorant of true metaphysics they
could not possibly become well acquainted with the
virtues, and what was called by so fine a name was
frequently nothing more than an aberration of the will.[2]

Thus it is really for its close union with science that
Cartesian morals is distinguished throughout. Still,
the pure and simple statement that it is derived from
science, especially the science of natural things, could
not be made. In all its phases it makes use of science
for the attainment of its object : the complete determination of will by reason. The full realisation of
reason is the end : all else is but the means. In all
things, said Descartes,[3] what we must seek after is
the *bona mens* ; nothing else deserves to be taken
into consideration except in so far as it contributes
thereto.

[1] Letter to the Princess Elizabeth, 15th June 1645, Garnier, iii. 192-3.
[2] *Méth.* i. 10.　　　　　　　[3] *Reg.* i.

KANT

"Was uns zu thun gebührt, dess sind wir nur gewiss."—KANT (1782).

THE philosophy of Kant is one of the most important facts in the history of the human mind. Kuno Fischer, the well-known historian of modern philosophy, affirmed that it represents nothing less than a revolution of like nature to that wrought by Socrates when he brought mankind back from the study of the world to the study of self; indeed, it sets before the human mind the task, not of discovering the principles of being and forming a conception of the universe, but rather of looking for the conditions of knowledge itself, the origin of our representations and judgments, and their importance. Windelband shrewdly said that the rationalism of Kant is the concentration in a living unity of all the motor principles of modern thought.

Kant's philosophy, in fact, was the beginning of the development of German philosophy, strictly so called. From Fichte or Schelling on to Wundt or Riehl, there is not a single German philosopher who does not either continue or elaborate Kantian ideas. But even outside of Germany, Kantianism exercises an influence that grows greater and greater the better it is known. Though refuted by some, it is accepted by the rest and is one of the essential factors of contemporary philosophic thought. In France, particularly, it attracts not merely a keen historical interest, but a theoretical one as well.

There exists a very flourishing French neo-criticism and scarcely a single philosophic dissertation appears in which Kant's point of view is not discussed, whilst its action makes itself felt even in literature and social life.

It is no easy task to set forth the true nature of a doctrine dealing with present-day preoccupations and controversies. The safest course to pursue will be to leave on one side the many developments it may have undergone, and look upon it, as far as possible, from the philosopher's own standpoint.

I.—Biography

Kant was a contemporary of Frederick the Second and the French Revolution. His principal works appeared between 1770 and 1797. Though he valued the triumphs of right more highly than those of might, yet he would never agree to separate freedom from order and discipline. The moral environment, in which his thought developed, was Pietism on the one hand, and the philosophy of the eighteenth century on the other. Pietism, which is opposed to abstract, theological Protestantism, set practice before dogma; it extolled feeling and the spirit of devotion, interior piety and the private, individual interpretation of the Scriptures. The philosophy of the eighteenth century, the philosophy of enlightenment (*Aufklärungsphilosophie*), as it was called in Germany, teaches that all the evil from which mankind suffers, is the result of ignorance and of the bondage that succeeds it, and also that the progress of enlightenment, in itself alone, procures happiness and its ensuing liberation.

The life of Kant may be divided into three main periods, that correspond to the different phases of his philosophic development: 1st, childhood and youth from 1724 to 1755, a period of study and preliminary essays ; 2nd, the years he spent as *Privatdozent*, from 1755 to 1770, immediately preceding his critical work ; 3rd, his professorship, from 1770 to 1797, devoted to criticism and the development of his teachings.

Immanuel Kant was born in Königsberg on the 22nd of April 1724. This town, in which the whole of his life was destined to be spent almost without a break, was a large commercial centre to which there flocked a considerable number of Jews, Poles, English and Dutch. Here the philosopher found ample material for psychological and moral observations. Königsberg, a university town, was likewise the centre of intellectual and political life in the Duchy of Prussia.

The family of Kant was of Scotch origin. His name was spelt Cant, which, as it was pronounced *tsant* in German, he changed to Kant. His father was a saddler, poor and of stern morality. His mother, Anna Regina Reuter, says our philosopher, was a woman of considerable intelligence and lofty ideals ; she was an earnest and devout Pietist, though her religion was free from both mysticism and fanaticism. Kant was the fourth in a family of eleven children. The importance of and respect for everything that was religious and moral was inculcated on him from his earliest years. He quietly acquiesced in this influence and retained a keen and pious memory thereof throughout life.

At the age of nine he entered the Collegium Fredericanum, the master of which was Franz Albert Schulz, professor of theology at the University of Königsberg. Schulz was Kant's first master. An ardent Pietist, he put his entire soul into his teachings. From him Kant learnt to regard interior piety as superior to reasoning, and practice as more important

s

than dogma. It may be noted that he invariably spoke with respect and gratitude of his Pietist masters. Was it the philosopher, or was it the former Pietist, who, in 1782, wrote in the epitaph of Lilienthal, the minister who had married his parents, the line :

Was uns zu thun gebührt, des sind wir nur gewiss ? [1]

Kant spent seven years at the Collegium Fredericanum. He was devoted to Latin and to Roman stoicism, which he looked upon as the religion of discipline. Right to the end of his life he adopted as his motto these lines of Juvenal :

Summum crede nefas animam praeferre pudori
Et propter vitam vivendi perdere causas.

In 1740, at the age of seventeen, he entered the University of Königsberg, intending to study theology. His idea at the time was to become a minister, but he quickly changed his mind. At first he attended the classes of Martin Knutzen, professor of mathematics and philosophy. Knutzen was his second master, and he too was a Pietist. Although a disciple of Wolf in philosophy, he was opposed to dualism, and came round to the genuine teaching of Leibnitz, according to which representative and motor force participate in and imply each other.

Kant was indebted to Knutzen for his acquaintance with the works of Newton, who may be called his third, and perhaps his principal master. The New-tonian philosophy was to Kant an experimental proof of the possibility of an *a priori* knowledge of nature. Henceforth it was his object to explain this possibility, and along that line to become, in a way, the Newton of metaphysics.

[1] What duty calls upon us to do, of that alone are we certain.

Knutzen did much to turn Kant from theology to philosophy. And, by degrees, he dropped the strict orthodoxy of his Pietism, retaining nothing but its moral rigidity.

Unable to obtain a living on the fees from his lessons, Kant became a private tutor in 1746, in which capacity he remained for nine years. He was thus brought into connection with foreigners and the nobility, and began to take considerable interest in foreign literature and politics. He went into society, anxious to show himself a worthy citizen.

This the first period of his life concluded with the anonymous publication of his *Universal History of Nature and Theory of the Heavens* (1755), a work that prepared the way for the theory of Laplace on the formation of the heavenly bodies.

After obtaining *promotion* by the writing of a dissertation on fire, and *habitation* by one on the first principles of metaphysical knowledge, he was appointed *Privatdozent*. He taught mathematics, physics, the theory of fortification, pyrotechnics, logic, morals, and philosophical Encyclopedism. His teaching was full of life. Whatever his subject, he spoke as one possessed of special knowledge, the result being that he met with considerable success. Between 1760 and 1769 he also lectured on natural theology, anthropology, criticism of the proofs of the existence of God, and the doctrine of the beautiful and the sublime.

Here we find the influence of Rousseau, whose works were then becoming known and being considerably discussed. Kant devoured Rousseau's books and was thus brought to take a passionate interest in moral problems, the combat against prejudice, and the return to nature and reason. Rousseau taught him, he tells us, not to despise man's natural tendencies. Physical science *a priori* as a fact was what he had found in Newton ; Rousseau now made him see morality as a fact. These facts he purposed to analyse.

With the object of thoroughly investigating moral questions, he read the English moralists : Shaftesbury, Hutcheson and Hume. Shortly afterwards, about 1762, he became acquainted not only with the moral but also with the metaphysical theories of Hume. This initiation proved to be a psychological moment in the development of his thought. "Hume was the first," he says, "to shake me out of my dogmatic indolence and start me on a fresh line of investigation in the domain of speculative philosophy." He adds immediately afterwards : "Of course, I was careful not to accept his conclusions." To his mind, Hume's skepticism was adequately refuted by the reality of moral action. His object was to do justice to Hume's criticisms in so far as they were well founded without agreeing with his conclusions, to steer his course safely between the Scylla of skepticism and the Charybdis of dogmatism. A slight clue which he found in Locke (book 4, chap. 3, § 9, etc.) proved the starting point of his own theory. And so Hume's influence, though certainly considerable, manifested itself in Kant as a note of warning or a stimulus for reflection. There is no proof that Kant passed through a phase of skepticism ; it was to escape from Hume's skepticism that he sought to take a stand outside traditional dogmatism.

It may be that his transcendental idealism drew its inspiration from the teaching of Leibnitz, now set forth in all its purity in the *New Essays*, which appeared in 1765. Leibnitz demonstrated how the principle of innateness may be held, whilst considering experience as indispensable to the formation of knowledge. Kant's forms and categories, however, are quite different from the Leibnitzian virtualities.

To become an ordinary professor, Kant wrote and defended a dissertation in Latin on the form and principles of both the sensible and the intelligible worlds (1770). He was appointed to the University of Königsberg by Frederick II., at a salary of 400 thalers (60 pounds sterling). From that time he refused all invitations from other Universities. He now lectured publicly only on logic and metaphysics, and privately on natural law, morals, natural theology, anthropology and physical geography. His ability as a professor was wonderful ; he did not teach his pupils philosophy, he rather trained them to become philosophers. His lessons were simple, clear and attractive ; he reserved all abstruse deductions and special terminology for his books intended for scholars. On moral subjects he spoke with warmth and conviction ; his eloquence was virile, leaving a profound impression on the souls of his hearers.

The problem of the criticism of human knowledge was not long before it captivated him. How can we explain why ideas, conceived of *a priori*, conform with things that exist outside of ourselves ? At first he thought he would be able to answer the question in a few months : he spent twelve years on it. Even then he allowed himself only four or five months to put his thoughts into words, for fear of delaying the solution too long. It was at Riga, in the beginning of 1781, that the *Critique of Pure Reason* appeared, one of the pillars of human thought. Kant was then fifty-seven years of age. The originality and purport of his book were not at first understood. No one cared to regard him as anything else than a Platonic dreamer or a Cartesian idealist; Hamann called him a Prussian Hume. Kant stoutly explained his position in a treatise entitled : *Prolegomena to all Future Metaphysic that may present itself as Science* (1783), and also in the preface to the second edition of the *Critique* (1787). Sure of his principles, he concentrated his efforts more and more exclusively on developing their consequences, finishing his work of criticism, and establishing on this basis a complete doctrine of speculative and moral philosophy. His writings devoted to this task appeared between 1785 and 1797.

His reputation began to increase. In 1790, Fichte, then quite a young man, forwarded him his *Aphorisms on Religion and Deism*, along with an enthusiastic letter. Schiller studied his teachings on esthetics and induced Goethe to do the same. J. P. Richter recorded his opinion that Kant was not so much a light of the world as an entire system of dazzling suns. His fame spread to Holland and England. His dissertation on eternal peace, published in 1795, was translated into French.

The government accorded him its esteem and protection. Once only was he near receiving a check in the promulgation of his doctrines : when writing on religious subjects. In 1792 he had sent an article on the root evil in human nature to the *Berlin Monthly Review*, and the Board of Censors had authorized its insertion. A second article, however, on the struggle between the good and the evil principles, was not accepted. Now, Kant had still two more to bring out. Refused by the Board, he applied to the Faculty of Theology, who granted the *imprimatur*. The four dissertations appeared under the 'title, *Religion within the Limits of Reason alone* (1793). The government grew alarmed at the success of the book, and on the 1st of October 1794 Kant received a letter asking for an explanation and commanding him never again to write on the subject of religion. Outwardly Kant yielded, and gave a written promise not to teach or write on religion "as a loyal subject of His Royal Majesty." When the king, however, died in 1797, he regarded himself as released from his promise.

In other respects he lived quietly enough, though he was very sympathetic towards the French Revolution. This sympathy is a special characteristic of his moral make-up. He looked upon the Revolution as an effort to establish the organisation of human societies on reason. Even after 1794 he persevered in his political convictions though he despaired of a favourable issue to events in France itself. To the very end he believed in the justice and practical value of theory ; in right, as a principle ; and in eternal peace, as the practicable goal of politics. Behind personal disputings he saw the conflict between history and philosophy, between the positive and the rational ; in all things he relied on the triumph of reason.

After the year 1790 his intellectual powers began to decline, and in 1797 he resigned his professorship. All the same, he continued to work right on to the end. The book on which he was engaged was to be his *chef-d'œuvre*, his object being to explain the transition from the metaphysics of the science of nature to physics. This work, which he left unfinished, was lost ; it has been found recently. Kant's last year of life was marked by ever-increasing feebleness of body. He died on the 12th of February 1804. His last words were : *Es ist gut* (It is well). His funeral took place amid universal homage and admiration. The body was interred beneath the arcades of Königsberg Cathedral. Several statues were erected in his honour, the most famous being the one by Rauch in Königsberg. Kant was a man of small, short stature, only a little over five feet in height, with poorly developed bones and muscles, a narrow, almost concave chest, the right shoulder joint slightly displaced, high forehead and fine blue eyes. A cast of his head was taken by Knorr, and his remains were exhumed in 1880.

Kant lived for philosophy alone. He held no political office and never married. All the same, he did not consider it possible to be a philosopher, without at the same time being a man, and so regarded it as necessary to come into contact with the realities of life before attempting to understand and regulate them. In his loftiest aspirations he was careful not to overstep the limits of this terrestrial world of ours. His object was to live here below in accordance with his own principles, which he looked upon as absolute and followed out to the letter. To his mind, the reconciliation of law and independence was to be found in reason ; by it he determined to form his opinions and control his life. In politics he professed liberalism, but would not admit of any separation between liberty and order, whilst he maintained a conscientious respect for established power. In religion he was a rationalist, though he deemed it right to uphold the spirit of Christianity, and valued the work done by the positive religions. In philosophy he attacked dogmatism, though rejecting skepticism. In morals he repudiated all exterior laws, though obeying an interior command of greater severity than the laws he rejected. Boldness in speculation, respect towards practical life and the material order of things : such were his distinguishing traits.

Kant was a thinker more than a writer. Some of his earlier works such as the *Observations on the Beautiful and the Sublime*, the Methodology of the *Critique of Pure Reason*, and, speaking generally, the passages in which he expresses his moral convictions, manifest a facile, pleasing and vigorous style. In metaphysical analysis, however, his style is complicated, laboured and redundant, and often only the more obscure from the fact that the author has made every effort to be clear. Kant's work is a thought seeking its form. In more finished shape, would it have stirred the human intellect to the same degree ?

The following is a chronological list of Kant's principal works, written, for the most part, in German :

Thoughts on the True Estimate of Living Force (*Vis Viva*), *and an Investigation into the Proofs of Leibnitz and other Mechanical Philosophers thereon* (1747). Kant, in this work, reconciles the doctrines of Descartes and Leibnitz with each other, as regards the measurement of the force of a moving body.

Has the Earth, from its Origin, undergone any Modifications in its Rotatory Motion ? (magazine article, 1754). Relying on Newton's principles Kant clearly shows that the speed of the earth's rotation must have diminished.

Is the Earth growing Old ? A research made from the physical standpoint (article, 1754).

A Universal History of Nature and Theory of the Heavens, dealing with the System and Mechanical Origin of the Universe, in accordance with Newton's Principles (1755), a famous work that appeared anonymously, with a dedication to Frederick II., and serving as a kind of prelude to the exposition of the world-system, published by Laplace in 1796.

Brief Account of some Thoughts on Fire (in Latin) (1755).
Heat, like light, is a vibratory movement of the ether.

A New Explanation of the First Principles of Metaphysical Knowledge (1755), a thesis in Latin ; written to obtain the right to be appointed *privatdocent*. It deals with the principles of contradiction and determinative reason.

Three dissertations *On Earthquakes that took place at Quito and Lisbon in 1755.*

Physical Monadology (1756), Latin thesis ; Kant defended this thesis with a view to a professorship which he did not obtain. In it he transformed the monad of Leibnitz into a physical atom.

Explanatory Remarks on the *Theory of the Winds* (1756), a precise explanation of periodical winds.

A New Conception of Motion and Rest (1758).

A Few Thoughts on Optimism (1759). Kant claims that everything is good if we regard things as a whole. At the end of his life he repudiated this work, inspired by Leibnitz.

The False Subtlety of the Four Syllogistic Figures (1762). The first figure alone, he affirmed, was pure and primitive.

An Attempt to Introduce into Philosophy the Notion of Negative Quantities (1763). Real opposition, in which the two terms are equally positive in themselves cannot be reduced to logical opposition, in which one of the terms contradicts the other.

The only possible Foundation for a Demonstration of the Existence of God (1763). The possible, regarded not in its form but in its matter or data, presupposes existence, and, in the final analysis, the existence of a necessary being.

An Essay on the Evidence of the Fundamental Propositions of Natural Theology and Ethics (1764), a work written for a competition inaugurated by the Berlin Academy. Kant obtained only the *accessit*, the prize being awarded to Mendelssohn. Both contrast philosophy with mathematics, and Kant concludes that the methods employed in the latter are not suitable for the former.

Observations on the Sentiment of the Beautiful and the Sublime (1764); a work on morals and criticism.

Programme of Classes for the Winter Session (1765-1766). The education of the various faculties of the mind should precede the acquiring of knowledge. In this treatise a critical propensity begins to show itself.

Dreams of a Spirit-seer (or Clairvoyant) explained by the Dreams of Metaphysic (1766, anonymous). This work was inspired by Swedenborg's visions. Kant here appears in a skeptical and somewhat inconsiderate vein, *à la Voltaire*. The only difference between illuminism and metaphysics, to his mind, is that the former is the dream of sentiment, the latter that of reason ; one is no better than the other. Let us not claim to know the unknowable.

Grounds for distinguishing Positions in Space (1768). A refutation of the Leibnitzian theory which posits things before space, this latter being reduced to nothing but a concept. According to Kant, we must admit the existence of universal, absolute space.

Form and Principles of the Sensible and the Intelligible Worlds (1770), a dissertation in Latin, written in order to obtain the right of being appointed professor of logic and metaphysics. Kant breaks away from dogmatism as regards sensible—though not intelligible—knowledge.

Letters to Marcus Herz, from 1770 to 1781. Kant endeavours to find some mean between idealism and realism.

The Different Human Races. The races are varieties that have become stable. A true history of natural beings would doubtless reduce many so-called species to the position of simple races, the offshoot of one common species.

The Critique of Pure Reason (1781). Theoretical knowledge implies both intuition and necessary connection. As we can realise the first condition only with regard to sensible things, these latter are the only ones we can know theoretically. In 1787, Kant published a second edition of the *Critique*. Whether the changes in this second edition refer to the substance or only to the form is a much-disputed question. Rosenkranz, Schopenhauer and Kuno Fischer agree that a thorough modification took place, tending to restore the " thing-in-itself," which, they alleged, the first edition had abolished. According to Kant himself, the second edition merely emphasises the realistic side of the doctrine, an aspect that had been disregarded by certain readers. Kant's affirmation may very well be maintained. The first edition did not abolish the " thing-in-itself," but rather the theoretical knowledge of the " thing-in-itself," a very different matter.

Prolegomena to all Future Metaphysics which may present itself as Science (1783). This short work gives an analytical exposition of the doctrine which the *Critique of Pure Reason* had set forth synthetically, and rectifies the mistakes made with reference to certain points in this doctrine.

Notion of a Universal History in a Cosmopolitan Sense (magazine article, 1784).

Answer to the question : What is enlightenment ? (magazine article, 1784). Enlightenment, says Kant, is the emancipation of the intelligence.

An Account of Herder's work entitled : Ideas on the Philosophy of the History of Mankind (magazine article, 1785). Kant rejects the doctrine of the essential unity of nature and freedom.

Foundations of the Metaphysics of Morals (1785 ; 4th edition, 1797). Here Kant determines and affirms the fundamental principle of morality.

Metaphysical Elements of Natural Science (1786 ; 3rd edition, 1800). In this work the axioms of pure physics are given.

Conjectures on the Beginning of Human History (1786).

Corporeal Medicine in so far as it comes under Philosophy, a discourse in Latin (1786 or 1788).

The Employment of Teleological Principles in Philosophy (article, 1788).

Critique of Practical Reason (1788 ; 6th edition, 1827). A determination of the nature of the moral law, and of the kind of adhesion that practical principles allow of.

Critique of Judgment (1790 ; 3rd edition, 1799). Here Kant deals with the basis and value of the ideas of beauty and finality.

Illuminism and the Remedies against it (1790). Dissertation on Cagliostro.

The Failure of all Philosophic Effort in Theodicy (1791).

Religion within the Bounds of Reason only (1793; 2nd edition, 1794). The deduction or legitimation of religion. Only what relates to morals is founded on religion. We must tend to make religion purely rational.

The Commonplace Remark: " That is all Right in Theory but Worthless in Practice" (magazine article, 1793). Kant rejects this well-known aphorism not only as regards morality, but also with reference to political and human right.

The Influence of the Moon upon the Weather (article, 1794).

Eternal Peace, a Philosophical Essay (1795). Eternal peace Kant regards as the goal of the historic development of mankind, and that, not from sentiment, but from the idea of justice.

Metaphysical Principles of the Theory of Right (1797; 2nd edition, 1798). The theory of right or legality as deduced from the criticism of practical reason.

Metaphysical Principles of the Theory of Virtue (1797; 2nd edition, 1803). The theory of morality, also as the result of criticism. These two latter works bear the title: *Metaphysics of Morals*.

Contest of the Faculties (to this work is added an article that appeared in 1797: *The Power of the Mind to Master its Morbid Feelings by Will alone*) (1798). This was the conflict of the Faculty of Philosophy, representing rational truth, with the three other Faculties: Theology, Law, and Medicine, representing the positive disciplines.

Anthropology Treated from the Pragmatic Point of View (1798; 2nd edition, 1800). Pragmatic anthropology is the art of using men for one's own purposes.

Logic, a work published by Jäsche (1800).

Physical Geography, published by Rink (1802-1803).

Paedagogics, published by Rink (1803). Notes taken from several lectures delivered by Kant on this subject.

Transition from the Metaphysical Principles of the Science of Nature to Physics, an unfinished work, written between 1783 and 1803, first published by Reicke between 1882 and 1884 in the *Altpreussische Monatsschriften*, and then,

more completely, by Albrecht Krause (1888). Here we
have the progress of deduction proceeding from the metaphysics of material nature to experimental physics regarded
as a science, *i.e.* as a system.

Kant's Reflections on Critical Philosophy, published by Benno
Erdmann (1882-1884).

Letters. About a hundred, nineteen of which were addressed
to Marcus Herz.

II.—THE ANTECRITICAL PERIOD

On the 20th of August 1777 Kant left it on record
that his investigations, hitherto professional and frag-
mentary, had finally taken systematic form and brought
him to the idea of the whole.   Thus, in the first place,
the development of Kantian thought shows a long
period of formation, during which works of different
kinds were undertaken for themselves alone without
reference to a general standpoint, and afterwards
brought together with a view to being reconciled with
each other.   And so Kant's thought progresses from
the parts to the whole.   His main idea is arrived at by
a process of synthesis.   This first period extends to
the time of his elaboration of criticism, *i.e.* up to and
including the year 1770.

The starting-point of Kantian thought is, on the
one hand, a substratum of Christian, and more especially of Pietistic beliefs, faith in duty, the cult of moral
intention, conviction of the superiority of practice over
dogmatism ; on the other, a very clear, keen sense of
science, the determination to be guided, so far as a
knowledge of nature is concerned, only by the evidence
of experience and mathematical reasoning.   Henceforth Kant is principally concerned with the connection between science and religion ; this, too, after both

have been developed in his mind independently, each according to its own method.

During the antecritical period Kant meditates in turn on the divers objects presented both by his studies and by the circumstances of life.

From 1747 to 1755 he is a Leibnitzo-Wolfian, though with a tendency to accentuate the difference between the mathematical and the real.

With Newton, he studies the mechanism of the heavens, from 1754 to 1763. Like him, he determines to employ experience only in conjunction with mathematics. Newton, however, did not state the problem of origins. Kant believes that the method which has established the present system is capable of going back to the genesis of this very system : the forces that preserve must also be the forces that have created. He undertakes to trace not only the possible but the real, the actual history of the formation of the world.

In the beginning was one homogeneous, elementary matter, moved by forces of attraction and repulsion : a gaseous chaos. This matter was maintained in a state of extreme tenuity by being kept at a very high temperature. In obedience to the forces contained within itself this chaos is subjected to a movement of rotation. Purely as the result of these physical conditions the homogeneous becomes differentiated. Rotation occasions the formation of nebulae, which themselves acquire a rotatory movement. In turn these nebulae, as the result of the centrifugal force, produce rings, and these rings represent the orbits of future planets. Then the rings break, and collect together again in planets. Satellites are formed in the same way.

The scientific value of this theory is now recognised even by such men as Helmholtz (*Mémoire sur la conser-*

vation de la force, 1847) and Faye (*Revue scientifique*, 1884).

The theory was the result of purely scientific considerations. Kant, however, at once confronts it with the teachings of religion. Religion, he says, has nothing to fear from a doctrine which, though dismissing accidental and extrinsic finality, as met with in the works of men, implies, on the other hand, a fruitful and essential finality, which alone is truly worthy of God. Besides, who will ever be able to say, "Give me matter and motion and I will make a snail"? At its very lowest stage life is immeasurably superior to mechanism ; it is a witness to God.

Following on Wolf, Kant studies the relations between possibility and existence (1755). The principle of contradiction is the law of the former ; the principle of determining reason, irreducible to that of contradiction, is the law of the latter. Determining reason is either antecedently determining and a reason of existence, or subsequently determining and a reason of knowledge. Antecedently determining reason alone gives us complete science. From these principles Kant deduces the impossibility of explaining, solely by the analysis of their distinctive essence, either change or the real connection between substances. All relations between substances must come from without. Thus, succession has its foundation in an external action which constitutes the reality of the world, whilst coexistence is based on an extrinsic connection which implies the existence of God. And so, speculating on Wolr's metaphysics, Kant ends in a deduction of the principles of Newtonianism. His system at this period may be defined as realistic mechanism dependent on natural theology.

Dealing with the relations between philosophy and mathematics, as did his contemporaries (1756-1764), Kant neither admits that the concepts of the mathematicians, infinite divisibility, an absolute plenum, the exclusive mechanism of all notion of force, are intelligible to the understanding, nor that these concepts are meaningless and devoid of real value. Though a stumbling-block to the logician, mathematics is none the less the key of the science of nature, as Newton proved. The problem is to reconcile mathematics with transcendental philosophy, not to sacrifice the one to the other. Now, if we analyse the conditions of mathematical speculation, and those of philosophic speculation, we find that in both cases the object is a synthesis, but that in the former it is built up by the mind, and in the latter it is given to the mind. Hence, the method that suits the one is useless for the other. Everything referring to dimension will be dealt with mathematically, but if we would know qualities and existences, we shall use experience and metaphysical systematisation, along with Newton. There are two certainties, two outlooks upon nature : that of mathematical proof and that of experience. These two paths of knowledge, starting from opposite poles, can never meet.

Yielding to the influence of the aesthetician Baumgarten, Rousseau and the English philosophers, Kant takes up the questions of taste and morals (1763-1766). His method consists in taking, as his starting-point, an impartial observation of human nature. We must proceed, he says, from what is to what ought to be. His observation, however, in spite of himself, is tinged with metaphysical analysis. In the given he is about to discover the absolute. What he thinks he ought

T

to observe is not so much ideas and things as the inner movements of sensibility. Taking this point of view, he is led to make a profound distinction between the beautiful and the sublime. This distinction introduces enlightenment and precision into literature and art. Thus, it is the province of tragedy to be sublime, that of comedy to be beautiful. The distinction likewise applies to morals. True virtue is sublime ; good qualities : a kind heart, the sense of honour, modesty, are only beautiful. The spring of virtue is the sentiment of the beauty and dignity of human nature, regarded as a motive of action. This principle must be understood in a formal sense : it consists essentially of an obligatory rule. This principle, too, is impossible of demonstration ; and it is good that it should be so. Providence has not willed that knowledge indispensable to our happiness should depend on subtle reasoning ; it has entrusted such knowledge to natural common sense.

Swedenborg's claim that he held direct communication with spirits, affords Kant an opportunity to examine the value of metaphysics, so far as it also affirms the possibility of becoming acquainted with suprasensible existences (1763-1766). Metaphysics seems to meet with unexpected confirmation in the facts affirmed by illuminism. It is apparently justified by the theory it advances thereof, as Newtonianism is justified by the explanation it affords of the experimental laws of motion. Unfortunately, illuminism can be explained in a far simpler and more satisfactory manner, as hallucination caused by certain organic disturbances. Might it not then possibly happen that metaphysics had a like origin ? What if it were, after all, a mere hallucination of the understanding, endowing the phantoms of sensible hallucination with an apparently logical existence ? All the same, we must beware of leaping to the conclusion that metaphysics is altogether inane. In one scale of the balance it places the hope of a future life. Now, we could not will that this weight remain actionless on our mind. What we do know, is that we can expect nothing from experience calculated to confirm our moral and religious beliefs. But these beliefs need no experimental confirmation ; they both will and ought to be free. In a word, the result of our examination is that we must offer the following new definition of metaphysics, one alike favourable to practice and imposed upon theory : metaphysics is the science of the limits of human reason.

Kant, like Leibnitz, studies the nature of space and time (1768-1770). Several facts of experience, including the real existence of symmetrical figures, prove that geometrical space is no mere consequence of the relations between things in point of position, but rather the basis of the possibility of these relations. The reality of absolute space being thus established, Kant asks himself how space is possible, *i.e.* conceivable without contradiction. Space and time are known *a priori* ; at the same time they are intuitions. How can these two characteristics be reconciled ? The only way of doing so, is to regard space and time as the conditions imposed on the human mind, by its very nature, for the perception of sensible objects. Space and time do not concern things as they are in themselves, but only as they appear to our sensibility. The " critique " idea has come to birth, but Kant applies it, so far, only to sensible or mathematical knowledge.

It was through Hume's influence that Kant's thought, which had hitherto wandered over all kinds of subjects, was finally to become concentrated and steadied (1762-

1780). Hume's dialectic made such an impression on Kant's mind that he soon thought of nothing else than solving the difficulties raised by the famous skeptic. In this task his true originality was shown, and there blossomed forth the idea which was to be the soul of his philosophy. Kant had long ago pondered on the relation between cause and effect, he soon saw the element of strangeness in a connection which could not be analytical, and yet was necessary. Still, he did not think of criticising its legitimacy. It was Hume who roused him out of his dogmatic calmness, proclaiming that the concept of causality—a concept foreign to reason, formed by nothing but imagination on the occasion of a mere habit and under the influence of some obscure instinct—could have no object outside of ourselves. Kant refused to follow Hume in the deductions the latter claimed to found on this analysis of his. Indeed, what would become of the freedom of the will, the condition of moral determination, if there existed for us nothing but phenomena; and what would become of science itself, the knowledge of things as necessary, if causality were nothing more than a subjective connection? In Kant's mind, science and morals are given, as are also the characteristics peculiar to them; it is the part of philosophy to explain their possibility or conditions, not to discuss their reality.

And so Hume's thesis was not a doctrine, but rather a problem, a starting-point for Kant. How comes it to pass that a relation, the terms of which are heterogeneous, should also be posited as necessary as valid for things? This was the question to be answered.

First, he had to satisfy himself that the principle of causality did not proceed from experience, for in that event its necessity would have been radically unintelli-

gible. Having noticed, however, that many other
concepts, such as those of substance, mutual action, etc.,
held the same position as the one with which Hume had
grappled, and having succeeded in determining the exact
number of these concepts by means of a single principle,
a thing impossible in the case of concepts of experience,
Kant from that time regarded it as established that the
concept of cause may be acknowledged to have an origin
a priori. And yet, can there conceivably be concepts
that are at once *a priori* and synthetical! Have we
not here two incompatible characteristics? This was
Hume's idea, and so he gave up the problem, discarding
causality in favour of experience. The reason was that
he shared a prevailing error of the age upon an important point closely connected with the question : the
nature of mathematical judgments. These latter he
regarded as analytical, and so refused to consider them.
In reality, they are synthetical ; and as their character
of necessity and apriority is indisputable, and even undisputed, they afford an instance of the effective union,
within our knowledge, of apriority and synthetic connection. There is nothing, therefore, to prevent the
judgment of causality from being both synthetic and
necessary.

Nevertheless, it is not enough for it to be necessary
in the sense that mathematical judgments are necessary.
Necessary, in the sense of causal connection, means :
applicable *a priori* to real things. How is such a
property possible ? If objects were produced by the
understanding, or ideas by objects, the agreement between
concepts and things would afford no difficulty ; but such
is not the case : mind and things form two distinct
worlds. Then how does the mind come to have the
right to dictate laws for things? It acquires this right,

answers Kant, from the conditions of experience itself, both inner and outer : no other explanation is possible.

This view, the origin of transcendental deduction, is the goal of the regressive movement occasioned by Hume's criticism. It includes the formula of Kant's criticism, and the central idea of the system he is now to build up.

III.—Criticism

The Kantian criticism of pure reason is strictly a theory of science. As Newton sought for the principle governing the system of celestial bodies, so Kant seeks for the principle governing the system of our knowledge. Science is given, just as the universe is given ; philosophy does not ask whether it is possible or not, but how it is possible, *i.e.* conceivable without contradiction.

Science consists of two disciplines, mathematics and physics, and the union of the two ; we must take these facts into account. Mathematics consists of *a priori* synthetic judgments, *i.e.* judgments in which the subject is attached *a priori* to a predicate not contained in it. It is the same with physics. Ever since the time of Newton, the certainty of physics, which deals with things themselves, is in no way inferior to that of mathematics, which deals only with relations of dimension. How are these characteristics intelligible, whence do they proceed, and what is science, considered in its generating principles ? It is the object of Kant's investigations to answer these questions.

And it is the province of philosophy to institute these investigations. Now, the inviolable principle philosophy gives us in this matter, is the following : all our knowledge has its starting-point in experience. We have to discover if, from this principle, there can be deduced the theory of science, as given to us. Thus, the problem resolves itself into the following question : " What is experience ? Is it an irreducible unity, or can analysis discern different elements in it ? Of these elements, are there any *a priori* ? Will these *a priori* elements account for the necessity proper to the judgments of science, and in what way ? "

In experience, an object is first given, secondly thought. How is that possible ?

For an object to be given to us, it must be presented in space and time. Are the notions of space and time supplied by experience ? No, for before experience, we know that the objects given will be given in space and time. Consequently, they are *a priori* elements. What is their nature ? Are they concepts ? No, for space and time are objects that are integral, homogeneous, and infinite, characteristics opposed to those offered by the objects of the concepts. Space and time are substrata of the things and objects of intuition. Then, are they suprasensible realities outside of ourselves ? No, for the conception of two infinite nonbeings as substances is impossible. After all, the representation of space and time can only be an intuition resting on the form of our sensibility. Space and time are our way of seeing things.

But then, if such is the case, are not our ideas of place and duration purely subjective ? With such a doctrine, what is to become of the truth of mathematics ?

The objection is groundless, for, as a matter of fact, it is in dogmatic theories, isolating the sensible from the mathematical, that the agreement of the one with the other is undemonstrable. Mathematics is justified if regarded in its true nature as a system of *a priori* synthetic judgments, when once objects are capable of affecting us only by becoming subject to the laws of time and space. Doubtless we cannot say that things, in themselves, possess modes of being that we can only explain as forms of our power to feel. But we know, *a priori*, that every object of our sensibility will conform with mathematics, and that is sufficient to insure the objectivity of this science. Transcendental ideality and empirical reality are the two characteristics of time and space. They explain and determine the possibility of mathematics.

This is the explanation of the first condition of experience : there is a second. For an object to be given is not sufficient, it must also be thought. Does thought imply *a priori* elements ?

Thought consists in setting up between two terms an objective relationship of subject and predicate, *i.e.* in affirming that the one, really and of necessity, belongs to the other. This is what takes place, for instance, when we say that one thing is the cause or substance of another. Such a connection cannot be supplied by experience, which gives nothing necessary. Therefore, it is known *a priori*, though in what way ? If we consider logic as it has been conceived of ever since the time of Aristotle, we note that it supplies many necessary connections, but yet is unable to determine one term as being a real subject regarding the other. In every declaration relative to existence, there is something more than simple logic. To affirm of an object that it is a cause, is to go beyond the limits of its concept. Now, we are without that intellectual intuition of the whole, which alone would enable its parts to be disclosed by a process of analysis. We proceed, in discursive fashion, from the parts to the whole. On what principle, then, do the different relations that constitute thought, depend ?

Apart from those we have had to reject, there remains only the understanding itself, or the faculty of judging. As relations of dimension are, at bottom, only the forms of our sensibility, so qualitative relations of things cannot be anything else than the categories of our understanding.

If this is so, the logical function of the understanding will enable us to detect and systematise all the concepts that control judgments of existence. For, on both sides, it is the province of the understanding to unify ; the extent of this unification alone causes difference. The table of the modes of logical unification thus supplies a model for the table of categories.

The following is the logical table of judgments : 1st, from the standpoint of quantity : universal, particular and individual propositions ; 2nd, from the standpoint of quality : affirmative, negative and indeterminate propositions ; 3rd, from the standpoint of relation : categorical, hypothetical and disjunctive propositions ; 4th, from the standpoint of modality : problematical, assertorial and apodeictic propositions.

The following is the transcendental table of the concepts of understanding : 1st, from the standpoint of quantity : unity, multiplicity, universality ; 2nd, from the standpoint of quality : reality, negation, limitation ; 3rd, from the standpoint of relation : inherence and subsistence, causality and dependence, reciprocal action ; 4th, from the standpoint of modality : possibility or impossibility, existence or non-existence, necessity or contingency.

This is the system of concepts or categories by whose aid we unite our representations of things. As these

concepts are only the modes of action of our understanding, in themselves they are devoid of all content.
They can find a use only if they are supplied with
matter, and the only matter at our disposal is sensible
intuition.   Have concepts, then, only a subjective
value ;   and whereas transcendental esthetics or the
analysis of sensibility may have pronounced for mathematical realism, will the analysis of the understanding
or transcendental logic have to confine itself to that
logical idealism which resolves things into modes of
thought ?

Here we have the famous transcendental deduction
whose object is to establish the objective value of the
categories, *i.e.* the possibility of obtaining, by means
of the categories as they have been determined, the
knowledge not only of our way of thinking, but of the
things themselves.   This possibility will be demonstrated if it can be proved that the categories are themselves the condition of the existence of realities, from
our standpoint.   Categories apply to things, if things,
to us, are possible only by their means.

According to our condition, in order that there may
be knowledge of a thing, there must be distinction
between subject and object: " I think " should accom-
pany all our representations.   For such a condition to
be possible, however, there must exist between the
two terms a relation analogous to that between positive
and negative quantities in mathematics, a relation of
opposition on a common ground.   The subject being
a unifying action, the object must be a unified multiple.
And so it is because things are unified, and unified for
the subject, that they can be presented as an object.

Now, how could this condition be satisfied, were
not the multiple unified by the subject itself?   Doubt-

less the empirical consciousness does not perceive this formation of the object. The operation takes place in the depths of transcendental apperception implied by the empirical consciousness ; and when the particular I is posited, it finds the object ready formed before it, and takes it for a brute thing. This thing, however, is the work of thought, therefore thought, in each of us, recognises its own laws therein. Thus the categories are necessarily applied to the things themselves, so far as they exist for us ; consequently they have an objective value.

Again, as the only intuitions at the disposal of our understanding, for the forming of objects thereof, are our sensible intuitions, and as the latter do not represent things as they are in themselves, but only the exigencies of our sensibility, one consequence of our human condition is that even our intellectual knowledge is unable to attain to the absolute, it remains confined to the world of experience. Empirical realism, and transcendental idealism are allied and correlative terms.

Thus, on the other hand, we find a place reserved for the suprasensible itself. Indeed, the concept of the "thing-in-itself," whilst limitative of the claims of our science, enables us to conceive of a world other than the one with which we are acquainted, and therefore susceptible of being freed from the conditions of our knowledge, and especially from the necessary connection which is opposed to freedom. We are permitted to superpose the noumenon on to the phenomenon.

It is essentially this doctrine that contains the philosophic revolution wrought by Kant. Instead of admitting, as appearances would seem to indicate, that thought gravitates around things, Kant, like a modern

Copernicus, causes things to gravitate around thought. From this point of view, he says, the disorderly and the inexplicable give way to the orderly and the intelligible. The agreement between the laws of nature and the laws of our mind is no longer either an insoluble problem or an object of faith : it is a scientifically demonstrated truth. And this revolution, which guarantees the objective value of science, is equally favourable to morals, which latter, in the field opened up by criticism, can now be developed unhindered, in conformity with the laws proper to itself. "It was only by abolishing learning," says Kant, with reference to the so-called knowledge of the suprasensible, "that I could find room for belief."

It is not enough, however, to lay down that, in order to be thought of and to become objects, the divers elements of intuition must be brought under the concepts of the understanding. How will concept, the one and universal, unite with phenomenon, the diverse and particular ? How shall we be brought to apply to intuition any one category rather than any other ? A middle term is here necessary.

This middle term is supplied by a faculty intermediary between understanding and sensibility : viz. imagination. In the form of the inner sense, *i.e.* in temporal intuition, imagination traces out, *a priori*, frames into which phenomena are capable of fitting, and which indicate under what category they are to be brought. Kant calls these frames *schemata of the concepts of pure understanding*. Each category has its own schema. The schema of quantity is number, that of substance is the permanence of the real in time ; that of causality, the regular succession of phenomena, and so on. The observance of regular succession, for instance, is a signal to us that the category of cause is being employed.

Still, the schemata are not yet sufficient to objectivise phenomena, because they only call forth the employment of a given category, without justifying this operation. But they make possible *a priori* synthetic judgments which complete the elimination of the subjective. These judgments are the principles of pure understanding. Understanding forms them *a priori*, by determining the conditions of an objective employment of the schemata. They are: the principle of quantity: "All intuitions are extensive dimensions"; the principle of quality: "In all phenomena, sensation, as well as the real which corresponds thereto in the object, possesses an intensive dimension, a degree"; the principle of relation: "All phenomena have a necessary connection in time." The principle of modality indicates the way in which a thing should agree with the conditions of experience, in order to be possible, real, or necessary. The proof of these principles consists in showing that, without them, the meaning of the schemata remains indeterminate; that the sensible can be determined and objectivised only by the intellectual. Thus, succession, for instance, instead of itself founding causality, can be regarded as objective only if it is founded thereon.

On reaching this stage, Kant was enabled to accomplish the second of the two tasks he had set himself: that of justifying physics and its alliance with mathematics. The first two principles—so-called mathematical—establish the application of mathematics to the science of nature. The second two—so-called dynamic —establish the physical laws strictly so called. In their entirety, the principles of pure understanding constitute the first distinctive features of natural philosophy. This theory, whilst being the metaphysical justification of Newtonian science, was the starting-point of that speculation which, with Schelling, enjoyed so dangerous a renown, under the name of the philosophy of nature.

Up to this point, Kant has analysed sensibility and understanding. There remains reason, properly so called, the object of which faculty is the complete unification of knowledge. Its syllogisms infer the unconditioned as their starting-point. So we see that reason is the faculty of the ideas, or concepts, of the total synthesis of the conditions.

From what precedes, we find that the ideas of reason have no real object. Going beyond all possible experience, they can be nothing but regulative, non-constitutive principles of knowledge. The illusion, however, which makes us believe in their objectivity, is natural, as is that of the man who believes the moon to be larger at its rise than at its meridian. To destroy this illusion it is not enough to demonstrate the falsity of our opinion ; its origin must be disclosed, it must be shown that, in this domain, in contradistinction to what takes place when dealing with objects of possible experience, it is wholly illegitimate to pass from the logical to the real ; and that the dialectic which lies deep hidden in dogmatic metaphysics must be denounced.

Reason thinks it can build up : 1st, a rational psychology, on the idea of the soul-substance ; 2nd, a rational cosmology, on the idea of the world as absolute reality ; 3rd, a rational theology, on the idea of God as the absolute basis of the possibility of being in general. In each of these domains it is mistaken regarding its own power.

When inferring the existence of an absolute subject from the reality of the thinking being, it illegitimately passes from a unity of form to one of substance, and commits a paralogism.

When attempting to determine the absolute existence it attributes to the world, reason becomes involved in insurmountable antinomies. Indeed, it proves, with like rigour, by the absurdity of the contradictory proposition, that the world both has, and has not, limits ; that it consists of simple parts, and is divided *ad infinitum* ; that freedom exists and that nothing free exists ; that there is a necessary being, and that there exist only contingent beings. The very production of these antinomies proves the illegitimacy of the point of view that gives birth to them, that is, of the supposition of a world existing in itself. In the first two antinomies, thesis and antithesis are alike false. In the latter two, they become true of each other if we have recourse to that distinction between phenomenon and noumenon called forth by analysis of the understanding. The free and the absolute are possible in the world of noumena, whereas natural causality and contingency hold sway in that of phenomena.

Finally, when reason speculates on perfect being, it gratuitously converts into a reality, a substance, a person, the ideal in which it unites all the modes of being possessed by finite things. Consequently, the reasonings it forms to prove the existence of this supreme person will not hold together. The ontological argument, the basis of all the rest, wrongly considers existence as a predicate, which can be obtained from a concept by analysis : existence is the position of a thing outside of thought and is absolutely inaccessible to analysis. To this error the cosmological argument adds the affirmation of a first cause in the name of the principle of causality, and this principle, just in so far as it is vouched for, excludes the possibility of a first cause. Lastly the physico-theological argument, or the argument of final causes, adds to the defects of the first two the false comparison of the world to a work of man, and the arbitrary transition from an "architect" God to a perfect "creator" God.

The general cause of this dialectic of our reason is our natural disposition to believe that the conditions of our thought are also the conditions of being, that the laws of our knowledge are the laws of reality. Criticism alone can dispel this illusion ; but the necessity of criticism is seen only in the consequences of this very illusion. The ideas of our reason correspond to nothing real : none the less are they useful as excitative and regulative principles. They forbid our halting in our search after causes. We cannot begin with God, but our efforts should tend in his direction.

And so criticism is established, wherein Kant sees the goal of the education of reason. The human mind began, and was compelled to begin, with dogmatism, or a blind belief in the absolute existence of the objects of our thoughts : Leibnitzo-Wolfianism is the complete expression thereof. Then came skepticism, excellently represented by Hume, who inferred, from the vices of dogmatism, the impossibility of knowing reality and the absolute subjectivity of knowledge. But skepticism is only a warning to mistrust dogmatism. Criticism, or the science of our ignorance, forbids us to speculate on the nature of things as they are in themselves ; at the same time, it withdraws experience from imagination and the individual sense, to make it an object common to all human intelligences and consequently substantial and real to ourselves. At the same time, criticism frees being in itself from the *fatum* which the presumption of the understanding caused to lie heavy on it ; it makes conceivable a world wherein freedom and the moral laws would hold undivided sway. The advantage is twofold, being both practical and speculative ; it attests to the providential harmony of our needs with our powers of knowing.

The "critique" of pure reason has explained the possibility of science ; in the same way, the possibility of morals must now be explained. We are not trying to find out if morality is possible, since it exists, but rather on what it rests and what its meaning is. Here, too, a sane philosophy can recognise no other starting-point for knowledge than experience, but this experience must be analysed.

The general idea afforded, in this connection, by common reason, is the concept of good will. Is this concept altogether empirical ?

When examined, it is found to imply the idea of a law which ought to be observed for itself, without regard for the consequences of the actions it enforces. This law is not a hypothetical imperative, dependent on such or such an end to be attained : it is a categorical imperative. It can be formulated only in the following terms : act in such a way that you would wish the maxim of your action to be set up as a universal law. Now, such a principle does not proceed from experience, it is known *a priori*.

Can we find its origin ? If we try to discover under what conditions a practical principle may be universally obligatory upon us, we shall find that it ought to imply no object or matter as a mobile of the will. Indeed,

U

given the faculties we possess, there are none other than empirical objects as far as we are concerned, the only matter at our disposal in the practical order of things is pleasure or the satisfaction of the love of self ; and pleasure cannot supply a universal, obligatory principle. The intention of our will, alone, depends entirely on ourselves and fulfils the requisite conditions. Law, then, is a purely formal principle which implies nothing else than itself and a will free to accomplish it. It has its root in the autonomy of the will.

But even in this, is it not illusory? Detached from things and referred to the subject, is it not purely subjective? Can we escape from idealism in the practical, as we have done in the theoretical order of things?

To deduce the moral law from the conditions of experience is impossible, since every object of experience ought to be separated from moral determination ; but, on the other hand, the moral law itself establishes a deduction from freedom. If I ought to, it is because I can. Moreover, if speculative reason has had to be debarred from knowing freedom, it has none the less regarded it as possible, even theoretically ; and thus the moral law has a basis in the reality of things, as this reality is theoretically known to us, viz. in that region of existence to which the knowledge of things as phenomena refers us. If the moral law is the *ratio cognoscendi* of freedom, the latter supplies the former with its *ratio essendi*.

So far, however, we have only reached a principle, a formal law. Now, morality also offers us concepts, the two principal of which are those of good and evil. Can we search into and understand these concepts? After eliminating all empirical matter, we have to deduce fresh matter from a principal posited as purely formal.

The course we must take is apparently paradoxical.
Is it not duty that is deduced from good, and not good
that is determined by duty? The ancients, in their
search after the sovereign good, constantly followed the
first, the dogmatic course. Now, willingly or unwillingly,
it came about that they founded morals on empirical
data. It could not be otherwise. From good, one
cannot deduce duty, unless this good is already moral
good, and it is only moral if there has previously been
instilled into it the very duty it is desired to deduce
therefrom. On the other hand, it is possible, by means
of duty, to determine good; it is possible for law
posited as primary, to find a suitable object in the
sensible world itself, the only one we can affect. For
this sensible world not only does not clash with the
universality characterising the moral law, but is itself
subject to universal laws. Good, therefore, is the realisation in the sensible world of a form of universality
capable of being the symbol of practical reason.

This doctrine of Kant's rejects mysticism as well as
empiricism. Though the principle of determination
ought to be obtained from the world of noumena, it is
in the world of phenomena that morality will be realised
and practised. And the very principle of determination will not remain unrelated to nature. There exists
a feeling which is within nature and which likewise
goes beyond it, and that is respect, a special affection
aroused by the idea of law in a soul endowed both with
sensible tendencies and with reason. Respect is the
moral mobile. The inclination it enshrouds, and which
comes from the will, does no harm to the disinterested
practice of duty.

And so the given morality is explained and defined
in all its elements: mobiles, concepts, and principles.

Here, too, we had only to go back from experience to its conditions, in order to explain whatever is absolute in our knowledge, without detracting from the general principle of modern science and philosophy.

And not only does criticism thus insure the foundations of morals, it also discloses the spring and reason of religious beliefs from the very point to which this investigation has brought it. Reason requires the full performance of duty, it exacts the union of virtue with happiness. How can such an object be realised ?

The necessity of answering this question leads us on to theoretical propositions that cannot be demonstrated as such, but are inseparably bound to practical truths of an absolute character. These propositions Kant calls *postulates*. They are three in number :

1. Freedom : necessary in order that man may determine himself, apart from all sensible attraction, in accordance with the laws of a purely intelligible world. Doubtless, freedom does not intervene in the course of phenomena, which would cease to be objects of possible experience if the law of cause and effect were violated in them. It is complete and entire, however, in the world of noumena, in which it establishes personality and creates within each of us an intelligible character, of which our empirical character is the symbol.

2. Immortality : necessary in order that indefinite progress may be realised, without which the perfect adaptation of our will to the moral law is inconceivable.

3. God : necessary in order that we may establish that agreement which reason demands, between morality and happiness, and the principle of which is contained in neither the one nor the other.

Thus, morality leads to religion, not as to some theoretical science explaining the nature of things, but rather as to the knowledge of our duties in so far as they are divine commands.

And so criticism, continuing its progress, gradually re-establishes all the suprasensible existences it had overthrown. Is it self-contradictory in doing this? By no means ; since it no longer regards these existences in the same manner. The criticism of pure reason has demonstrated that such objects cannot be known theoretically, *i.e.* by the aid of intuitions which determine them. This result subsists. The criticism of pure reason, however, did not prevent our conceiving of objects above experience, on the contrary it allowed and invited this. On the other hand, the criticism of practical reason in no way shows us the world shut out from us by the criticism of pure reason, it does not give us an intuition thereof, but offers us, as connected with the existence of duty, the objects on which theoretical reason could not declare itself. It brings us to say, not : It is certain there is a God and immortality ; but rather : I will there to be a God, I will my being, in one aspect, to be free and immortal. That is not a matter of science, it is a practical, pure, and rational belief. We can neither see the object nor deduce it from what we see ; we can only conceive of it. How fortunate this inability ! For were we in possession of the missing faculty, instead of duty tempering and ennobling our will, God and eternity, with all their awful majesty, would ever be before our eyes, and would reduce us, through fear, to the condition of marionettes, making the proper movements but devoid of life or moral worth. " The mysterious wisdom by which we exist is no less admirable in the gifts it has refused than in those it has granted to us " (*Critique of Practical Reason*, Part i. Book ii. Chapter ix.).

Criticism has explained the existence of science and morals. To complete the different orders of our knowledge, it remains for us to examine the notions of taste and finality. Will experience be able to supply us with their principle and their limits ?

The experimental datum here considered is judgment ; not determining judgment, which proceeds from the general to the particular, but reflecting judgment, which rises from the particular to the general. This judgment is that which affirms the existence in nature, not only of laws in general, but of certain determinate laws. It calls for a special principle which can be only the following : just as the universal laws of nature are based in our understanding, which prescribes them to nature, so, as regards empirical and particular laws, everything takes place as though they also had been dictated by an understanding that purposed to make intelligible and objective the very details of the phenomena. This reason of particular laws may be sought for, either in the agreement of things with our faculty of knowing, *i.e.* in the beautiful, or in the agreement of things with themselves, *i.e.* in finality.

Appreciation of the beautiful cannot be explained by sensation alone, as Burke would have it. The beautiful is not the agreeable ; it is disinterested, the object of a real judgment. Nor is it explained by reason alone, according to Baumgarten the Wolfian. The beautiful is not the perfect : it dwells only in the form, not in the matter, of the object, and it pleases without aiming at pleasing but solely by reason of its harmony, by a kind of endless finality : in a word, it has something of feeling in its nature. Formed *a priori* and being subjective at the same time, what is the origin of the judgment of taste ?

It can only be explained as the working of an aesthetic common sense, or the faculty of perceiving some agreement between our sensible faculty of knowing and our intellectual faculty. Those objects are beautiful, before which our imagination finds itself, of its own accord, satisfying our understanding. The beautiful is the feeling that our faculties are at play, somewhat analogous to a physical pastime, wherein the spontaneous observance of a rule freely laid down in no way trammels the free expression of activity. Consequently, the beautiful dwells only within ourselves ; it has no other origin or rule than the special sense in which sensibility and understanding meet each other.

From the beautiful, properly so called, that we are now analysing, we must distinguish the sublime, as being another species of the same genus. Whereas the beautiful object is the adequate sensible realisation of the idea, the sublime object utterly routs the imagination, which spends itself in vain attempts to represent an idea transcending it. There are no images, but only symbols, of the infinite. The substratum of the sublime and the beautiful alike can therefore be nothing else than our suprasensible nature, and the need of agreement between that nature and our sensible nature.

But then does not this analysis result in the judgment of taste being denied all objective value ? Such would be the case, had the objectivity of the beautiful to consist, in our mind, of some property of things in themselves : such an objectivity, however, is an illusion. The sense of taste that we have found, has an objective import, in so far as it alone makes intelligible the characteristic of beauty that we attribute to objects, and in so far as this very sense should be considered identical in all beings capable of sensibility and discursive understanding.   The universality of the faculty is sufficient to establish the objectivity of the operation.

But if we now consider things of taste, especially art, whose existence is given, our doctrine will supply the theory thereof.   Art is a product of intelligence, and ought to appear a product of nature ; it has an object and ought to seem not to have one ; it punctually observes rules and does this without manifesting effort. All these characteristics are explained as soon as man possesses a faculty wherein the understanding, which thinks and rules, coincides with the imagination, which sees, feels, and invents.   The spring of genius is discovered in the general essence of man.   And it is also seen that the more human the object of an art, the more sublime that art is.

Moreover, the ideality of the beautiful is the only doctrine that enables us to solve the antinomy to which the judgment of taste gives rise.   We discuss about the beautiful, and yet we cannot account for it by demonstration.   This would be incomprehensible, did the beautiful belong to things in themselves.   But then, on the other hand, the beautiful could not, like time and space, be enclosed within the sensible world.   We discuss about the beautiful and yet we cannot demonstrate anything, because the judgment of taste is based on a principle connected both with concept and intuition, on an indeterminate concept : that of a suprasensible substratum of phenomena.   The beautiful is the symbol of moral good, and it is towards this good that taste dimly leads us.

The second principle of particular natural laws is derived from finality.   Do there really exist in nature harmonies that cannot be explained by mechanism or the system of causes and effects ?

Wherever finality is only exterior, consisting only in the utility of one being with reference to another, the mechanical explanation is sufficient, for this agreement of different beings with one another is far from being the rule in nature. But there is one case in which finality, being internal, cannot be explained by the hazards of mechanism: the case of organised beings. That which is living produces itself, both as species and individual, and the parts thereof are conditioned by ·the very *ensemble* which is to result therefrom. The effect here is the cause of its cause ; the cause is the effect of its effect. Such a relation goes beyond mechanism, such a being is an end, as well as a product of nature. How is that possible ?

In vain does dogmatism attempt to reply either by hylozoism, which looks upon nature as intelligent, or by theism, which weaves the action of intelligence into the tissue of phenomena : the former attributes to matter qualities opposed to its essence ; the latter vainly claims to pierce the designs of God. Organisation, the internal finality, is not cognisable in its cause. Finality, to us, can be nothing but ideal : it is our way of looking upon a certain class of phenomena.

Is such a doctrine a purely negative result? By no means.

Some knowledge of nature is implied if we simply know that, in certain of its products, nature cannot be known by us. This principle is instructive, either in its restrictive or its positive bearing. It is regulative, not constitutive. In this capacity it serves science. Though it does not make the production of things more intelligible, all the same, it supplies anticipations by which we are enabled to discover the particular laws of nature. It sets up beacon-lights throughout infinity.

So far as metaphysics is concerned, only such a conception of finality enables one to escape from the traditional antinomy of mechanism and teleology. On the ground of being in itself, wherein both systems are placed, neither the first is able to explain what it calls the illusion of finality, nor the second to prove that the transcendent explanation of it is necessary. On the other hand, the principle of final causes becomes unassailable when there is only one point of view upon things.

And it opens up to our conception, if not to our knowledge, a perspective upon the absolute itself. Indeed, how do we come to posit the idea of an end as the cause of a phenomenon? The impossibility of deducing the particular from the universal comes from the fact that understanding and intuition are separate in us ; our concepts are void, our intuitions powerless to connect themselves into laws. Then how can we affirm the existence of particular laws? The problem is solved as follows. We can conceive that the difficulty in our way would be non-existent to a mind in which understanding were one with sensibility : to an intuitive understanding. Such a mind, instead of proceeding from the parts to the whole, as does our discursive understanding, and, consequently, seeing a contingent result in the whole, would proceed from the whole to the parts, and, in a flash, would see the latter in their necessary connection. To this mind, mechanism and finality would coincide. Now, once the idea of such an intelligence is conceived of, our understanding, in order to approach it in its own way, substitutes for the whole the idea of the whole, and posits this idea before its intuitions as the cause of the special relations that unite them. To the employment of the notion of an end is thus linked on the conception of an intuitive understanding, as a possible foundation, in the absolute, of the sum total of the harmonies of nature.

This deduction from teleological judgment determines the use we ought to make of it.

As regards the explanation of the phenomena of nature, we have the right, as far as possible, to assume the mechanical point of view, but we cannot do this on all occasions with like success. In the fact of life we are brought in opposition against an invincible barrier. We cannot picture to ourselves living bodies as capable of coming from inorganic matter. Doubtless, it is not inconceivable that from one common, originally organised, matter, all living bodies might have issued by purely mechanical changes. In this way, the explanation of things would be the province of mechanism; their origin, that of teleology. Indeed, the comparison of organic forms enables us to conjecture the relationship of all that lives, and encourages us to hope, however feebly, that it will be possible to refer them to one common origin. Then one could picture to oneself the womb of the earth as giving birth, first to creatures ill-suited to the conditions of their existence, and then to these same creatures as becoming more perfect, generation after generation, until finally the creatress, in a state of congealed ossification, so to speak, limited her productions to a certain number of clearly defined and henceforth immutable species. This is a brilliant hypothesis of reason, but apart from the fact that so far experience does not seem to warrant it, instead of excluding, it would imply as a condition of its consistency the primordial life of the universal womb.

As regards the general conception of the world, we have the right to complete by thought the unification to which teleological concepts tend, provided we place this ultimate end outside the sphere of sensible phenomena. And as this end can be only a being that has within itself the object of its activity, and consequently, is capable of positing ends and using nature as a means, man alone, not as a part of nature, but as intelligence and will, can be the end of the universe. We must not, like Rousseau, expect nature to satisfy our longings, to give us happiness ; that is out of her province, and she will play us false. But she will not belie the expectations of the man who, through her, endeavours to realise moral good.

Finally, in the matter of our conception of God as the principle of finality, it has not been without purpose that men, at all times, have been influenced by the argument of final causes. This argument well expresses man's impression when he sees the order of nature : the aspiration towards something that goes beyond nature. We must always speak of this argument with respect, for it is the most persuasive, popular, and potent one of all. To be really solid and sound, however, the argument must be understood in its true meaning. Not as an architect is God revealed to us by the world, but rather as the condition of an agreement between nature and morality. In trying to discover the attributes needed to play this part, we shape for ourselves a moral theology which leads us on to a moral religion.

IV.—The Metaphysical Doctrine

Criticism is not the abolition of metaphysics, it is the introduction to metaphysics as a science. In realising the plan it here marks out, the method to be followed is the one inaugurated by the famous Wolf. We know that

transcendental logic does not break through the framework of general logic : it fills it in. We shall find metaphysics changing its meaning without changing its form.

Human reason is legislative in two ways : by its
understanding, in the domain of nature ; and by its
will, in the domain of freedom. Hence the idea of a
double metaphysics : of nature and of morals. There
are no others.

Kant deals first with the metaphysics of the science
of nature.

Corporeal matter, being alone lasting, can alone give
rise to metaphysics. The latter seeks amongst the
sensible data or properties of matter, for some object
to which the synthetic laws of understanding are
applicable, and this it finds in motion. Once this
single result has been obtained from experience, metaphysics pursues its course, proceeding *a priori*.

Determined solely by the notion of quantity, motion
is nothing but dimension in time and space : it does not
yet imply cause of production or of modification. In
this connection it gives rise to *phoronomics*, which we
now call kinematics.

Determined, besides, by the notion of quality, it
envelops an intensive dimension or force, as the cause
of its existence and of our sensible affections. The
theory of force *is dynamics :* the essential element in
this portion of Kantian metaphysics. We admit as
many simple forces as it is necessary to posit, in order
to distinguish movements in a straight line, consequently we admit a force of repulsion and one of
attraction. From the first, there results divisibility
ad infinitum ; from the second, a limitation of the first.
These two forces are solidary : solidity, which the

Newtonians found themselves compelled to add on to attraction, unless it be an occult quality, implies a repulsive force. Matter results from the equilibrium of the two.

Determined by the notion of relation, matter assumes properties which are investigated by *mechanics*, properly so called. Here, Kant establishes the law of the persistence of material substance, the law of inertia and that of action and reaction.

Finally, regarding modality, we have to find out the rules followed by the mind when distinguishing possible, real, or necessary motion : this is *phenomenology*. Rectilinear motion is only possible, it appertains to phoronomics ; curvilinear motion is real, and appertains to dynamics ; motion conceived of as communicated by a mover to something movable is of necessity determined as regards existence and speed ; it appertains to mechanics.

From these metaphysical principles Kant endeavoured to pass on to physics itself. Physics would evidently be constituted as a science, if only we could determine *a priori* the forces that produce sensation. Now, we see from the *Critique* that these forces, being bound to the life of the mind, must, after all, be of the same nature as the mind. They can be nothing else than the action exerted upon our empirical I by our spontaneity, *i.e.* our understanding. And it is because this action is transcendental that, in our endeavours to picture to ourselves the cause of our sensations, we imagine things outside of ourselves in space. Henceforth, the principle of the deduction of material species is in our hands : it is none other than the principle of the functions of the subject itself. It is in this way that Kant, by the light of the cate-

gories, undertakes the deduction of the different kinds
of forces, of first matter or ether, of bases or specific
matters. In all probability, he would have reached a
rational deduction of the system of the world itself,
such as Newton had constituted it.

The second and last part of metaphysics is the
metaphysics of morals.

In the moral as in the physical order of things, it is
the task of method to bring the given empirical conditions under the laws of reason, and thence deduce the
complete system of fundamental laws. Moral legislation has a double object in view : action and its mobile.
Harmony of action with the law is *legality*, that of the
mobile is *morality*. This distinction results in the
division of the metaphysics of morals into the theory of
right and the theory of virtue.

Right consists of the whole of those conditions that
are universally required in order that the free-will of
each individual may be reconciled with that of the rest.
External free-will commands respect, because it is the
form of moral freedom, the latter being realised only
by action and action implying a connection with something external. Consequently the science of right is
distinct from, though dependent on, morals.

There are two essential principles that control the
development of the theory of right : 1st, right is altogether based on the suprasensible nature of man so far
as it is manifested in time, *i.e.* on personal dignity ;
2nd, legal restraint is legitimate, so far as it is necessary for suppressing the obstacles that one will may
arbitrarily set up against the development of the rest.
The consequences of these principles are as follows :—

So far as *private right* is concerned, there belongs of
necessity to each man such a portion of freedom as is

compatible with the freedom of the rest of mankind. But here we can deal only with freedom regarded in its external existence. This external expression of freedom is what is called *possession*.

There are as many kinds of rights as there are of possessions.

The first has reference to things, and gives rise to *real right*. This right is not a relation between the owner and the thing, it is rather one between persons. How can its realisation be legitimate ? On the one hand, possession in common is the primitive right ; on the other, the given fact is individual property. Here we should have an insoluble antinomy, if possession in common were regarded as a fact that has existed historically. It is not a fact, however, it is the command of reason. Consequently, the actual fact does not go against a previous realisation of justice. Till further orders, it is the only effective realisation of the principle that attributes things to persons. None the less should it be sanctioned by a contract between wills for it to become juridical ; all appropriation, in the state of nature, is only provisional.

The second kind of possession refers to the actions of persons, and creates *personal right*. This is realised by contract, the value of which lies in the stability and simultaneity of suprasensible wills.

The third kind of possession refers to persons themselves and creates *real personal right*. Its domain is the family. How can a person become a thing ? Here we should have an intolerable contradiction, if the owner of the person did not restore that person's dignity, by also giving himself, re-establishing by an act of freedom the moral order which is threatened by nature. Thus, marriage is the only legitimate relationship between the sexes, for it alone safeguards the dignity of the woman.

As regards *public* or *civil right*, Kant lays it down as a principle that, since the natural state of mankind is war, it is necessary to constitute a civil society in order to make possible a *régime* of right. The laws that create such a *régime* are divided into *political right, the right of nations and cosmopolitical right.*

Political right rests exclusively on the idea of justice. Sovereignty originally belongs to the people ; the State can only be the result of a contract, by which men give up their natural freedom, to recover it intact under a legal *régime*. But this contract is not an historical fact, it is an idea of reason : this is the point of view that both citizens and legislator must adopt, in the performance of their respective tasks. Consequently power must be obeyed without inquiring into its origin. However vicious a social form may be, it is not a falling away from a primordial state of justice : it is the degree of reality that the idea of right has been able to reach in the world of time. To amend it by reform is legitimate, but not to overthrow it by revolution.

If such is its principle, the State has, for its mission, to guarantee the natural rights of man. It will trouble itself about morals only in so far as they interest public order. It will respect religious beliefs, but will resist political influence on the part of the Churches. It has the right to abolish all privileges which are only facts devoid of rational foundation.

The realisation of the idea of the State requires the division of power into legislative, executive and judicial power. The most important of these is the legislative, which ought to be the full complete expression of the collective will. Government is more or less despotic in proportion as it departs from the representative system. The republic, an ideal, rational form, is a government that is representative in its three powers. In practice, Kant, as became a loyal subject of Frederick II., recognises an autocratic *régime*, wherein power, thanks to the generosity of the prince, is in conformity with the philosophical principles of right.

Ever relying on the idea of justice, Kant regards penal right as based not on utility but on reward ; he defends the death penalty against the sentimentality of Beccaria.

The right of nations extends to States—with certain modifications—the relations which public right sets up between individuals. Their original condition is war,— not a *régime* of right. In order that juridical relations may be established between them, they must form and maintain, in accordance with an original contract, an alliance or federation, by which they undertake not to intervene in internal discords, and also to unite for mutual protection against external attacks.

Finally, cosmopolitical right insures for each man the power to enter into communication with all. Nations should allow foreigners access to their territories. Colonisation is a right ; all the same, it should not violate any acquired right : injustice is not permitted, even with the object of extending the domain of justice.

Right comes indefinitely near to morals, without being able to attain to it. It requires that it be possible for the rule of our external actions to be set up as a universal law : morals puts forward the same demand as concerns the maxim itself, the internal principle of our actions. Thus, the duties of virtue differ from those of right, both in their object,—for they determine the intention, not the act, whereas the duties of right determine the act and not the intention ; this is expressed by saying that the latter are strict and the former accommodating ;—and in their motive, for the subject imposes them upon himself, whereas duties of right are imposed by external compulsion.

What are the ends that are, at the same time, duties ? There can only be two : one's own perfection, and the happiness of others. I ought to aim after my own perfection, not happiness : whereas, I ought to aim after the happiness, not the perfection of others. As a matter of fact I can neither make myself happy, nor can I work out the will of others ; whereas the determination of my will does concern me, as also the condition of the rest of mankind.

The detailed list of duties will comprise nothing referring to family or State. Kant sees in these communities only juridical relationships, so he has already said all he wished about them, in the theory of right. Morals will be essentially individual and social.

We have duties only towards ourselves and other men, not towards God or the animal world. For we can be under obligation only towards persons who are objects of experience to us : and one or the other of these two conditions falls through, in the case of beings superior or inferior to ourselves.

Respect for human dignity, in oneself and in others, is the one preëminent duty. This duty admits neither of conditions nor of temperament : it is absolute and immutable. Love of one's neighbour, and benevolent feelings in general, can become duties only in so far as we are dealing with active benevolence, not with the sympathy of complaisance or pathological love.

From these principles proceed such maxims as the following :—Allow no one with impunity to trample your right under foot. Never incur a debt, without giving security. Lying, whether to others, or more especially to oneself, is moral suicide. Meanness is unworthy of man ; he who crawls like a worm cannot complain if he is trampled upon. The violation of the duty of love is only a sin, that of the duties of respect is a vice ; for in the latter case man is insulted, in the former he is not. Moral gymnastics is not mortification, it is the will practising to overcome one's inclinations so as not to be hindered by them, and joyfully exulting in its regained freedom.

Naturally following on the metaphysics of morals, comes religion, not as implied, but as demanded by morality. Religion consists in looking upon moral laws as though they were divine commandments. It cannot increase our knowledge either of God or of nature ; it ought not to aim at this. Its sole object is to extend the ascendency of the moral law over the will.

Thus understood, it is in conformity with and sanctioned by reason. But the positive religions add on to the moral postulates and the law, traditional and statutory elements : it is important for us to find out how far this addition can be justified by reason.

If we examine the Christian religion : an excellent form of religion, we find four essential ideas in it : that of original sin, that of Christ, that of the Church, and that of worship. What value have these ideas?

In the dogma of original sin lies concealed a philosophic truth. There are two characters in each of us: the empirical and the intelligible. The vices of the one, whilst attesting an innate tendency towards evil, indicate a radical failing in the other. This failing consists in reversing the order which ought to regulate the relations between sensibility and reason ; in placing the latter at the service of the former. Morality, to the one who has been guilty of this failing, cannot from that time be anything else than conversion, a new birth, as it is called in Christian theology. In this sense, dogma is justified.

The idea of Christ, too, is accepted by criticism, if by Christ we mean the ideal of the human person. This ideal descends from heaven to earth, not historic-ally, of course, but in the sense that, whilst belonging to the intelligible, it is manifested in the sensible world. This ideal redeems us, for whereas punishment affected the guilty man, it is the man who is converted by the conception of the ideal, the new man, who suffers and struggles in order to free the former man from evil. The good man takes upon himself the sins of the wicked, and stands in his place before the judge.

The Church, also, is recognised by reason, so far as it is an association whose members mutually fortify themselves in the practice of duty, both by example and by the declaration of a common moral conviction. In itself, it is one, like rational faith, but human weak-ness demands that there be added to this faith, in order to make it sensible, various historical dogmas that claim a divine origin. Hence, a multiplicity of churches, and antagonism between heretics and ortho-dox. The history of the Church consists entirely of the struggle between rational and positive faith ; and the goal to which it is advancing is the effacement of the latter by the former.

Finally, worship itself is a rational matter, provided it be assigned a place in moral intention and in the realisation of that intention. All that man thinks he can add on to virtue in order to honour God is but false worship and vain observance. The consequence of the illusory value attributed to this false worship is the subordination of the laity to the Church, and all the evils to which this subordination gives rise, such as hypocrisy and fanaticism. The positive faith the Church enjoins has, for its true object, to make itself superfluous. This faith has in the past been necessary as a vehicle ; it remains useful until mankind comes of age. Once this time arrives, however, the leading strings of tradition become mere fetters. The very ecclesiastic who, as a minister of religion, is bound down to symbols, as a scholar has the right to examine dogmas : to decree the unchangeableness of statutory faith would be an outrage on human nature.

V.—APPLICATIONS OF THE METAPHYSICAL DOCTRINE

It is Kant's constant preoccupation to unite concrete reality to practice. His principles, obtained by metaphysical analysis from the given itself, ought rationally to reconstitute and govern the given. In the material order of things, he sought the transition from metaphysics to physics ; so also in the moral order he again descends from idea to action.

In this connection, the history of mankind is his principal theme. He purposes deducing its main phases, not describing them. Here, too, he makes a distinction between the natural and the moral history of man ; the latter having its beginning in the former.

On the subject of natural history, Kant deals with the question of races. Is there a distinction amongst the human races, of such a kind that one of them should have the right to claim for itself alone the dignity of manhood and reduce the rest to a state of slavery ? The question is answered by a consideration of origins. Fecundation is possible between human beings of all races ; consequently they have one identical origin and form only one species. Races are stable varieties ; unalterable by intermixture and transplantation. They have become differentiated by adapting themselves to climatic conditions. As there are four climates, so there are four races : the white, the yellow, the black and the red. In the formation of these races, external causes have played an indispensable *rôle*, but these alone could not have brought about stable changes ; they merely developed the internal dispositions of the species. The real cause of the existence of races, is man's capacity for adapting himself to external conditions.

In answer to the attacks of Forster, who would explain life by none but geological causes, Kant, from the year 1788 onwards, affirmed the necessity of a special, immaterial principle as alone conforming to the requirements of criticism. To attribute to matter a power of organisation which observation could not find in it, is to reject the guiding clue of experience. Doubtless Forster's explanation is neither absurd nor impossible, but it goes beyond our means of knowing. The only finality we can grasp is in ourselves, in our conscious activity ; nothing authorises us to admit that an unconscious thing has the power of acting with a view to an end. We do not know what causes life, but we explain it by finality : this is the point of view taken by criticism.

Whereas the natural history of man goes back to his origin, moral history considers his end. The philosophy of history finds its principle in the idea of this end, as natural philosophy does in the idea of attraction. Now, the development of reason, the essence of man, cannot tend to anything else than the establishment of a *régime* of freedom, *i.e.* to the realisation of justice. Consequently the historian ought to find in facts the various phases of the realisation of justice.

History begins when man becomes a moral being, *i.e.* when he acts by will instead of by instinct. His primitive state was one of innocence ; his abode, paradise. He formed one with nature, wherein his will was buried. The awakening of his will showed itself by a desire for rule, an act of pride, rebellion against the nature to which he was united. Original sin is freedom's first step. From that time, a new life begins for man. In order to dominate nature, he must work. From work there arise discord, society, property, civil inequality : civilisation has succeeded a state of nature. What does this new condition stand for ? Had human activity no other end than individual happiness, then Rousseau would be quite right in longing for a return to the paradise of innocence. But what man wills is to be free, and effective freedom can be found only in the disinterested agreement of wills, on the ground of reason. Now, civilisation, the conflict of wills, is the necessary antecedent of their reconciliation. The reign of justice, the source of moral harmony, is the third phase of universal history.

In the realisation of this progress of freedom, the will is not left to itself. It is aided by nature ; consequently, progress is constant and has the character of a natural law. A law beneficent and necessary, for were man to believe that his works perish wholly with himself how could he keep alive an earnest desire to work for the good of mankind ? Nature stirs up man to quit nature ; she stimulates his freedom. She is an artist, a providence, capable of bringing forth good out of evil. She makes men selfish and violent, and violence engenders war ; but war calls a judicial *régime* into existence. She separates men through differences in constitution, language and religion ; but these differences render universal domination impossible. Whilst evil succumbs, sooner or later, to the contradiction within itself ; good, which reason substitutes therefor, when once established, continues and increases, because it is in harmony with itself. For logic is the one supreme force. At first, man wills union, and believes himself wise ; but nature knows better what is suitable for him, she wills a state of war.

The first object of this collaboration between nature and will, is the establishment of the rational State, a combination of freedom and legality. The second object is the establishment of an Amphictyonic council of nations, ensuring the maintenance of peace. Without such an institution, mankind cannot advance to its goal. War is a return to a state of nature. In the ideal of reason is implied the idea of eternal peace. If this object is unrealisable, then Rousseau is right in advocating a return to a savage state. Better barbarism than culture without morality.

But is not this a purely theoretical conception ? Will real humanity accept such views ? Has not Hobbes shown that the real man is influenced only by interests, not by ideas ? Such a doctrine must be utterly rejected ; the belief must not gain ground that what is good in theory can ever be impossible or evil in practice. What, indeed, is not practical is that unlimited power Hobbes confers on sovereigns, and the rebellion he admits of in subjects.   Interests, certainly, in the State, should have a place of their own, but does it follow that principles should be excluded ?   Can one not be both as wise as the serpent and as harmless as the dove ?   To the man who guards against both idealism and empiricism, the real and the ideal, instead of excluding, include each other, and politics ceases to be incompatible with morals.   There is a practical means of bringing the former into harmony with the latter : publicity.   Whosoever thinks he can be useful to his country ought to seek publicity.   Now, only what is in conformity with justice can bear publicity.   Here as elsewhere, universality is the point of contact between the real and the rational, the form and token of truth.

According to this theory, what is the present phase of the history of the human species?   It is the phase of enlightenment (*Aufklärung*), and its characteristic is the emancipation of the intelligence.   Man, reflecting upon himself, finds that there is a contradiction between his reasonable nature and his position as a minor : he makes an effort to liberate his reason.   *Sapere aude* is his motto.

The progress of enlightenment cannot be realised by overthrowing political institutions, by revolution, which has no other result than the substitution of new for old prejudices.   Personal reflection alone can truly enlighten a man.   Consequently freedom to think and make known his thoughts is the condition of the progress of enlightenment.

How can this freedom be reconciled with the rights of the State ?   Here, a distinction must be made between man as a citizen of a limited community, and man as a citizen of the whole world.   In his dealings with the members of his community, man is bound to submit to the statutes by which it is governed ; but as a citizen of the world, he is free. As such a person, indeed, he speaks from the summit of reason, for the generality of reasonable beings, whereas as a citizen of a State, he limits his action to some particular place and time. Only by identifying itself with the universal does the will attain to freedom. Therefore each citizen will unresistingly pay taxes, though retaining the right to dispute such payment. The teacher, as an official, will respect such symbols as are recognised in his own country ; but as a scholar, he will have the right to criticise all doctrines. In accordance with these principles, the rights both of legislators and of citizens are clearly defined.

And so, fully maintaining the harmony of nature and of freedom in the moral history of man, Kant guards against asserting that progress is a mere development of natural powers. To his mind, the Leibnitzian theory of Herder is radically erroneous. In nature dwells the means ; but the end, which is the spring of progress, can come only from moral reason, superior to nature. This is why the moral ideal can never be expressed by the individual as such ; it cannot be represented except in the whole of mankind. True history is, of necessity, universal. Certainly, the individual is a reality, but in the whole, there is something that goes beyond it, and only by union with the whole can it attain to freedom.

Not content with expounding his general views as to the ends of human activity, Kant, in some things, deals with practice proper. We here refer to his ideas on education and university instruction.

It is impossible for education, in its present state, to satisfy him. It neglects the will, drills and over-burdens the mind instead of moulding it for reflection. Here a radical reform is necessary. The pedagogic theories of Rousseau, the practical attempts of Basedow come just at the right time to support his criticism. He is passionately in favour of these innovators, and demands the organization of elementary schools as the indispensable condition of reform. But he remains himself, even on this ground, subordinating all authoritative direction to moral ends.

The body, he tells us, ought to be hardened and exercised, subjected to such discipline as will make it the powerful and obedient auxiliary of the mind. Let the child grow up in perfect freedom, but at the same time teach him to moderate his movements : one cannot accustom oneself too early to live according to rule.

As regards the intellect, a sane education awakens and guides the mental faculties instead of loading the memory with facts. There are two exercises of the faculties : the one, which is free, is play ; the other, which is imposed from without, is work. The latter is obligatory in itself, and, in instruction, it could not be replaced by the former. The faculty of intuition should be formed before the understanding. Thus, all instruction will at first be intuitive, representative, technical. A beginning may be made with geography. So far as it has the cultivation of the understanding for its object, instruction will be Socratic and catechetical. It will go to the root of things, and make the pupil really master of his knowledge. A robust intellect is the condition of a will that is free.

Paedagogics has the formation of the moral personality as its end. Here education is needed, for virtue is not innate. This education comprises moral instruction and its corresponding practice.

Moral instruction is catechetical. Aiming at demonstrating obligatory laws, it proceeds by principles, not examples : if examples come in, that is only in order to prove the principles to be really applicable. Kant left in writing a fragment of moral catechism, wherein the pupil, prompted by questions, discovers for himself moral conceptions of life.

Practice, or moral ascetics, cannot create morality, which must come from ourselves ; it does, however, produce in man the disposition that favours morality. It aims at a hardening process, for effeminacy or indolence is opposed to virtue. Instead of destroying the will, it strengthens it. It makes us masters of ourselves, contented and happy. Moral education tends to develop the inner aversion to evil, self-esteem and dignity, the domination of reason over the senses. It does not reward, but it punishes. It never humiliates, lest it make the child despise himself, except when he has been guilty of that one fault which effectively degrades mankind, to wit: falsehood. In all things it puts forward the moral motive, the law of duty itself, certain that this motive, when set forth in all its purity, will be more powerful than any material stimulus, any assurance of benefit or harm.

With paedagogics we may compare the question of university instruction. On this point, too, the *Critique* throws fresh light. A University consists of four Faculties : Theology, Law, Medicine, the so-called superior Faculties, and Philosophy, the so-called inferior Faculty. Between the first three and the fourth, conflict naturally arises. The object of the latter, indeed, does not differ from those of the former, but the one studies from a universal and theoretical point of view what the others study from a special and immediately practical one. This gives rise to jealousy and rivalry. Each of the two sides, claiming the whole realm of knowledge, repels the other as a usurper. The title of superior, borne by the first three Faculties, is nothing less than the superiority that tradition attributes to the positive over the rational. Is this hierarchy justified ?

The conflict between theologians and philosophers is based upon the use to be made of the holy Scriptures. The *Critique* does not deny the legitimacy and utility of the sensible vehicle of religious truth ; but it claims for reason the right to distinguish, in the Scriptures, between the moral and eternal substratum, and the sensible outer form, made up of narratives and contingent circumstances. To understand the Scriptures is to interpret them in a moral sense. Theology presupposes this mode of interpretation, and so cannot condemn it. How, indeed, does it distinguish true from false revelation, except by the rational idea of God. How can it maintain the divine character of consecrated texts, in detail, except by making frequent use of an allegorical, moral interpretation?

The conflict between philosophers and jurisconsults is based on respect for law : the *Critique* shows that legality has a good foundation, consequently it condemns the revolutionary spirit. But, in addition, it claims the right to examine existing laws. And who can refuse it this right? Jurisconsults, in order to attain to their practical ends, need to know whether mankind is going backwards or forwards, or remaining stationary. Now, this is a question that cannot be solved empirically : it concerns reason. And reason answers it by postulating

indefinite progress in the name of the moral law. But
what if the commandment is only an idea incapable of
realisation! Experience, under the guidance of reason,
removes the doubt. Beneath our very eyes, we can see
where reason and history coincide. There is one fact
which is at the same time an idea. This fact is the
French Revolution. Whatever comes of this enter-
prise, writes Kant in 1798, whether it succeeds or fails,
it stirs up a sympathy that is akin to enthusiasm in all
who witness it by reason of the object it has in view :
now, a purely moral ideal is alone capable of affecting
the soul of man in this way. The Revolution is the
effort of man to create a rational State, it is the
eternal entering into time. Such a phenomenon, once
witnessed, can never be forgotten.

The problem for philosophers and doctors to
solve, is whether the art of healing depends on
experience alone, or whether reason has any share in it.
Now, the *Critique* demonstrates that reason may be
will, and that will bears some relation to phenomena.
Reason, then, must also possess a healing virtue. And,
indeed, man can do a great deal in modifying his
physical condition by the sole exercise of his will.
Here, Kant relates his personal experience : by moral
force, he is able to keep himself free from hypochondria,
and even to master spasmodic states. Once the disease
has entered, the will may be unequal to the task before
it, but at all events it can do much to prevent it, and
keep the body in a state of health. The will is the
first condition of health. Far from reason ever being
the servant of experience, it is the latter that, under all
circumstances, borrows from the former its truth and
possibility.

VI.—Kant's Influence

The Kantian philosophy had difficulty in making a way for itself in the field of thought already occupied by the Leibnitzo-Wolfian, the English, French and popular philosophies, without counting the increasingly flourishing positive sciences. Kant did not deceive himself as to the strange novelty of his work, which met with its first favourable reception at Iéna, thence spreading by degrees all over Germany and finally throughout the world. Not only was metaphysical speculation renewed, as it were, thereby : most of the departments of intellectual activity felt its influence.

In Germany, the history of Kantianism forms an important element in the general history of ideas and sciences.

Amongst its first opponents may be cited : Selle and Weishaupt, followers of Locke ; Feder, Garve and Tiedemann, electics ; Platner, Mendelssohn, Nicolai and Meiners, representatives of popular philosophy ; Ernst Schulze, the skeptic ; Jacobi, the philosopher of belief, and along with him, Hamann ; Herder, who reconciled nature with history. The main reproach these philosophers bring against Kant is that the affection or action of things on sensibility, implied by his system, is made impossible by the abolition of all casual connection between " things-in-themselves " and the feeling subject. Consequently, the system was alleged to be fundamentally contradictory.

Among Kant's immediate disciples may be mentioned Johannes Scultz, the first commentator on the *Critique of Pure Reason* ; Karl-Leonhard Reinhold ; Krug ; Fries, who attempted to give criticism a psychological basis; Salomon Maimon, who deduced from consciousness both the matter and the form of our representations and so abolished the "thing-in-itself"; Beck, and Bardili.

Whether in the way of development or by combining with foreign elements, Kantianism gave birth to a number of important systems. The philosophies of Fichte, Schelling and Hegel are so many stages, as it were, in a connected line of thought dealing with the problems he raises. The subjective idealism of Fichte deduces the theoretical from the practical I, regarded as originally unconscious, and so makes of none effect the concept of the "thing-in-itself." Schelling objects to call I this first principle of Fichte, for, in reality, it is neither subject nor object: to his mind, the principle is absolute identity, no less superior to the I than to the not-I, an identity that is first realised as nature and afterwards as spirit: his system is objective idealism. Hegel establishes, defines and methodically develops the principle of this new idealism. The absolute cannot be absolute identity, otherwise it would be immovable: it must of necessity be spirit. Its movement is the methodical effort it makes to remove the ever-recurring contradictions developed by reflection deep in its own nature. The philosopher's dialectic gives itself up to the objective movement of concept and thus brings forth in succession: logic, the philosophy of nature and the philosophy of spirit. Idealism has become absolute.

Apart from this somewhat organic development, several German systems sprang from a fusion of Kantianism with other doctrines.

Schleiermacher, placing Spinoza, Plato and Christianity alongside of Kant, compares being and thought, and regards space, time and causality as forms both of things and of knowledge. God becomes the unity of the universe. Supreme good, the unity of the real and the ideal is, in morals, substituted for the purely formal principle of Kant.

Herbart draws upon Kant, the Eleatics, Plato and Leibnitz. Like Kant, he sees in philosophy the criticism of experience. According to him, however, the "thing-in-itself" is not inaccessible. It is obtained in its true form, if we eliminate from the data of experience all the self-contradictory and consequently subjective elements found therein. It consists of a plurality of simple beings with no real relation to one another : it is we ourselves who introduce relations and a process of becoming.

Like Kant, Schopenhauer limits space, time and causality, to phenomena ; but instead of considering the independent reality of our representation as incapable of being known, he places it in will, as given by internal perception.

All the same, the difficulties inherent in these divers systems, more particularly the foolish claim— set up by absolute idealism—to build up in detail the laws of nature, very quickly brought these developments of Kantianism into disfavour. It was considered that Kant's system of thought had been perverted by his successors, and that the line of reflection must be picked up just where Kant had dropped it. Such was the idea of an important school of philosophers, called the Neo-Kantian, especially after a famous lecture by Zeller on the theory of knowledge, published in 1862. They proposed either to defend Kant's own principles, or to develop them—without considering the great metaphysical systems that have sprung therefrom—in a manner strictly suited to the spirit of our times. The principal members of this school were : Lange, Cohen, Liebmann, Bonna Meyer, Paulsen, Krause, Stadler, Riehl, Windelband, Schultze. Most of them, along with Lange, insisted especially on the distinction between knowledge and belief, corresponding to that between phenomena and " things-in-themselves," so far as this distinction guaranteed the possibility of science, whilst at the same time limiting it. Philosophy ought to be a theory of knowledge, not a conception of the world. Moral things may be a matter of faith, not of science. With few exceptions, including Paulsen, these philosophers put in the background, or even neglected the moral and religious part of Kant's work, and emphasised the critical and antimetaphysical part.

Apart from philosophy, Kantianism in Germany has long since left its mark on the majority of intellectual disciplines.

Following on Kant, Schiller entered into philosophic speculations on esthetics, endeavouring to define the connection of beauty with nature and morality.

In theology, Kant initiated a moral rationalism that long held sway. Even of recent years, Ristchl, the theologian, has returned to Kant, protesting against the metaphysical fancy which claims to know the suprasensible.

In jurisprudence, the Kantian theories of natural right are found as leading ideas in the works of Hufeland, Schmalz, Gros, Feuerbach, Rehberg and Zachariae.

In science, Kantianism has exercised a varied influence according to the way in which it has been understood. Radically idealistic in interpretation— though, truth to tell, this interpretation was repudiated by Kant—there came into being the famous philosophy of nature, which, bringing matter entirely within the compass of unconscious thought, boldly deduces the phases of its development from the laws of the formation of consciousness itself. On the other hand, the Kantian theory of experience, as the sole origin of knowledge, is accepted by many modern scholars in quest of a rational justification of their own methods.

In mathematics, the Kantian point of view is characterised by the admission of synthetical *a priori* principles, or extralogical rational principles, and in particular by the negation of the metageometrical space of the Leibnitzians, as an object of possible intuition.

In the psycho-physiology of the senses, the negation of Johannes Müller, who maintains, in opposition to empiricism, the primitive character of the representation of space, is based on transcendental esthetics.

Finally, Kantianism exercises considerable influence over the political life of Germany. It represents the idea that reason, even in politics, is the true norm, and commands man to act in accordance with the universal idea of duty and humanity : a highly philosophical doctrine, which has certainly not altogether given way to that of historic right and an exclusively national ideal.

In other countries besides Germany, the influence of Kant's philosophy is still great, though more tardy in making itself felt, and less profound in the impression it has made.

In 1773, Kant began to be appreciated in Strasbourg. In 1796, the translation of his works into French was begun. In 1799, Degérando sets forth his system. Mme. de Staël speaks enthusiastically of the man she looks upon as an apostle of sentimental spiritualism.

In 1818, Victor Cousin lectures on Kant's morals ; in 1820 he expounds on the *Critique of Pure Reason*. In his own theory of reason, he is indebted to Kant for several of his ideas. After being thus utilised in doctrines based on other principles, such as electicism, positivism, and independent morals, Kantianism was studied and developed for its own sake, especially by Renouvier, Janet, Lachelier, and Pillon. Renouvier, Pillon, and Dauriac advocate, under the name of *criticisme*, a doctrine which, in contradistinction to German Neo-Kantianism, emphasises the excellence of Kantian morals. They directly subordinate theoretical to practical reason, looking upon the will as the first principle of all certainty ; and not only that, but, doing away with the noumenon, they set up natural laws as ultimate reality, and, following on phenomena, they prepare a place for the initiative of freedom. Under Kant's inspiration, also, M. Secrétan, of Lausanne, limits the rights of science, and places above it belief in freedom. In divers forms and degrees, Kantianism even now-a-days is to be found in most of the doctrines whose aim it is to reconcile science with morals, without injuring either.

In England, Kant's influence was mainly felt by Hamilton and the agnostics. Combining Kant's doctrine with that of Reid, Hamilton maintained that the representation of the absolute was impossible for a mind limited to human knowledge. Spencer's agnosticism, also, though dependent on positivism, owes much to the Kantian antinomies. In the realm of psychology the revolutionist school claims to be the reconciler of Kantian apriorism with Locke's empiricism. At the present time, Kant is scrupulously studied for his own sake. In the translation of the *Critique of*

Pure Reason which Max Müller published in 1881, he declares the work to be an Aryan monument as precious as the Vedas, and says that throughout all time it may be criticized but never ignored.

In Italy, the *Critique of Pure Reason* was translated in 1821-1822, and José del Perojo translated it into Spanish in 1883.

Looking at the matter from a general point of view, what was the historical *rôle* of Kant ? What relation has his philosophy with present-day speculation?

Kant's main purpose was analogous to those of Socrates and Descartes. Socrates undertook to show that practice, even regarded as the end of human activity, cannot exclude science, because in reality it implies this latter. Descartes grants that a commencement be made with universal doubt : this doubt does not abolish certainty, but rather creates a foundation for it. Kant, in turn, declares that experience is the starting point of all our knowledge. Are we to conclude that reason is a mere word ? By no means, for experience is based on reason. And in the very development of the doctrine, analogy follows its course. Deduced from practice, the science of Socrates is limited to morals and the objects connected therewith. Cartesian certainty at first extends only to thought, the condition of doubt ; it restores the objects that doubt had overthrown, only in so far as they are capable of being connected with thought. Kantian criticism, likewise, allows to persist only that in *a priori* notions which is required for experience ; it makes the possibility of this latter the norm of the entire use of pure reason.

Like Socrates and Descartes, Kant contends that his

method is constructive rather than destructive. Science, limited as regards " things-in-themselves," is at all events the abode of certainty. Idealism melts away before empirical realism. Nor is this all : criticism is to give even better results. The very deduction that establishes science allows morals to stand by its side, without risk of offending it. True, morals also must put up with limitation. It must be based on an exclusively formal principle, the simple notion of duty. But here again, criticism restrains only in order to secure. Morality may be absolute and remain practical, if it has no other object than the determinations of the will that is free. The insoluble antinomy of mysticism and eudemonism vanishes in the system of rational autonomy.

Indeed, throughout Kant's philosophy, it is reason that creates as well as destroys, that supplies principles to replace those it has abolished. In Descartes, it had already discovered within itself, in its faculty of intuition, that principle of certainty which it found neither in the senses nor even in demonstrations. Kant shows us reason making an inventory of its content, and finding, in its very constitution, all the principles necessary for science and morals. Naturally, it does not suffice unto itself, the absolute goes beyond it. Its science, consequently, is relative ; its morals, in application, limited to endless progress. None the less does reason offer man all the resources he needs to realise the ideal of mankind, for it is freedom and, at the same time, law.

Such being the essential elements of Kantianism, this philosophy stands at the term of the rationalistic development which began with Descartes. Reason, according to Kant, drives to the utmost limits both its renunciation of the comprehension of absolute being and its efforts to provide, by the principles it finds within itself, for the intuition in which it is lacking. One more step in either direction, and rationalism will lose itself either in skepticism or idealism. Kant, whilst shutting himself up in the world of time, claimed that he found in the heart of reason, which forms part thereof, a means of converting this world into a symbol of eternal being.

Such is the historical signification of his work. Regarded theoretically, it is of supreme interest, even in our days.

The human mind, influenced by the positive sciences and by philosophy alike, asks itself more than ever what is our relation to the reality of things, and whether or not it is possible to know that reality. Now, transcendental idealism has an answer to give to this question. Beyond phenomena, according to Kantianism, we can yet grasp the laws of thought by which phenomena are conditioned, and constitute philosophy as a theory of knowledge ; but as for forming an ontological theory of the universe, as the ancients did, we must give up all ambition in this direction : a plain solution, and one of grave consequence, finding much support in present-day science.

On the other hand, the progress of the positive sciences, in extent and in certainty, makes us wonder if whatever interests man cannot at least be dealt with according to the methods of these sciences, and if morals itself cannot be assimilated thereto. Kant answers this question with his stern dualism, limiting science in order to give it a basis, and establishing morals in the domain opened up by this very limitation. Now, neither the sovereignty of science in the practical order of things, nor the theoretical impossibility of freedom, are, even in these days, sufficiently clearly demonstrated for it to be possible to relegate to the past the Kantian solution.

As regards the philosophy of science, Kantianism deals just with those problems that increasingly occupy the modern mind. How can experience alone afford certainty, how can the knowledge of a law, in the exact meaning of the word, be purely experimental in its origin ? Aristotle taught that the general, so far as it is known by experience alone, necessarily includes exceptions, and that only intellectual knowledge can have universal value. And this has been the classic doctrine up to the present. Descartes, however, had already declared that there is a true science of phenomena, that what is transitory in its nature may be reduced to immutable essence ; and science, in its onward march, has been increasingly unconscious of Aristotle's objection. And yet, what right have we to reject a doctrine which seemed to be evidence itself ? How, and in what sense, can a fact be a law ? Kant accepted this question as modern science states it ; it is the object of his doctrine of forms and categories to answer it. The solution is a profound one ; it cannot be avoided by any who persistently determine, without fearing contradiction, to unite experience with certainty.

Kant's system of morals, too, is far from having become foreign to us. We are at present, as regards action, in a position similar to that in which science places us as regards being. We accept only facts, and yet we cannot renounce certainty, law, belief in duty. We are determined to reject every motive of action adopted from the idea of a suprasensible world, and yet we claim to maintain a system of absolute morals, a doctrine of obligation. Are we not, then, almost prepared to appreciate a philosophy which actually brings duty out of the very heart of experience, and holds aloof from mysticism and utilitarianism alike ?

And if, in social, religious and political questions, we are troubled by the conflict between history and reason, between what is and what ought to be, between form and idea, between fact and right, between the national ideal and the human one, do we not thereby find ourselves somewhat in the same position as Kant when he was investigating the relations between theory and practice and reconciling the necessity of nature with the sovereignty of reason in his doctrine of moral progress ?

Not in vain, then, was it that Kant endeavoured, both in the sphere of action and in that of knowledge, to adopt that point of view of the universal, at once real and ideal, which is also the point of view of reason : his doctrine thereby receives a lofty, positive character, such as could not be met with either in the pure generalisations of experience or the dreams of imagination. It is not the mirror of a single epoch, nor even the expression of a nation's thought : it belongs to the whole of mankind.

INDEX

331

THE END